POWER AND POLITENESS BETWEEN NATIVE AND NON-NATIVE SPEAKERS

MUSTAPHA TAIBI

POWER AND POLITENESS BETWEEN NATIVE AND NON-NATIVE SPEAKERS

MUSTAPHA TAIBI

Common Ground

First published in Champaign, Illinois in 2011
by Common Ground Publishing LLC
as part of the On Diversity series

Copyright © Mustapha Taibi 2011

All rights reserved. Apart from fair dealing for the purposes of study, research, criticism or review as permitted under the applicable copyright legislation, no part of this book may be reproduced by any process without written permission from the publisher.

Library of Congress Cataloging-in-Publication Data

Taibi, Mustapha.
Power and politeness between native and non-native speakers / Mustapha Taibi.

   p. cm.

Includes bibliographical references and index.
ISBN 978-1-86335-842-2 (pbk. : alk. paper) -- ISBN 978-1-86335-843-9 (pdf : alk. paper)
1. Intercultural communication. 2. Politeness (Linguistics) I. Title.

HM1211.T35 2011
303.48'2--dc22

                        2010045610

Cover image: Phillip Kalantzis-Cope

Table of Contents

Introduction 1

Chapter 1: Theoretical background 5
   A. An overview of communication 5
      1. Communication and interaction 5
      2. Intercultural communication 7
      3. Communication between native and non-native speakers 11
   B. The concept of face 14
      1. Definitions 14
      2. Brown and Levinson's Theory 17
      3. Criticism of Brown and Levinson's framework 22
   C. The concept of power 25
      1. Power in social sciences 25
      2. Power in linguistics 27
      3. Sources and manifestations of power 28
      4. Symmetry and asymmetry in face and power 33

Chapter 2: An empirical study 37
      1. Introduction 37
      2. Hypothesis 38
      3. Methodology 42
      4. Transcription 48
      5. Analysis 51

Chapter 3: Analysis of two interactions 55
   A. First interaction 56
      1. Transcript 56
      2. Context and participants 62
      3. Topics and conversation structure 64
      4. Politeness strategies 67
      5. Power manifestations 76
          5.1. Amount of speech 76
          5.2. Simultaneous speech 78
          5.3 Topic control 84
          5.4. Questions 85
              Conclusion 86

B. Second interaction 88
　1.Transcript 88
　2. Context and participants 92
　3. Topics and conversation structure 92
　4. Politeness strategies 95
　5. Power manifestations 97
　　　5.1. Topic control 97
　　　5.2. Amount of speech 98
　　　5.3. Simultaneous speech 99
　　　　Conclusion 101

Chapter 4: Overall findings 103
　I. Background 103
　II. Phatic communion in openings 105
　III. Topic negotiation and decision making 122
　IV. Signs of power 130
　1. Lexical assistance and error correction: knowledge asymmetry 130
　2. Topic control 133
　3. Amount of speech 140
　4. Interruptions 142
　5. Supportive minimal listener responses 146
　6. Questions 148
　V. Face relationship 152
　Introduction 152
　1. Attention to one's interlocutor 153
　2. In-group solidarity 154
　3. Conversational joking 157
　4. Complimenting/praising 159
　5. Face-boosting and face-threatening acts 161

Conclusion 165

Further research 169

References 171

Index 185

List of Figures

Figure 1: Native–non-native communication in relation to intercultural communication and communication in general. 11

Figure 2: Possible strategies to do an FTA 18

List of Tables

Table 1: Strategies of positive, negative and off-record politeness 21

Table 2: Possible combinations of assumptions and their symmetrical or asymmetrical results 35

Table 3: Some of the politeness strategies in Annie and Susana's interaction 75

Table 4: Amount of speech in Annie and Susana's conversation 76

Table 5: Distribution of simultaneous speech (back-channel utterances and interruptions) between Susana and Annie 78

Table 6: Politeness strategies in Catalina and Tracy's interaction 96

Table 7: Distribution of questions at the opening stage between native and non-native participants 121

Table 8: Topic and subtopic tabling 136

Table 9: Distribution of amount of speech among native and non-native speakers 140

Table 10: Distribution of interruptions between native and non-native speakers 144

Table 11: Rate of interruptions by native and non-native participants. 145

Table 12: Distribution of Supportive Minimal Listener Responses between native and non-native participants 147

Table 13: Distribution of questions between native and non-native speakers 149

Table 14: Types and distribution of questions in the 20 conversations 151

Table 15: FBAs and FTAs performed by native and non-native participants 163

Introduction

When two persons meet and start interacting, they usually take into consideration their respective situational and interpersonal contexts in order to determine what contents to express and what words, register and tone to use. As human beings and, therefore, rational and sensitive communicators, we tend to be careful about what we say, when and how we say it, depending on where we are and where we stand in relation to the addressee or the audience. If we appear to forget this or fail to behave appropriately, we are likely to be reminded by our addressee (who may say, for example, "Watch what you're saying!", "Don't speak to me like that!", "Nobody has ever spoken to me like that!", "I'm afraid what you're saying is inappropriate", etc.).

In order to avoid being reminded, rebuked or punished by such utterances or actions, we tend to behave ourselves: we follow social and cultural rules to avoid conflict and to avoid losing friendships or harming relationships. We know, and generally abide by the rule, that insulting other people is rude, impolite and possibly risky. We know that, at least in some cultures, one should greet one's friends and acquaintances when one sees them; otherwise they will likely be offended. We know these rules, we assume them and we act upon them so as not to offend others or cause affront, and to gain or maintain our society's good opinion of us. In sum, in order to survive socially, we comply with certain implicit rules.

Both the social actor and the rest of society have a self-image they need to preserve to maintain understanding and harmony. However, this understanding and social and interpersonal harmony are not always maintained. Sometimes, if one is angry or depressed, one may suspend the application of social rules and insult or be rude to others, which is a form of disruptive behaviour. This kind of behaviour may be excused or may be responded to, and, generally speaking, is later remedied by apologising and explaining the circumstances that led to it. Other times, if the addresser and the addressee are intimate friends or one is the other's subordinate, some "disrespectful" behaviour may be tolerated and, therefore, no offence is taken and no "revenge" is called for. Sometimes the "aggressor" is no longer interested in the "victim" or does not mind damaging their relationship or good opinion, so they can afford to blatantly criticise, insult and damage the other's image. Obviously, if there are no constraints, the other party may respond with similar behaviour. Once again, the interpersonal, situational and social context determines the kind of action social actors are allowed or required to take. It determines whether interpersonal harmony is worth maintaining and, if so, how it should be maintained.

Part of this social context is the interpersonal relationship between the social actors: whether it is intimate or distanced, equal or unequal. Depending on which is the case, the two participants may appear either close to each other or detached, as status equals or as a superior and subordinate.

It is this kind of relationship that is of interest in this book, which offers an empirical study of communication between native and non-native speakers of English. Language learning has been studied from structural, psychological, social and cultural perspectives. Much has been said about whether second-language learners are equipped with the same "devices" as the ones they developed when they acquired their mother tongue. Equally, much has been written about mother tongue transfer, communicative and structural approaches to language teaching and language learning, linguistic versus communicative competence, the differences between native and non-native language use, and so forth (see Ellis, 1985, for an overview of research into these issues). What is of interest in this study, however, is a related yet distinct issue: interaction between native and non-native speakers in terms of self-image, social harmony, conflict and relationships of equality/inequality. The study examines the interaction of "face rituals" and power (a)symmetry and the resulting linguistic and communicative surface manifestations. To study these aspects, twenty dyadic, face-to-face conversations between native and non-native speakers of English were recorded. These were later analysed from a pragmatic perspective to compare the politeness strategies and power manifestations in the speech of native and non-native participants.

The first chapter provides a general theoretical background, beginning with an overview of the three key concepts in this research, namely communication, face and power. First, some background will be provided about communication in general and intercultural communication in particular, and focusing more specifically on interaction between native and non-native speakers. Subsequently, some definitions of the concept of "face" and its relevance to face-to-face interaction are reviewed, with special emphasis on Brown and Levinson's (1978/1987) theoretical framework of politeness. This is followed by an overview of some theoretical questions regarding the concept of power in social sciences in general and linguistics in particular, including the material and abstract grounds for power and its reflection in communication and behaviour in general. The relationship between face and power is also explored, as are the face and power a/symmetries that result from different social variables.

The second chapter provides a general description of the study on which this book is based: research aims, hypothesis, methodology and the linguistic and communicative aspects used as analysis tools. The third chapter consists of a qualitative and quantitative study of two samples of the twenty recorded conversations and offers an example of data representation, description and analysis, using the transcription code, analysis tools and theoretical interpretation discussed in the section on methodology. The fourth chapter broadens the scope of analysis to include all the recorded data, thus providing a general report about the results of the study in terms of face strategies and power relationships between native and non-native participants, using statistics of conversational aspects such as amount of speech, interruptions, topic control and politeness strategies. Finally, an interpretation and explanation for the results is provided. The conclusion recapitulates the content of the study and the ensuing results, followed by a discussion of possible shortcomings and suggestions for further research.

Chapter 1
Theoretical background

A. An overview of communication

1. Communication and interaction

As Fernandes (2005:44) defines it, communication refers to "the process by which a person, group, organization (the sender) transmits some type of information (the message) to another person, group, organization (the receiver). The simultaneous sharing and creating of meaning through human symbolic action". Interaction, on the other hand, refers to an "exchange of communication in which communicators take turns sending and receiving messages" (Fernandes, 2005:140). As has been mentioned above and as Fernandes' definitions seem to suggest, to be able to transmit information and build a two-way channel between at least two people, we need a code or language, in conjunction with two opposite and complementary processes, namely encoding and decoding. The first process includes "all activities required to transform information into some behavioural response" (McCall and Cousins, 1990:16). It is a process of transforming concepts and knowledge about reality into a sign system that can be understood by one's interlocutor. The second process, on the other hand, "embraces all those activities necessary to transfer raw sensory data into what we experience as meaningful information" (McCall and Cousins, 1990:16). In other words, it is the direct opposite of encoding, as decoding is the process of receiving the encoded message and deciphering it according to our shared code or knowledge about the world around us.

Despite the above assertion, referring to "a shared code or knowledge" may be overly presumptuous, for "mutual knowledge must be certain, or else it does not exist; and since it can never be certain it can never exist" (Sperber and Wilson, 1986:19-20). Indeed, when we refer to communication between two people or two entities, we presuppose that communication takes place between "a Self different from an Other" (Dolitsky, 1984:183). At the same time, achieving this communication is conditioned by the existence of mutually shared concepts and knowledge that can be made use of to bridge the gap and reduce the difference between Self and Other (Dolitsky, 1984:183). It seems, therefore, that human beings are trapped in the dilemma of difference in their personal conception of how the world is organised and, at the same time, the need for shared concepts, knowledge, a code (or whatever it may be called) to make communication possible.

To overcome this hurdle, human beings tend to translate from their world or idiolect into that of their interlocutor(s) and vice versa, which practically can be termed a type of bilingual communication (François, 1982). This implies a continuous cognitive shift from the Self and the Self's perspective to that of the Other and the other way around (Dolitsky, 1984:183). This continuous movement, it should be understood, does not occur between two stable entities; rather, as interaction develops, one's conception of the other and their position is subject to continuous modification (Dolitsky, 1984:183) and, therefore, one should take the new position or state into consideration before proceeding with subsequent communication. As such, communication seems to be a continuous awareness of and adaptation to one's interlocutor.

Such awareness and adaptation mean that each participant in the interaction is conscious of who they are speaking to and, for this very reason, tries to make their own message easy for their interlocutor to understand. Even when communication is successful, the process of awareness and adaptation does not stop; rather, every new step, position or piece of information is incorporated into the accumulated knowledge about one's interlocutor and acted upon during the subsequent stages. On the other hand, if communication fails or misunderstanding arises, the speaker (and the addressee) try to "enact a repair" (Dolitsky, 1984:184). In other words, they try to identify the source of misunderstanding or lack of understanding in order to adopt measures or use other procedures or channels to achieve understanding and communication.

Both participants in the interaction make an effort to keep the communicative channel free from obstacles. Every communicative interaction is a collaborative act requiring the efforts of both interlocutors (Mey, 1979).

To sum up, the act of communication presupposes or requires the following:
- Awareness of the fact that Self is Self and Other is Other, for "identity between interlocutors leaves nothing to communicate" (Dolitsky, 1984:183).
- A desire to reduce the difference between oneself and the other and create a link between the two.
- A minimum amount of knowledge about the Other, for without this knowledge speakers would be speaking to "stereotypes, illusions, images, or projections of themselves, everything and anything except their interlocutor" (Dolitsky, 1984:192).
- Willingness to adapt to and accommodate one's interlocutor at every stage of communication, and the ability to assimilate and incorporate new information throughout the building-up process of communication.

In addition to assumptions and knowledge about one's interlocutor, one makes use of the linguistic code acquired (in the case of a mother tongue) or learnt (in the case of second or foreign languages), and at the same time takes into consideration the physical, interpersonal, institutional, social and cultural context in which the interaction takes place. This context can include a variety of aspects of which the following are but examples:
- The physical place and surroundings (a classroom, a street, a shop, etc.)
- The presence or absence of audience or overhearers.
- Whether the encounter/meeting is casual or formal.
- Whether the encounter takes place by chance or has been arranged.
- The level of intimacy between the participants and their personal, professional and institutional relationship.
- Their respective social status.
- Any new or exceptional circumstances (such as sickness, promotion, accident, etc.).
- Time constraints (being busy or in a hurry, for instance).

2. Intercultural communication

In spite of the difficulty defining intercultural communication and distinguishing the concepts referred to by terms such as interethnic communication, interracial communication, cross-cultural communication, etc. (Knapp, Enninger and Knapp-Potthoff, 1987), generally it can be said that intercultural communication is any instance of communication between people from different cultural backgrounds. However, this definition does nothing but shift the focus from the term "intercultural" to "culture" itself, as the question arises: What does "culture" consist of and when can we consider an "entity" as one culture on its own which is distinguishable from others? It is commonly assumed that very early in life one learns discourse patterns and cultural norms of behaviour and expectations (Scollon and Scollon, 1981:28), but what can hardly be agreed upon is when a specific discourse pattern or cultural rule or expectation can be considered as belonging to the same or a different culture. Furthermore, no individual member of a (cultural) group is absolutely representative of the characteristics associated with their group (Scollon and Scollon, 1995:157). Individuals may embody some of their group's characteristics but not others, and they can also embody the characteristics of different (age, gender, professional, social, cultural, etc.) groups at the same time. As Scollon and Scollon (1995:157) put it, "we all are simultaneously members of multiple groups."

If it is assumed that every individual is different from every other individual, that everyone has their own conception of the world and their idiosyncratic idiolect or way of speaking (François, 1982; Dolitsky, 1984), it will ensue that every person constitutes a culture in their own right. However, to avoid such an extreme interpretation of difference, which would only lead to the conclusion that communication is impossible, we often rely on common sense and stereotypes to generally define what constitutes a different culture. As in the case of the demarcation point between dialect and language (the difficulty in determining whether two linguistic codes are variations of the same language or different languages), we can always resort to commonly perceptible large entities such as continents, nationalities, race, etc. Indeed, for the purposes of this book it is sufficient to assume that people belonging to large entities such as "Spain", "Britain", "The United States", "Morocco", "Latin", "Anglo-Saxon", "Arab", etc. can be easily identified and assumed to be culturally different, whatever the degree and areas of difference may be.

The existence of these large chunks and of the cultural differences among them is reflected in common and widespread stereotypes, for the latter are the (over-generalised) result of contrasting and detecting differences between one group and another, one culture and another (Scollon and Scollon, 1995:158). Because they are over-generalised, these stereotypes are not reliable. However, this does not deny the existence of deep differences between cultures in some significant aspects, such as the following, as summed up by Scollon and Scollon (1995:127):

1. *Ideology:* history and worldview, which includes:
    a. Beliefs, values, and religion

2. *Socialisation:*
    a. Education, enculturation, acculturation
    b. Primary and secondary socialization
    c. Theories of the person and of learning

3. *Forms of discourse:*
    a. Functions of language:
        - Information and relationship
        - Negotiation and ratification
        - Group harmony and individual welfare

b. Nonverbal communication:
      - Kinesics: the movement of our bodies
      - Proxemics: the use of space
      - Concept of time

4. *Face systems:* social organisation, which includes:
   a. Kinship
   b. The concept of the self
   c. Ingroup–outgroup relationships
   d. *Gemeischaft* and *Gesellschaft*"[1]

This cultural difference means that, in addition to the difficulties and problems commonly experienced even among people belonging to the same social group or culture, there may arise other problems, difficulties, misunderstandings and even breakdowns as a result of the application of different cultural norms and the enactment of distinct cultural expectations. This is because different cultures have different "assumptions about the presentation of self and the distribution of talk" (Scollon and Scollon, 1981:28), have different practices and interpretations of some conversational phenomena such as interruption and silence (Murata, 1994:390), they order the interaction principles in different ways (Escandell, 1995:47) and they have different uses and interpretations of nonverbal cues or signs such as touching, eye contact, smiling, etc. (McCall and Cousins, 1990:67). All these and a large number of other differences make it much more likely that intercultural encounters result in misunderstanding, conflict and negative stereotyping (Scollon and Scollon, 1981: 28; McCall and Cousins, 1990:67).

To illustrate misunderstanding in intercultural encounters, Scollon and Scollon (1995:122) put forward the following short exchange between two businessmen; one American and the other from Hong Kong:

Mr Richardson: By the way, I'm Andrew Richardson. My friends call me Andy. This is my business card.

Mr Chu: I'm David Chu. Pleased to meet you, Mr Richardson. This is my card.

---

1. The two terms mean community and society, respectively. They were used by Ferdinand Tonnies (1971) to claim that the problems of modern European societies are the result of breaking up with traditional medieval social organisation, which was based on solidarity (*Gemeischaft*), common history and traditions. In modern Western society, on the other hand, social structures and relationships are based on *Gesellschaft*. That is to say, they are rational, contractual and instrumental (Scollon and Scollon, 1995:135). In cultural and discourse systems too there is a division between family/kinship/community-based systems and goal-directed/instrumental ones, in which one joins the group or corporation willingly to serve one's purposes. This difference may (and very often does) have consequences for business, interpersonal and international relationships, as different assumptions may lead to misunderstanding or conflict (Scollon and Scollon, 1995:136–137).

Mr Richardson: No, no. Call me Andy. I think we'll be doing a lot of business together.

Mr Chu: Yes, I hope so.

Mr Richardson (reading Mr Chu's card): "Chu, Hon-fai". Hon-fai, I'll give you a call tomorrow as soon as I get settled at my hotel.

Mr Chu (smiling): Yes. I'll expect your call.

With this example the authors show how relatively "small" or "insignificant" aspects of verbal and nonverbal communication such as forms of address and smiling may be sources of communication breakdown and interpersonal, professional or intercultural misunderstanding. The example also illustrates the extent to which "insignificant" surface behaviour—in this case address terms and smiling—is a reflection of deeper and fundamental differences between cultures in the conception of interpersonal relationships, in-group/out-group relationships, the function of language, worldview, etc.

Indeed, even apparently universal nonverbal signs such as smiling and laughing can give rise to misinterpretation because of differences in the underlying cultural norms and orientation. For cultures which perceive language use as a means "to promote individual welfare or the transfer of information" (Scollon and Scollon, 1995:143), smiling is likely to be interpreted as pleasure and satisfaction; for cultures which make use of language "to promote interpersonal or group harmony", on the other hand, the same nonverbal sign is likely to be used when this harmony is threatened (Scollon and Scollon, 1995:143), for example, when the situation is embarrassing, when there is bad news to be communicated, etc.

This is why in the above encounter, as Scollon and Scollon (1995:123) explain, the Asian businessman's smile is misinterpreted as a sign of satisfaction, while it is actually a sign of embarrassment and unease in an awkward situation in which his American interlocutor calls him Hon-fai, a name used only by a restricted group of relatives, to which the American businessman obviously does not belong. In addition, something similar happens when the American businessman insists his interlocutor should call him "Andy". For American businesspeople it is important to have an equal-to-equal, solidarity-based (friendly) relationship to make things go smoothly in business. This is why they usually prefer to use solidarity address terms from the very beginning or shortly after meeting. Asian people, on the other hand, have a more complex system of address terms and for business relationships they would not prefer to use first names.

This is but a simple example of what can happen when two untrained persons from different cultures meet and start interacting. So many aspects of communication and worldview are acquired in the social and cultural context in which one is born and develops that differences are likely to arise and to cause misunderstandings, communicative difficulties and even conflict.

3. Communication between native and non-native speakers

Communication between a native person and a non-native one is part and parcel of intercultural communication. Indeed, it can even be affirmed that every instance of native–non-native communication is an instance of intercultural communication, but not vice versa (see Figure 1 below). For, the very fact of learning and using a language other than the mother tongue means that the speaker has their original language, which they acquired as an infant in a given social and cultural context, and another language they learnt in the same or a different country, but necessarily through a different cultural context, for language itself is a manner of perceiving and shaping the world. On the other hand, not all instances of intercultural communication are between native and non-native speakers. Think, for example, of an Australian native speaker of English and a British English speaker: their interaction can perfectly be called intercultural, as the two people belong to two geographically distant and culturally different countries, but it obviously cannot be considered native–non-native, as the two interlocutors in question speak English as their mother tongue.

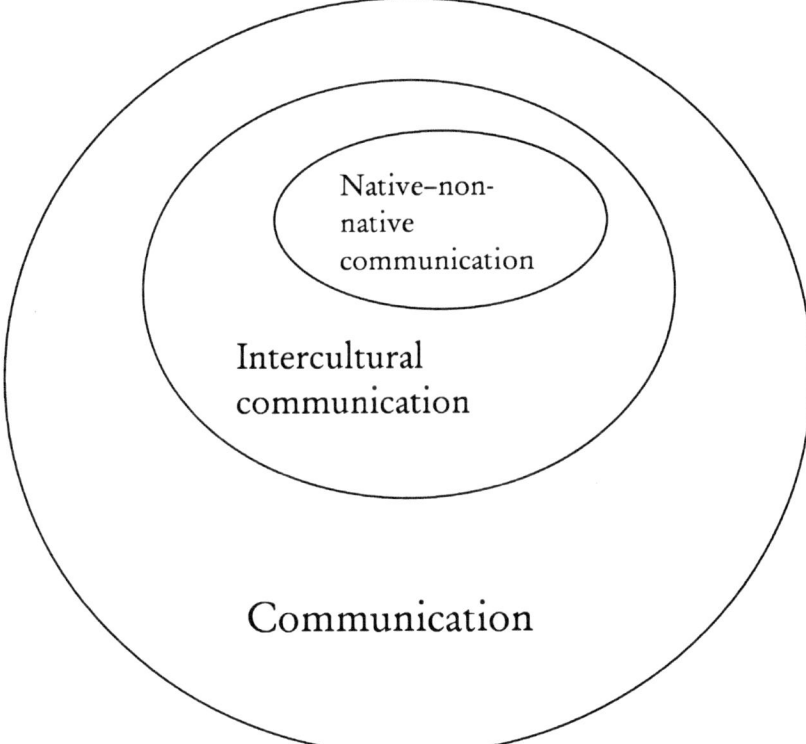

Figure 1: Native–non-native communication in relation to intercultural communication and communication in general.

As has been pointed out above, communication between two people who do not share the "same" culture is likely to give rise to communicative problems or a communication breakdown. Similarly, communication between native and non-native speakers of a language is likely to result in similar problems, because it is an instance of intercultural communication, in addition to others specifically resulting from the interlocutors' different levels of linguistic and pragmatic competence in the language used as a medium of conversation.

Indeed, when we think of a non-native speaker, we tend to have in mind a person who learned a language following a process and some (conscious) strategies which are totally or partially different from the (subconscious) mechanisms and processes used or followed by an infant acquiring their mother tongue. If, in addition to this, we assume as true the claim that at a certain age the mental capacity to learn a second language is no longer the same, it follows that, independently of the context in which the language is learnt, the non-native speaker will not always be able to reach the same linguistic (this including pronunciation) and pragmatic knowledge or competence as a native speaker (see Ellis, 1985 for a review of research about second-language learning).

There is a continuum (called "interlanguage" by Selinker, 1972, as cited in Ellis, 1985:47) of levels of linguistic and communicative competence which a language learner can go through, and there are different stages at which they may stop or "fossilise" (Selinker, 1972, as cited in Ellis, 1985:47). These stages are more or less equivalent to the levels into which second-language learners are classified, such as beginner, pre-intermediate, intermediate, upper intermediate, advanced or similar denominations. The point or stage at which a learner may fossilise depends on a variety of factors, such as the following:
- The learning context: at school in a country where the language is not spoken or in real life in a place where the language is spoken.
- The starting age: it is not the same for, say, a ten-year-old boy/girl and a middle-aged man/woman.
- The purpose for which the language is learnt.
- The learner's motivation and their attitude towards the language, the people who speak it and their culture.
- Aptitude.
- Personality, etc.

(For more details about the effects of each of the above factors, see a review of relevant research in Ellis, 1985).

Still, independently of how high a level the learner may reach, and except for some cases in which both aptitude and circumstances make it possible to attain a native-like competence, learners in general tend to fail to reach "complete" target language competence and fossilise at a stage in which at least some linguistic aspects or rules are different from those of the target language system (Selinker, 1972, as cited in Ellis, 1985:48). It goes without saying, therefore, that this means that learners who interact with native speakers would be using a linguistic and communicative system which is, at least slightly, different from that of the native speaker. This, in addition to ("purely") intercultural difficulties, is likely to create a communicative situation where participants face practical problems of encoding and decoding, and where the native person and their non-native counterpart will have to be in a continuous "negotiation of meaning", trying to overcome not only cultural differences but also "communicative difficulties which are always likely to arise as a result of the learner's limited L2 [second language] resources" (Ellis, 1985:141).

In the interaction between native and non-fluent (non-native) speakers the accent and the limited L2 linguistic and communicative resources of the latter are easily noticed by the former. This awareness often gives rise to a communicative phenomenon called "speech accommodation" by Giles and Smith (1979). In its broad sense Speech Accommodation Theory addresses the social cognitive processes which affect or determine the individual's perception of the communicative context and their communicative behaviour (Giles *et al.*, 1987:14). Specifically, the theory attempts to explain the converging or diverging speech shifts or changes which take place during social interaction. According to the interactant's perception of the situation and their relationship with their interlocutor(s), they will either converge or diverge. Interactants are likely to make an effort to converge with their interlocutor when they are interested in projecting a likeable self-image and they are likely to diverge when their interest is in maintaining their group identity or expressing a disassociating or negative attitude. Convergence is usually carried out through a set of linguistic and communicative strategies intended to "adapt to each other's speech by means of a wide range of linguistic features, including speech rates, pauses and utterance length, pronunciations and so on" (Giles *et al.*, 1987:14). Divergence, on the other hand, is the accentuation of speech differences between oneself and one's interlocutor (Giles *et al.*, 1987:14).

In the particular case of native–non-native interaction, converging accommodation, clearly, is not only motivated by the desire to be accepted or liked, but also by the very fact of limited resources and relatively lower competence associated with the non-native speaker. Understandably, the non-native speaker may adopt the native interlocutor's accent, for example, to make a positive impression. However, relatively greater convergence tends to be carried out by the native speaker for intelligibility purposes. Bearing in mind that non-native speakers, especially non-fluent ones, find it difficult to follow/understand native speakers' "real life" speech, this convergence consists of the native speaker adapting their speech/language (vocabulary, constructions, pronunciation, speech tempo, etc.) to their non-native partner in order to make comprehension and communication possible. This phenomenon has been observed and studied by many researchers (e.g. Freed 1978 and 1981; Bradford *et al.*, 1980; Long, 1981 and 1983; Perdue, 1984; Snow, Eeden and Muysken, 1981; and Gass and Varonis, 1985, all of whom are referred to in Smith *et al.*, 1991:174), who have found that native speakers slow down their speech rhythm, simplify their vocabulary and constructions and make use of "strategies such as rephrasing, elaboration and confirmation checks" (Smith *et al.*, 1991:174) when they are interacting with non-native interlocutors.

However, without denying the existence of the accommodation phenomenon, Smith *et al.* (1991) claim there are also cases in which there is a tendency towards "counter-accommodation" or divergence, that is to say the use of strategies aimed at discouraging and limiting communication rather than making it possible and easy, especially for the non-native party. This claim is based on Gass and Varonis (1985) and Harding (1986), who argue that foreign talk (the native speaker's accommodation to non-native speakers) is difficult, fatiguing and even frustrating, one reason being that sometimes the effort made by the native participant is not rewarded by understanding on the non-native interlocutor's side. Furthermore, Harding (1986) claims, native speakers do not only assume the responsibility to lead the communication and make the necessary adjustments, but also have to be careful not to threaten or damage their non-native interlocutor's self-image, which makes the burden even heavier and the option of giving up more likely. This provides some foundation for Smith *et al.*'s (1991:185) counter-accommodation, as native speakers "will use a variety of accommodation devices when conversing with a non-fluent speaker. But when accommodation demands too much extra effort, speakers may instead use strategies designed to limit communication". Giles *et al.* (1987:25) seem to support this view, as converging accommodation, in their opinion, should not be expected in all contexts, but only in those where rewards (e.g. approval or compliance) outweigh costs (e.g. effort or possible loss of group identity).

Thus interaction between native and non-native speakers, in addition to communicative problems inherent to intercultural contact, is likely to give rise to an additional difficulty, at least when the non-native speaker is not fluent, which has its origin in insufficient linguistic and communicative competence.

B. The concept of face

1. Definitions

As Ho (1975) and Mao (1994) claim, the notion of face seems to have Chinese origins: it is a literal translation of *miánzi* and *liân*. Its first appearance in English, Mao claims, was among the English community in China, namely in their use of the phrase "to save one's face". The phrase was used to mean preserving "one's credit, good name, reputation" (Mao, 1994:454). "To save one's face", Mao explains, "refers to the ways or strategies the Chinese commonly adopted in order to avoid incurring shame or disgrace".

However, regardless of its origins, it seems that "face" is a widely, if not universally, used word or concept. In English , in addition to "save one's face", there are expressions such as "to lose face" and "to give face", both of which are originally Chinese idioms, Mao claims. In Spanish *"salvar la cara*" means the same as "to save face". In Standard Arabic, a language which is historically, linguistically and culturally unrelated to Chinese and English, there is an idiom which may be translated literally as "to save face water", meaning to save one's image, reputation and to avoid embarrassing situations. In regional varieties like Moroccan Arabic "face" is referred to in expressions such as "you/he don't/doesn't have face", used to describe someone who humiliates themselves, for example, by going back to another's home after being offended there, or by making a request again to someone who had already, and maybe repeatedly, refused to satisfy a previous request. The existence of this concept in different societies and cultures, as shown through the above examples and as demonstrated by Brown and Levinson (1978/1987) in the case of English, Tamil and Tzeltal, by Scollon and Scollon (1981) in the case of the Athabaskan Indians and Anglo-Saxon Canadians, by Mao (1994) for Chinese, and by Matsumoto (1988) for Japanese, etc., seems to support Brown and Levinson's claim that face is something universal, a claim that Janney and Arndt (1992:27) share and express clearly as follows:

> The desire to maintain face, and the fear of losing it, are universals transcending all cultural, ethnic, social, sexual, economic, geographical, and historical boundaries.

It is not only because of this but also because of the importance and influence of face considerations in human interaction, that the concept has been widely studied and thought-inspiring in linguistic studies, social anthropology, cross-cultural studies and other disciplines. Numerous attempts have been made in different fields of study related to communication in order to understand the nature of face, how it works, how it affects communication and interaction, how it is linguistically served and reflected, and in order to define it, study its manifestations and come out with generalisations which link it to language, culture and social variables such as status, gender and ethnicity.

Goffman (1967), who is often referred to as the starting point in social interaction and face theory, defines face as the positive public self-image that every individual claims for themselves. It is a public self-image that everybody (who has it) needs to maintain and fears to lose, which implies that it can be lost or taken away because of misconduct, as it is socially dependent and sensitive:

> The term face may be defined as the positive social value a person effectively claims for himself by the line others assume he has taken during a particular contact. Face is an image of self delineated in terms of approved social attributes... (Goffman, 1972: 5)

> ... while his social face can be his most personal possession and the center of his security and pleasure, it is only on loan to him from society, it will be withdrawn unless he conducts himself in a way that is worthy of it . (Ibid:10)

Along the same line and in a more illustrative attempt, Goffman (1972:344), as cited in Werkhofer (1992:177), draws an analogy between the person concerned with preserving face and a schoolboy who must work hard in order to pass and must not cheat or "obtain ends by improper means"; otherwise, he will be penalised.

Goffman (1967:32) also draws an analogy between the behaviour intended to preserve face and religious ritual, between the "little ceremonies of everyday life" and religious ceremonies. Among the "little ceremonies" of interpersonal relations are the endeavours to respect the other's "personal preserve, by having the *virtual offence* in mind, that is, by being aware that one's actions or utterances might offend the other or trespass their territory (Goffman, 1971:138). This is why, for example, when we see somebody with whom we are acquainted we greet them in order to show that we noticed them, because failure to "notice" somebody (socially speaking, not literally) is likely to be interpreted as hostility or indifference, which constitute an offence or threat to the person's self-image—at least in most cultures. Similarly, when we want to interrupt somebody who is working in order to ask them for help or a favour, we follow certain ritual steps to make the intrusion as unintrusive as possible (e.g. by saying, "I'm sorry to interrupt, but it's something urgent" or "I know I'm a pain, but you are the only person I could think of", etc.). This is because we assume that the person whose help we are seeking has face (interests, privacy, a social or hierarchical position, etc.) and that our interruption carries an embedded potential offence.

More influential, but still inspired by Goffman, is Brown and Levinson's (1978/1987) definition and framework of face. Starting with the assumption that Grice's (1975) Cooperative Principle in conversation is philosophically valid, Brown and Levinson proceeded to complement it and account for its failures with an interactional theory that goes beyond the perception of conversation as a logical, effort-sparing transmission of information. Grice claimed that underlying human communication is a universal principle, namely the assumption that interactants will be cooperative, in the sense that they will subscribe to the information-exchange purpose of communication, saying what is relevant to the previous utterance and the context (Maxim of Relation), telling the truth (Maxim of Quality), saying as much as required (Maxim of Quantity) and presenting their contributions in a clear and straightforward manner (Maxim of Manner).

However, normal conversation is far from being a strict application and fulfilment of the above guiding maxims. Actually, if it were so, it would be tedious, predictable, non-creative and rapport-threatening (Lakoff, 1990). Grice's explanation or solution to the violations of his maxims, which are so common in everyday language use, is conversational implicature, the claim that the Cooperative Principle can be observed at a deeper level, a level that can be reached through the initial assumption that the interlocutor is willing to cooperate and through reasoning and "reading between the lines" or digging into the implicit. For instance, the person who initiates the interaction may ask the other, "Excuse me, what time is it?", to which the addressee may reply, *"The Unforgettable Encounter* has just started." At surface level the reply does not answer the question, and does not even seem coherent, because when we ask people to tell us the time, what we expect to get from them is something like "twelve twenty-five", "half past two", etc., not an utterance referring to something totally different and unpredictable in relation to the script of asking–giving the time. However, the first speaker, assuming that the second one is a rational and cooperative person, will try to find out the relevance of the reply by going beyond the surface level, that is by inferring the implicit message with the help of shared knowledge and background: "I know that *The Unforgettable Encounter* is a popular TV show, I know that it starts at 9:00 every night, so the person I have asked the time must mean that it is a little past nine."

What can give rise to conversational implicature and "not talking maxim wise", Brown and Levinson (1987:95) argue, can range from shirking the assumption of responsibility for straightforward statements to just a question of personal style. However, what is more important, the authors add, is the need to "give some attention to face"; the need to be aware and act according to the other's "desire to be unimpeded in one's actions (negative face), and the desire (in some respects) to be approved of (positive face)" (Brown and Levinson, 1987:13). Thus, when a speaker apparently violates Grice's maxims, and deviates from rational efficiency, most of the time it is because they want to be polite, that is, to avoid conflict by reducing the impact of their utterance (Brown and Levinson, 1987:13, 281). Due to the fact that it has been so influential and sometimes controversial, Brown and Levinson's theory will be dealt with in more detail in the following section.

2. Brown and Levinson's Theory

Inspired by Goffman (1967) and Durkheim (1915), and as an attempt to close the gap in Grice's theory, Brown and Levinson elaborated a face theory which assumes that human beings are not only rational, as Grice presumed when he coined his Conversational Principle, but also "face bearing" (Brown and Levinson, 1987:58). That is to say, for a conversation to develop satisfactorily, and in order to account for how that conversation develops, we need to assume that the parties involved in it are sufficiently rational to link means and ends, as well as have a self-image they want to maintain and project. Furthermore, face maintenance is a reciprocal activity, since the speaker's and the addressee's respective faces are interdependent and mutually vulnerable (Brown and Levinson, 1987:61). If one does not pay attention to one's interlocutor's face, the latter will most probably respond in a similar manner, provided status difference or other circumstances do not interfere. Like Goffman, Brown and Levinson assume that face can be "lost, maintained, or enhanced " (Brown and Levinson, 1987:61).

The pivotal notion in Goffman's theory is the "virtual offence", "the worst possible reading" of an utterance; that of Brown and Levinson's is the Face Threatening Act (FTA). An FTA is an "intrinsic potential impact that a specific communicative intention may have on a social relationship" (Brown and Levinson, 1987:281). And since at least some speech acts are inherently face threatening, the speaker may choose to do the FTA on record (baldly or with redressive action, the latter option being possible either with positive or negative face strategies), do it off record, or not do it at all (see Figure 2).

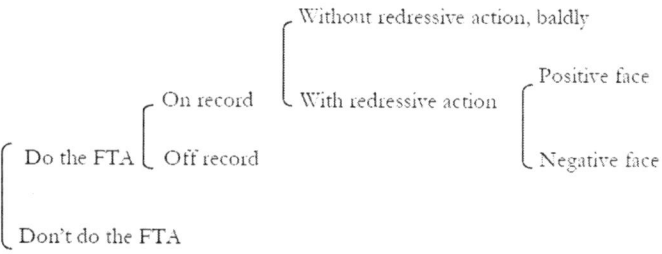

Figure 2: Possible strategies to do an FTA (Brown and Levinson, 1987:69).

The choice of one of the above strategies depends on three factors, according to Brown and Levinson, namely the relative power of the hearer (H) over the speaker (S), the social distance between the two and the rank of imposition. What is meant by power (P) is "the degree to which H can impose his own plans and his own self-evaluation (face) at the expense of S's plans and self-evaluation" (Brown and Levinson, 1987:77). This power can originate in one's "material control (over economic distribution and physical force) and metaphysical control (over the actions of others, by virtue of metaphysical forces subscribed to by those others)" (77). Distance (D) refers to a "symmetrical social dimension of similarity/difference" (76) which can be assessed culture-specifically (e.g. by the frequency of interaction, the language or dialect one speaks, kinship, neighbourhood, etc.). Finally, rank of imposition (R), refers to the degree to which an imposition interferes with "an agent's wants of self-determination or of approval (his negative- and positive-face wants)" (77). The authors do not claim that the three variables are the only significant and relevant factors, but they do claim that they "*subsume* all others (status, authority, occupation, ethnic identity, friendship, situational factors, etc.)" (80).

Therefore, assuming that some speech acts are inherently face threatening, Brown and Levinson claim that interactants will tend either to avoid them, if it is possible or judged convenient, or to modify or reduce their impact:

> In the context of the mutual vulnerability of face, any rational agent will seek to avoid these face-threatening acts, or will employ certain strategies to minimise the threat. In other words, he will take into consideration the relative weighting of (at least) three wants: (a) the want to communicate the content of the FTA x, (b) the want to be efficient or urgent, and (c) the want to maintain H's face to any degree. Unless (b) is greater than (c), S will want to minimise the threat of his FTA. (68)

Taking into consideration the kind of interpersonal relationship and other contextual factors (reduced to and summed up in P, D, and R), speakers will choose the most appropriate strategy to convey the intended content of their utterance. For example, in situations of emergency, where the communication of the message is more important than any other consideration, the speaker will communicate what they need to communicate clearly and straightforwardly, however face threatening it might be to the hearer. The same will probably happen if the speaker has greater power over the hearer and, therefore, assumes they have the "right" to threaten the hearer's face without running the risk of a face loss on their own side. If there is no power difference between the two parties and there is a considerable degree of intimacy (e.g. in the case of close friends or intimate work mates), the interlocutors are likely to use positive politeness strategies, or what Scollon and Scollon (1981) prefer to call "solidarity strategies". On the other hand, with the same power symmetry and with more social distance (e.g. in the case of newly introduced strangers), interactants will tend to use more indirect ways (the question of indirectness is controversial), that is, what Brown and Levinson call negative politeness strategies and what Scollon and Scollon (1981) prefer to call "deference politeness", to avoid the negative connotations of the word "negative". Finally, if the speech act is extremely face threatening and there is a risk of not being able to redress it, it will probably be expressed in an off-record manner, that is to say in a way that leaves "more than one unambiguously attributable intention so that the actor cannot be held to have committed himself to one particular intent" (Brown and Levinson, 1987:69). What this amounts to is that the speaker in question will try to shirk responsibility and avoid direct damage to the addressee's self-image by covering the potential FTA with a "coat" of other possible interpretations.

The importance of P, D and R as factors in human interaction has been widely supported by research (Grimshaw, 1980 and 1983; Lakoff and Tannen, 1979; Leech, 1977 and 1983). Still, Brown and Levinson, as has been mentioned above, admit that these are not the only factors underlying conversation. Indeed, it is impossible, they continue, to capture all culture-specific factors. This, however, does not undermine the importance and validity of the above factors (Brown and Levinson, 1987:16). Furthermore, Scollon and Scollon (1981:193) argue, P, D and R determine not only politeness phenomena in conversation but also "one's private identity", and consequently one's private and public behaviour. Lakoff (1990), in her classification of politeness strategies into distance, deference and camaraderie, seems to take into consideration these very three factors, though not explicitly. This is because distance and camaraderie can be seen as two extremes of the same scale/factor: (degree of) distance. More distance in Brown and Levinson's terms seems to be equivalent to distance strategies in Lakoff's, while less distance means camaraderie. Moreover, both distance and camaraderie take into account confrontation or conflict (or the absence of both). In the first (and also in deference politeness), interlocutors assume that conversation involves the risk of confrontation (because of the risk of imposition, Brown and Levinson would say) and, therefore, tend to avoid the risk. In camaraderie interlocutors assume that "interaction and connection are good in themselves", that "confrontation need not be feared", and that "nothing is too terrible to say" (Lakoff, 1990:38-39), precisely because the relationship between the two sides is intimate and close. Similarly, deference strategies are just a reflection of the power factor:

> Where distance politeness more or less assumes equality between participants, deference works by debasing one or both (depending upon whether the deference is mutual or unilateral. (Lakoff, 1990:36)

In other words, deference works according to which side of the interaction has more power, more freedom to impose on and "debase" the other; however, it should be borne in mind that the power relationship may be symmetrical.

The choice of one strategy rather than another is not only determined by P, D and R but can also be used intentionally to obtain a particular end. For example, a person who uses on-record strategies can be seen as outspoken or honest and can avoid misunderstandings. A person who goes off record can be considered tactful and can find a way to avoid responsibility for face-threatening acts. A speaker who uses positive politeness strategies can get closer to the addressee by conveying the idea that both belong to the same group (solidarity); an interlocutor who uses negative politeness strategies can show the respect and deference expected of them and can maintain social distance and thwart attempts to come closer. Finally, a person who chooses not to communicate the FTA can be seen as somebody who avoids offending others whatever the circumstances might be (Brown and Levinson, 1987:71–72). However, what should be kept in mind is that these strategies will not necessarily have the effect they are intended to: intention is one thing and effect might be quite another. For instance, a person who uses an on-record way of speaking in a situation that requires tact and emotional support will most probably appear as inconsiderate and heartless. Similarly, somebody who uses positive politeness with the intention to give the impression that they and the addressee are friends might be seen as intruding and disrespectful if their assumptions are not shared by the addressee or the audience, if any is around. It goes without saying that context—the personality of the interactants and the audience included—will determine what interpretation every strategy and every act will have (Brown and Levinson, 1987; Sperber and Wilson, 1986).

Brown and Levinson provide a list of possible strategies under positive politeness, negative politeness and off-record communication, which are reproduced in the following table:

Table 1: Strategies of positive, negative and off-record politeness (Source: Brown and Levinson, 1987)

POSITIVE POLITENE	NEGATIVE POLITENESS	OFF RECORD
- Claim common ground :	- Be direct :	-Invite conversational
* Notice, attend to H (his	* Be conventionally	implicature
interests ,wants, needs, goods)	indirect	* Give hints
* Exaggerate (interest, approval,	- Don't presume/assume	* Give association clues
sympathy with H)	* Question, hedge	* Presuppose
*Intensify interest to H	- Don't coerce H	* Understate
* Use in-group identity markers	* Be pessimistic	* Overstate
. Address forms	* Minimise the imposition,	* Use tautologies
. Use of in-group language or	Rx	* Use contradictions
dialect.	* Give deference	* Be ironic
. Use of jargon or slang	- Communicate S's want	* Use metaphors
. Contraction and ellipsis	not to impinge on H	* Use rhetorical questions
* Seek agreement	* Apologise	-Be vague or ambiguous :
. Safe topics	. Admit the impingement	Violate the Manner Maxim
. Repetition	. Indicate reluctance	* Be ambiguous
* Avoid disagreement	. Give overwhelming	* Be vague
.Token agreement	reasons	* Over-generalise
.Pseudo-agreement	. Beg forgiveness	* displace H
.White lies	* Impersonalize S and H	*Be incomplete, use ellipsis.
. Hedging opinions	. (avoidance of personal	
* Presuppose/raise/assert	reference in) performatives	
common ground	. (avoidance of personal	
. Gossip, small talk	reference in) imperatives	
. Point-of-view operations	. Impersonal verbs	
. Personal-centre switch: S to H	. Passive and	
. Time switch	circumstantial voices	
. Place switch	. Replacement of the	
. Avoidance of adjustment of	pronouns 'I' and 'you' by	
reports to H's point of view	indefinites	
. Presupposition manipulations	. Pluralization of the 'you'	
. Presuppose knowledge of H's	and ' I' pronouns	
wants and attitudes	. Address terms as 'you'	
. Presuppose H's values are the	avoidance	
same as S's values	. Reference terms as 'I'	
. Presuppose familiarity in S-H	avoidance	
relationship		
. Presuppose H's knowledge		

* Joke - Convey that S and H are co-operators: * Assert or presuppose S's knowledge of and concern for H's wants * Offer, promise * Be optimistic * Include both S and H in the activity * Give (or ask for) reasons * Assume or assert reciprocity - Fulfil H's want for some x * Give gifts to H (goods, sympathy, understanding, cooperation).	. Point-of-view distancing * State the FTA as a general rule * Nominalize - Redress other wants of H's * Go on record as incurring a debt, or as not indebting H.	

3. Criticism of Brown and Levinson's framework

Brown and Levinson claim that the notion of face is universal and, even after reviewing the relevant research following their original paper (1978), they still maintain (in the 1987 version) that their politeness framework is valid. According to the authors, although some of the findings of this research might be apparently challenging to some aspects of their framework, the latter and its predictions still hold, and the exceptions can be accounted for by the socio-cultural variables or different cultural ethos the two authors referred to in their work. By this they mean their distinction between negative politeness cultures, which tend towards deference and distance keeping, and positive politeness cultures, where impositions are considered relatively harmless and easy-going interaction and relationships are given more importance than power relationships or social deference (Brown and Levinson, 1987:245). In the same line of awareness of cultural differences, Brown and Levinson show they are aware of the fact that what constitutes an FTA in a culture might not be so in another, or at least not with the same rank of imposition (247). They also show their awareness of the cultural relativity of the importance of the hearer's or the speaker's face, the possible existence of cultures in which face needs can be superseded by other needs, and the existence of sub-cultures within the same culture, with their own ethos (e.g. the dominated and the dominant, women and men, etc.).

However, most of the criticism of Brown and Levinson's theory is related to cultural relativism. Starting from the notion of face itself, it has been argued that their notion is highly influenced by and based on Western cultures, hence its non-universality. In Western cultures the focus of interaction is on individualism, while in other cultures (e.g. Asian cultures) the focus is on group identity (Matsumoto, 1988; Ide, 1989). Mao (1994), after tracing the notion of face back to its Chinese origins (see above), draws clear distinctions between Brown and Levinson's face and the Chinese face. The former, Mao explains, is individual, while the latter is intimately linked to the community and determined by the participation of others. While in Brown and Levinson's framework negative face means freedom from imposition, in the Chinese culture there is no such desire but "the desire to secure public acknowledgement of one's prestige or reputation", which is the public image the society bestows on the individual (Mao, 1994:464–65).

Similarly, Ide (1989) argues that Japanese society is based on group membership and social hierarchy and that, accordingly, Japanese interaction is based on "the role or status defined in a particular situation" (1989:241). This is the case to such an extent that "social interrelationship is encoded in the Japanese language" (Mao, 1994:467), especially in its honorific system, which is deterministic, unlike Brown and Levinson's politeness strategy options. It is deterministic because the intuition about one's place in a given situation in relation to other participants and to social conventions (i.e. *wakimae* or "discernment") leaves no interactional choice of strategies. Rather, the linguistic output is determined automatically.

Because of this, Mao (1994:472) concludes that

> the Chinese and Japanese concept of face, and Brown and Levinson's characterization of face, are informed, respectively, by two different underlying forces. The first may be regarded as a *centripetal force,* as Chinese and Japanese face gravitates toward social recognition and hierarchical interdependence. The second may be regarded as a *centrifugal force,* because Anglo-American face spirals outward from individual desires or wants, and sees the self as the initiating agent.

In order to account for the two apparently opposed forces, Mao (1994:472) suggests "the relative face orientation", an alternative interactional construct which takes into account that face can be directed either towards an ideal social identity (e.g. in China and Japan) or an ideal individual autonomy (e.g. in Western cultures), depending on which of the two is more salient in a given culture.[2]

Werkhofer (1992:158) recognises that Brown and Levinson's framework is a classic in politeness research and an ambitious and complex theoretical system. Still, he criticises its adoption of Gricean elements. The Gricean theory and politeness theory, he claims, are incompatible; however, what Brown and Levinson (as well as Lakoff, 1973 and Leech, 1983) do is just add a politeness maxim to Grice's rational theory:

> And Brown and Levinson (1987:5) note that the Gricean postulates are "'unmarked' or socially neutral (indeed asocial)" and that they are "of quite different status from that of politeness principles". But if this is so, how, then, can the theory of politeness start from the presumption that "Grice's theory of

---

2. It is worth pointing out at this point that Western face is not only oriented towards individual autonomy, as may be understood from Mao (1994). Rather, it is also sensitive to the community where one lives and is socialised. For, on the one hand, individual autonomy is enacted in and through relationships and, on the other, the essence of face is how others (society, community) perceive the individual in question.

conversational implicature and the framework that gives rise to such notions is essentially correct?" (Werkhofer, 1992:161).

Due to the greater importance ascribed to the Gricean element, however, these social elements [social factors determining politeness strategies] and ...the whole aspect of politeness, appear to be of lesser, in fact secondary importance, less important that is than "true", and that means here "referential", communication. Thus that and how Gricean elements are built into and adapted to this construction make it a difficult, inherently contradictory one" (Werkhofer, 1992:162).

Another aspect of Brown and Levinson's theory Werkhofer criticises, or rather questions, is the capacity of the variables P, D and R to cover all the social and situational factors relevant to interaction. He also claims that they are so fuzzy and vaguely defined that they pose a problem of quantification (Werkhofer, 1992:175). Furthermore, Brown and Levinson conceive of these variables as "static entities" that determine politeness strategies, a conception that "neglects the dynamic aspects of social language use" (Werkhofer, 1992:176).

Bayraktaroglu (1991:26) argues that Brown and Levinson's FTA-based approach focuses on single activities (or acts) and their common characteristics, which are difficult to understand without an overall understanding of the mechanisms of conversation, as a whole, and of "interactional imbalance", a concept she borrows from Goffman (1972:19):

> When the participants in an undertaking or encounter fail to prevent the occurrence of an event that is expressively incompatible with the judgements of social worth that are being maintained and when the event is of the kind that is difficult to overlook, then the participants are likely to give it accredited status as an incident—to ratify it as a threat that deserves direct official attention—and to proceed to try to correct for its effects. At this point one or more participants find themselves in an established state of ritual disequilibrium or disgrace, and an attempt must be made to reestablish a satisfactory ritual state for them.

The key to this concept is disequilibrium. Bayraktaroglu argues that speakers in interaction do not have in mind only the face-threatening potential of their utterances, but also the "interactional reparation" that a given imbalance calls for (1991:31). Accordingly, she proposes an improvement rather than a challenge to Brown and Levinson's theory, in order to analyse and understand politeness features in conversation: as an addition to FTAs to self or other, she puts forward FBAs (Face Boosting Acts) of self or other. As its name suggests, a Face Boosting Act refers to an act that enhances or improves a person's self-image by attributing positive or valued qualities (e.g. skills, intelligence, beauty, etc.) to them. Therefore, according to Bayraktaroglu, face values fall into four categories:

1. Boosting the face of self: FBA/self (e.g. by boasting).
2. Threatening the face of self: FTA/self (e.g. by self-degradation).
3. Boosting the face of other: FBA/other (e.g. by compliments).
4. Threatening the face of other: FTA/other (e.g. by criticising or accusing). (15)

However, Brown and Levinson (1987:233-236) themselves are aware that conversational understanding cannot be achieved through analysis of single utterances, and that at least some FTAs can only be described with reference to the overall sequences or 'hierarchical plans' they occur in (e.g. the conventional refusal of an offer in the first time, followed by insistence and final acceptance). Because of this they posit the "balance principle":

> If a breach of face respect occurs, this constitutes a kind of debt that must be made up by positive reparation if the original level of face respect is to be maintained. Reparation should be of an appropriate kind and paid in a degree proportionate to the breach. (1987:236)

From the above quotation it can be seen that Brown and Levinson's balance principle echoes Goffman's (1972) interactional imbalance, referred to above. Their principle is apparently the same as Bayraktaroglu's, except that the latter is not limited to the "breach of face respect" but is extended to include Face Boosting. For Bayraktaroglu, face-boosting acts may also cause an imbalance and, therefore, require attention or balance redressing.

C. The concept of power

1. Power in social sciences

Power is one of those concepts that are widely used (in politics, discourse analysis, literature, psychology, everyday life, etc.) but seldom defined, and when they are defined, the definition is often vague. "In the entire lexicon of social concepts", Bierstedt (1950) says, "none is more troublesome than the concept of power. We may say about it in general only what St. Augustine said about time, that we all know perfectly well what it is—until someone asks us."

In social sciences there have been many attempts to define the concept; however, every attempt seems to be "armed with the terminology of a particular theological framework" (Harris, 1989:132), and every approach carries an "ideological commitment" (Lukes, 1974:34). Without going into the ideological differences between the Community Power Debate (e.g. Dahl), the Marxists (e.g. Marcuse and Gramsci), the Post-Structuralists (e.g. Foucault) and other schools, we can examine a few definitions to obtain a general understanding of "power". For Dahl (1957:203), "A has power over B to the extent that he can get B to do something that B would not otherwise do." The key to power, then, according to this author, is the ability to get (or make) and the fact of getting (or making) another person (or entity) (to) do something (they would not otherwise do). In other words, Dahl defines power as causality and agency: A causes B to act and thus A himself acts. This conception can easily be challenged by the following hypothetical case with which Clegg (1989:67-68) starts a critique of Dahl. Two householders live next door to each other. They are unconsciously under the observation of another neighbour of theirs who lives opposite them. The observer can see that whenever householder B is in his garden and householder A comes out to work in his, B goes inside his house. This pattern of A's appearance causing B's disappearance leads the observer to conclude that A has power over B (following Dahl's definition). It is obvious, however, that householder A may have no power over his neighbour and may not even be aware of the effect of his presence on B's behaviour.

Russell (1986) and Weber (1947) would argue that the absence of power in the above situation is due to the absence of intention on A's side, as power, Weber (1947:152) argues, is "the probability that an actor within a social relationship will be in a position to carry out his own will despite resistance, regardless of the basis on which this probability rests". It is, therefore, a will or intention that one is capable of carrying out, regardless of their counterpart's will or intention. Hence, there is the possibility of conflict caused by the opposition of wills, attempts to exercise power and acts of resistance.

Apparently similar to Weber's definition of power as 'the imposition' of one's will is Giddens' (1984:257) definition of the concept as "the capacity to achieve outcomes". However, Giddens curiously falls into a vicious circle of power–agency–action: starting from the belief that human agency is inseparable from and dependent on power, he defines power "in terms of agency, which is defined in terms of action, which in turn is defined as power" (Clegg, 1989:139):

> To be an agent is to be able to deploy (chronically, in the flow of daily life) a range of causal powers, including that of influencing those deployed by others. Action depends upon the capability of the individual to 'make a difference' to a pre-existing state of affairs or course of events. An agent ceases to be such if he or she loses the capability to 'make a difference', that is to exercise some sort of power. (Giddens, 1984:14)

The recurrence of the terms "capacity" and "capability" in the above definitions leads us to distinguish between power as capacity and power as exercise. Dahl (1968:413) distinguishes between having and exercising power in terms of "the presence or absence of a manifest intention". If a "causal agent" A manifests their intention to act in a certain way, which is pertinent to B's response, then we can say that A has power and exercises it. Indeed, Dahl attributes power only on the basis of its exercise/manifestation. Like Dahl, Wrong (1979) distinguishes between having and exercising power. However, unlike Dahl, he does not restrict the attribution of this social "asset" to agents who exercise it. Instead, he also conceives of power as capacity, or what he calls "dispositional" power (Wrong, 1979:6). A person, say a traffic police agent, can have/dispose of and exercise power (when there are cars in sight and the police agent gives them orders through gestures or signs) or merely have it without exercising it (when there are no cars in sight) (Clegg, 1989:83). This is a common-sense understanding and usage of the term "power", Barnes contends, as power is not always "something that is continually manifest and actual" (1988:2). Barnes provides four examples which are similar to the one of the traffic warden above: a powerful magnet, a car engine, a powerful body and a powerful office, all of which remain powerful when not in use.

The co-occurrence of "have" with "power" usually leads to conceiving of power as a "thing" which is possessed in a proprietorial sense. So much so that Marxists see it as an abstract commodity (Watts, 1991:59). Other theorists (e.g. Parsons, 1967:130) draw an analogy between power and money: if you have money you can get desiderata available in the market; and if you have power you can get desiderata in the political system. However, a better understanding of power may be achieved if it is conceived of relationally. "It is not a thing", Clegg (1989:207) says, "nor is it something that people have in a proprietorial sense. They 'possess' power only in so far as they are relationally constituted as doing so".

At the end of this section, and always bearing in mind what has been exposed above, it seems sensible to conclude with a conception of power that takes into consideration both the latent and manifest sides of this quality (power capacity and power exercise, respectively) and, at the same time, caters for a wide range of possible sources of power, a range that goes, for instance, from physical safety to self-image. It is, therefore, worth concluding with a comprehensive quotation from Dye (1990:4), which seems to include most, if not all, of the above aspects:

> *Power is the capacity to affect the conduct of individuals through the real or threatened use of rewards and punishments.* Power is exercised over individuals or groups by offering them some things they value or by threatening to deprive them of those things. These values are the *power base*, and they can include physical safety, health, and well-being; wealth and material possessions; jobs and means to a livelihood; knowledge and skills; social recognition, status, and prestige; love, affection, and acceptance by others; a satisfactory self-image and self-respect. To exercise power, then, control must be exercised over the things that are valued in society.

2. Power in linguistics

Away from the macro level and moving on to the interpersonal or interactional level in small groups, it can be seen that linguistics and communication researchers also tend to use the notion of power without defining what exactly they mean by it, or merely by providing some vague definitions. They often rely on the common-sense understanding of the reader, especially that power seems to be taken for granted. Furthermore, although the term "power" stands out as the most popular among researchers, there are also a variety of other terms, apparently equivalent but whose equivalence is questionable, to say the least (Spencer-Oatey, 1996:7). As a main term, Baxter (1984), Blum-Kulka et al. (1985), Brown and Gilman (1972), Brown and Levinson (1987), Holtgraves and Yang (1990), for example, use "power"; Beebe and Takahashi (1989), Cansler and Stiles (1981), Holtgraves (1986), Olshtain (1989) and Wood and Kroger (1991) use "status"; Trosborg (1987), on the other hand, uses the term "dominance"; and Leech (1983) uses "authority". As alternative or secondary terms, we can find "status" (e.g. Baxter, 1984), "dominance" (e.g. Blum-Kulka and House, 1989), "higher station" (e.g. Brown and Gilman, 1989), "social rank" (e.g. Cansler and Stiles, 1981), "equality/inequality" (e.g. Holtgraves, 1986), "authoritative status" (e.g.

Leech, 1983) (see table in Spencer-Oatey, 1996:8). However, there are some writers who distinguish between such apparently synonymous terms. Leet-Pellegrini (1979:11), for example, draws a clear distinction between the "bases" of power and its "social effects", that is, between "social power... as the potential influence of some influencing agent, O, over some person P. Influence is the change in cognition, attitude, behavior or emotion of P which can be attributed to O" and the manifestations of the exercise of power, like dominance, control, influence, etc. (11). Watts (1991:55) also distinguishes between power and dominance, the latter being just an "explicit expression" of the former. Still, confusion seems to persist in relation to the two terms "status" and "power":

> Dominance may be understood in terms of the hierarchy of status relationships as an explicit expression of power over others. Thus a dominant person in verbal interaction is generally taken to be one who is perceived by the other participants to assume, rightly or wrongly, a position of higher status and to act on this assumption in preventing others from achieving their interactional goals.

It is a confusion he later dissipates as follows:

> Status is a prerequisite of power but it is not necessarily co-extensive with it.

3. Sources and manifestations of power

When a participant or a social actor assumes a more "powerful" position in relation to another and the latter acknowledges this power differential, they usually do so based on some personal, social, cultural, political, economic, mythical, etc. considerations. French and Raven (1959) name six sources of power:

- *Reward power:* based on the belief that P- (the less powerful) can receive rewards from P+ (the more powerful) if they cooperate with them.
- *Coercive power:* based on the belief that P+ can control resources and facilitate or obstruct P-'s goal achievement. Therefore, P- must behave according to P+'s wishes in order to receive rewards; otherwise, they would be punished.
- *Legitimate power:* based on the belief that P+ (because of reputation, position or role...) has the right to impose or prescribe certain behaviour from P-'s side.
- *Referent power:* based on the desire of P- to be associated with P+ because of similarities between the two or because of P-'s admiration for P+.
- *Expert power:* as the name suggests, it is a power based on the belief that P+ has special expertise or knowledge in an area relevant to P-'s interests.
- *Information power:* based on the belief that P+ holds information needed by P- or is the key to have access to it (information gatekeeper).

It can be seen from the above that some bases may intersect with others, as is the case, for example, for reward and coercive powers or expert and information powers. It is worth noting also that the categorisation is too abstract.

In more practical field studies a set of variables and characteristics have been used or assumed as sources of power or status. Leet-Pellegrini (1979), for example, assumes that gender and expertise/knowledgeability constitute examples of such sources; Zimmerman and West (1975) use gender; Harris (1989) studies institutional power (in courts); Scollon and Scollon (1981) assume that ethnic identity (of Whites and Indians in their study) is also a source of power. Other sources may be social prejudice (Quasthoff, 1989), age, occupation, rank in a military or religious or other hierarchy, etc.

To study the reflection of power asymmetry in the social behaviour of people, there is a tendency to assume that certain patterns of behaviour are associated with the more powerful and others with the less powerful. More concretely, in linguistic studies there is a long tradition of assuming that interruption, holding the floor (talkativeness), topic tabling and control, questioning, directness, etc. are linguistic and conversational aspects that are more expected from powerful participants than their less powerful counterparts. Similarly, indirectness, taciturnity, hedging, recurrent hesitation (Ng and Bradac, 1993), supportiveness and assenting, the use of deferential terms and pronouns (Brown and Gilman, 1972), etc. are considered a reflection of a lesser position/status in relation to one's counterpart.[3]

Of all the above linguistic and conversational aspects, interruption (or turn-taking in general) is the one which is most commonly used as an indicative manifestation of power distribution. Starting from the assumption that for conversation to flow satisfactorily and efficiently there should be only one speaker at a time (Sacks et al, 1974), the overlap of two speakers is seen as a disruption or violation of the speaker's right and, therefore, as a possible exercise of power.

To understand this, it is worth reviewing the concept of turn-taking in the work of Sacks et al. (1974). The authors start off with the observation that for many types of social interaction (e.g. games, traffic, meetings, ceremonies, attending to customers at commercial establishments, etc.) to evolve smoothly, participants take turns. In everyday conversation, the authors claim, the same turn-taking organisation applies. In a conversation between two people, speaker-change occurs or recurs and, as a rule, only one party speaks at a time. If overlap (two speakers speaking at the same time) occurs, it is usually brief and it is normally repaired by one speaker (apologising and) giving up the floor. Turn length, turn order and conversational content are not fixed in advance. Similarly, the conversation may be continuous or discontinuous, and the number of participants may vary.

A speech turn, Sacks et al. (1974) claim, may be constructed using a single word, a phrase, a clause, one sentence or a sequence of sentences, as the following examples show :

---

3. This tradition, it should be pointed out, has been challenged by another school that considers linguistic and conversational differences as manifestations of sub-cultural differences and not necessarily signs of dominance or power asymmetry (Cameron, 1992b:14).

1. A: What's your name?
   B: Annie.
2. A: Do you like it?
   B: Very much.
3. A: When did he tell you that?
   B: When he was leaving.
4. A: I go out with my friends every weekend.
   B: I see mine every day.
5. A: Did you manage to repair it?
   B: Yes, it took some time to find out what the problem was, I had some trouble finding the necessary spare parts, but I finally managed to fix it.

The minimal unit to fill a speech turn, therefore, is one word or interjection and, theoretically, there is no limit to its length; it can go on and on using as many words, phrases, clauses and sentences as one wishes. However, since conversation and turn-unit are "interactionally managed", a turn is stoppable at certain points that Sacks *et al.* (1974) refer to as Transition Relevance Places. A TRP is the projected end of a word, phrase, clause or sentence. At such a point three alternatives can be enacted:

1. The current speaker may select the next speaker (e.g. by asking a question). In this case the selected candidate has the right and "obligation" to speak next.
2. A participant may self-select and start speaking. In the case of a group, if more than one speaker self-select, the first to start secures the right to continue.
3. The current speaker, seeing the addressee's lack of initiative, may continue speaking, bearing in mind that the same three possibilities may re-apply at the first or subsequent Transition Relevance Place.

If during the course of a speech turn of one participant (that is, before the completion point) another one self-selects, the current speaker has the right to consider this act as an interruption. However, whether this act (starting one's speech turn before one's interlocutor completes theirs) is perceived as an interruption or given another interpretation depends on a number of contextual variables, as the concept of Transition Relevance Place should be understood in functional and discourse terms, not only in lexical or syntactic terms. For example, if one's interlocutor is telling a joke, one cannot perceive a TRP at the end of every sentence; rather, the discourse structure of jokes makes us expect the "denouement" or the final funny turn. Moreover, the content of the "interruption" (Murray, 1985), whether it is intentional or not (Murata, 1994), whether it is supportive or competitive (James and Clarke, 1993), whether it causes the current speaker to lose the floor (Beattie, 1981), etc. are all factors that would determine the nature and perception of simultaneous speech.

Without embarking upon a detailed definition of interruption or distinction between it and supportive overlap, we can review some examples of studies which used it as an analysis tool. Zimmerman and West (1975), taking interruption as a manifestation of power, found that male participants tend to interrupt female ones more than the other way round, and so do high-status men with low-status ones, high-status women with low-status ones, and adults with children. Leet-Pellegrini (1979, 1980), in her study of the role of expertise and sex in dominance/control, expected males and experts to be more talkative (to hold the floor more) and more intrusive (to interrupt more often) than females and non-experts. That is to say, she expected that men and experts would be more powerful and women and non-experts more assenting and supportive. The findings of the study suggested that gender, especially when combined with expertise, was the determining factor in the perception and exercise of power (dominance, in her terms): men tended to interrupt more, in some cases even when they were non-experts, and women tended to be less competitive for the floor, sometimes even when they were the experts in their dyads. Her interpretation of this is that:

> Male socialization may be such that in a task-oriented situation, *even when framed as a co-operative venture*, the issue of competition arises early for males and that power is the first order relationship normatively constructed .... In other words, the threshold for eliciting dominance behavior is lower for males than females, especially for males interacting with other males on specific measures of conversational structuring. Thus, we are seeing the possible intrusion of male concern for dominance hierarchy and its absence in female concern. (1979:106)

Other studies (Scollon and Scollon, 1981; Bennet, 1981; Ferguson, 1977 and Zimmerman and West, 1975, among others) also coincide in the conclusion that the powerful party tends to interrupt and speak more, while the powerless are more easily interrupted and less talkative. However, other researchers, such as Watts (1991), question the methodological operationalisation of interruption, that is, the leap from the objective observation of interruptive behaviour to the arbitrary interpretation of that behaviour as dominating behaviour or power exercise:

> It is one thing to observe the phenomenon of a participant in an interaction intervening in the ongoing contribution of another, and we may, if we wish, even label this phenomenon "interruption", but it is an entirely different thing to assume without question that the phenomenon is a measure of "dominance" and "power" hierarchies... (1991:75)

This does not mean, however, that Watts does not assume that interruption can be used to enhance one's self-image/status in a conversation and that "interruptive behaviour is the most salient type of attempted exercise of power" (1991:249). The author only claims that to exercise power it is necessary to have the required status, and that researchers should take into consideration the perceptions of the social group being studied and the cultural relativity of interruption as a face-threatening act or as an exercise of power. He also argues that an attempt to restrict a speaker's opportunities to hold the floor (i.e. to interrupt them), is necessary but not sufficient on its own to constitute an interruption. To consider it as such, another component is necessary, namely evidence that the interrupted speaker's positive face was ignored (108).

On the other hand, simultaneous speech, most of which is considered instances of interruption by some researchers, can also have other functions, such as supporting (James and Clarke, 1993:239), which is quite the opposite of power exercise. For a participant who breaks into the present speaker's turn only to say, "That's right", "I totally agree with you" or to relate a story or anecdote that supports the present speaker's point cannot be said to be interrupting. Instances of works that have drawn attention to this are Bennett (1981), Edelsky (1993), Beattie (1982), Shultz, Florio and Erickson (1982), Kennedy and Camden (1983), Murray (1985, 1987), Tannen (1983, 1984, 1987a, 1990), Testa (1988), Moerman (1988), Coates (1989), Goldberg (1990) and Herman (1991). Whether an interruption serves the purpose of "snatching" the floor from the other participant, thus threatening their face, encroaching upon their right to speak, and exercising power over them, or is used to support the floor holder, show involvement and interest, can only be determined with the help of the larger context of the interruption, which includes the semantic content of the interaction preceding the instance of interruption, the social relationship between the interrupter and the interruptee, cultural background and the respective personal styles of the two participants, among other factors (James and Clarke, 1993:247). To this should be added the nature of the conversation or task the interactants are involved in, as interruptions might be signs of power exercise only in formal, task-oriented conversations and interactions in which there is competition or conflict (James and Clarke, 1993:244).

Interruption seems to be dominant in research into power-related conversational aspects; however, it is not the only manifestation of power. As has been pointed out above, other aspects such as amount of speech, topic tabling, topic control and questions may also reflect a status or power difference.

Speaking more than one's interlocutor is sometimes a right that a higher status bestows on its holder and, at least in some contexts, can lead to topic and conversation control, expressing one's point of view and, therefore, achieving one's communicative (or other) objectives, while leaving one's interlocutor in a disadvantaged position. Of course, it could be asserted that everything depends on the context and the content of the speaker's intervention, for by the mere fact of speaking extensively one may reveal one's weaknesses and appear less desirable and less powerful in the eyes of the listeners. Moreover, there are situations in which silence, not speech, is a privilege and a sign of power (Tannen, 1995:234). Still, what is intended is that at least in some contexts a larger amount of speech is a sign of self-confidence and assumption of competence and a higher status (James and Drakich, 1993:289-90), that talk is a means of enhancing one's position in a dyad or group (Watts, 1992b) and that amount of talk is the result of successful turn-taking and turn-maintaining and, therefore, a sign of dynamism and a characteristic of powerful participants and group leaders (Ng and Bradac, 1993:77).

Similarly, asking questions apparently compels the person who is expected to answer them to reply in a relevant manner, thus affecting their action, determining the course of the conversation and exerting a kind of control over them (Harris, 1983; Cameron, 1992b). This is clearly the case in some institutionalised situations such as court hearings, police questioning and oral examinations, because judges, police officers and examiners are institutionally authorised to conduct the course of action and to exercise control over their "subjects" through questioning and other strategies (Lakoff, 1990). However, there are other contexts in which the person who asks a question is not in a powerful position: a pupil who asks a teacher, a tourist who asks for directions, or a library user who asks a librarian for specific information, all these would clearly be in a dependent or powerless position because they need the information they seek by means of the question and because, as an expert who can help them, the person they are asking is entitled to some consideration (see French and Raven's expert and information powers above).

Topic control has also been treated in research as a possible manifestation of power and dominance or, at least, as a strategy through which status can be gained and objectives achieved (e.g. Collins and Guetzkow, 1964; Scollon and Scollon, 1981; Grimshaw, 1990; Watts, 1991). Although the concept of "topic" is slippery and almost impossible to define (Wardhaugh, 1985:139; Van Dijk, 1977:119), there seems to be a consensus about its vague definition as "what is talked about" (Moya Guijarro, 1998). The assumption that people talk about "something" and that, at least in casual conversations, they do not fix in advance what they are going to talk about (Sacks et al., 1974; Wardhaugh, 1985) leads to the conclusion that throughout conversation decisions are interactionally made and "topics" are tabled and are either accepted or rejected, talked about with enthusiasm for a long time or dropped immediately or after a short turn. Understanding power as decision making (Dahl, 1961), it seems clear why topic control (deciding what is talked about, conducting the course of topic development and expanding or curtailing topics according to one's interests) has been associated with power or dominance. It is because it allows the participant who chooses the topic to achieve their conversational or real-life goals. These objectives may range from solving an urgent problem to gaining status throughout the conversation by appearing knowledgeable (Watts, 1991:156) or making one's addressee perceive the situation or the world from one's perspective (De Beaugrande and Dressler, 1981).

4. Symmetry and asymmetry in face and power

We have seen that face and power are related to some extent. In addition to the degree of intimacy/distance and the face-threatening potential of a speech act, the choice of a politeness strategy rather than another is determined by the power relationship between the two participants. However, while face is everybody's need, power is only some people's "right" or privilege: while people in general have a self-image they want to maintain, nourish and defend, not everybody has enough status bases to claim, assume and exercise power. Still, there is something they have in common: both face and power have flexible boundaries that can expand or shrink according to the given relationship (of status, intimacy, formality, etc.) between the two participants. Thus, nobody's face can be said to be vulnerable to specific acts, such as criticising or ordering, independently of the situation and the performer of the acts, nor can anybody be said to hold and, therefore, have the right to exercise power, without specifying the kind of situation, interlocutor, etc. that is likely to allow such power perception and exercise. This is why a person can be extremely offended by a particular comment if it is made by a particular person, in a particular social or professional context, while they might overlook it or accept it kind-heartedly if it is made by another (more powerful or beloved) person or in a different context (where there is no risk of losing one's face).

Interactions, therefore, are the product of relationships: relationships of power, intimacy, formality, etc. Relationships, it goes without saying, can be either symmetrical or asymmetrical, and face and power relationships should be no exception. However, the universal assumption that every interlocutor has face seems to contradict this last statement. If everybody has a positive and a negative face, and all the interactants act upon this assumption, it follows that there is a symmetrical face relationship between the two parties to any conversation. In fact, Brown and Levinson (1987:61), among others, maintain that the reason why conversations and social encounters proceed smoothly is that participants mutually pay attention to and respect each other's face because of the "mutual vulnerability of face", hence a symmetrical/reciprocal relationship. However, when it comes to the flexibility of face and power mentioned above, it follows that one participant has more or less face, more or less power than the other. Due to differences of status, role, personality traits, etc. either one or both participants may rightly or wrongly assume that one's or the other's face needs or deserves more or less attention and deference. This is why in some relationships we find, for example, face-threatening acts, such as giving orders, going in only one direction. It is the same for the face-boosting acts of the other (one participant paying lip service and enhancing the other's positive face, while the latter does not respond reciprocally).

Symmetry or asymmetry in these relationships is the result of differences in outside social evaluations, that is, the common operations of summing up or subtracting points according to the score in socially significant criteria, and also of the personal assumptions of participants about themselves and others and the relationship between the two sides. Naturally, these assumptions may coincide or diverge. Thus, if A and B are interacting and A makes an evaluation of their bases of power, in other words "status characteristics" in the sense of "...any characteristic that is socially valued, is meaningful, and has differentially evaluated states..." (James and Drakich, 1993:286), and concludes that there is no power or status differential between the two parties, but keeps in mind that the lack of intimacy and, say, the short time of acquaintance make their relationship quite distant, A will probably tend to use negative politeness or off-record strategies so as not to appear as encroaching upon B's right of autonomy. If participant B makes a similar evaluation, comes up with a similar result and approaches or responds to A using similar face-preserving strategies (negative or off-record politeness), the outcome will most probably be a symmetrical relationship in which each party receives as much as they give and is treated on the same terms. Otherwise, if B, instead of coinciding with A in their assumptions about the situation and the relationship, sees that B is more powerful than A and, therefore, thinks B has the right to use bald on-record strategies, A will feel insulted and the observer or spectator of the interaction between A and B, in this case, will notice an asymmetrical relationship in which one party (A) loses face because they receive less face attention than they think is due. Similar problems can always arise as a result of differences in assumptions, especially about the relative power and distance. Scollon and Scollon (1981:186) illustrate this in the table reproduced below:

(As mentioned above, P stands for power, D for distance and R for rank of imposition. The new abbreviations S1 and S2 stand for speaker 1 and speaker 2, respectively).

Table 2: Possible combinations of assumptions and their symmetrical or asymmetrical results (source: Scollon and Scollon, 1981:186).

S1 assumption	S2 assumption	Result
+ P +/-D bald on record (asymmetrical)	+ P +/-D negative politeness/ off record	OK
	- P + D (no response)	Disagree on P, insult
	-P-D bald on record/ positive politeness	Insult to S1's +P
-P + D negative politeness/ Off record (symmetrical deference politeness)	+ P +/- D bald on record	Insult to S1's P
	- P + D negative politeness/ off record	OK
	- P - D (no response)	D is wrong, standoffish
- P - D bald on record/ positive politeness (symmetrical solidarity politeness)	+ P +/- D negative politeness	Confuses S1 about P/D
	- P + D (no response)	P or D is wrong
	-P - D bald on record/positive politeness	OK

Not only in such interaction problems is the importance of participants' assumptions evident, but also in smooth interactions, where nothing seems to go wrong. Similarly, not only can we find asymmetry in interactions in which different assumptions give rise to misunderstandings and disruption of diplomatic harmony, but also in the ones where social and interpersonal harmony is maintained and safe. This is because in many situations and relationships the very harmony, stability and lack of conflict is the result of an established, imposed or accepted asymmetrical relationship, an asymmetry that is sanctioned, institutionalised and perpetuated through socialisation.

In an interaction between a teacher and a student, for example, there may be an imbalance in the effort that each party makes to keep the other's face (the heaviest part, of course, corresponding to the less powerful, the student), an imbalance which means asymmetry (because what the teacher is institutionally allowed to tell the student, do to them or make them do cannot be responded to reciprocally). However, smoothness can still continue to be the dominant characteristic of the interaction between the two.

It is this kind of asymmetrical relationship that is of interest in the study on which this book is based: the extent to which one participant or group of participants makes use of communicative strategies and means, especially the ones that are socially significant and related to status characteristics, while the other participant or group has less access to such resources. This asymmetry, especially if maintained without any friction or conflict, is normally a reflection of (assumptions about) power and status differentials. This is because, during an interaction, when a participant is, for example, continuously interrupted or questioned without being given the right to do the same, this shows an asymmetrical power relationship that gives the interrupting or interrogating party more communicative rights and privileges, which, in their turn, have origin in institutional, social, organisational, or interpersonal qualifications.

Since the subject of the present study is face and power relationships in the interaction between native and non-native speakers, asymmetry in face-preserving strategies and in the use of communicative strategies with power connotations could be revealing. Other social attributes being supposedly equal, if the factor of nativity makes non-native speakers pay attention to their native interlocutors' face more than vice versa, or if this very factor gives native speakers the right to control the conversation, direct its course, decide what should be talked about, interrupt their non-native interlocutors more freely, etc., if such a manifestation is found, it will provide us with significant insight into native and non-native speakers' assumptions about their respective status and their relationship.

Chapter 2
An empirical study

1. Introduction

Like other studies investigating and analysing politeness phenomena and power relationships among specific communities, social groups, cultures, etc. (e.g. Leet-Pellegrini, 1979; Tannen, 1990 and 1995; Ulijn and Li, 1995; Watts, 1991; Harris, 1995; James and Clarke, 1993; Zimmerman and West, 1975; Brown and Levinson, 1978, etc.), the study reported in this book intends to tackle face and power relationships between members of two (culturally and linguistically distinct) groups in order to verify how face considerations are taken into account, how face attention is manifested in linguistic output and communicative strategies, whether assumptions about face and power are shared, and whether and how interactional patterns, if there are any, are based on such assumptions. The two groups referred to above are native and non-native speakers of English. It goes without saying that under both labels, "native" and "non-native", lies a set of different social classes, gender groups, cultural, regional and national characteristics. Under the rubric of native speakers of English we can find American, British, Australian or Irish speakers, Afro-Americans, Anglo-Saxon Americans, native speakers of Hispanic origins, second-generation immigrants in general who acquired English as their native language, and so on and so forth. Under the rubric of non-native speakers of English, because of the widespread use of this language as a foreign language all over the world, we can find a variety of cultures, ethnic groups and nationalities (Asian, African, European, South American; Whites and Blacks; Mediterranean, Sub-Saharan, Caribbean; Arabs, Latin and Slav people, etc.) and speakers of English with different personal and learning experiences with the English language and its native speakers (non-native speakers who have learnt the language in a country where English is a second or foreign language, people who learnt it in English-speaking countries, people who learnt it because of cultural influence and interest, people who learnt it out of a professional necessity, people who studied the language structurally, and others who learnt it functionally and in context, etc.).

This means that the two groups to which the participants in this study belong are too large to be dealt with in a wholly representative manner, and also that other factors and dimensions of self identity and group membership may be at play in the interactions to be studied and not only the nativity dimension. Since the self as "a psychological construct... is seen as an integrated, hierarchically organised set of self-attributes or components... that defines how an individual perceives him- or herself and influences perceptions and social behaviour" (Hecht *et al.*, 1993:36), and since membership is multidimensional (gender, racial, occupational, mental dimensions, etc.), it obviously follows that native and non-native participants will probably be acting upon assumptions based on aspects of their identity and group membership which are related to dimensions other than the nativity dimension. However, it should be kept in mind that not all identity traits are always significant and influential in all kinds of interactions and contexts (Hecht *et al.*, 1993). While job or position in a professional hierarchy, for example, may be determinant of how an interaction will proceed in a given situation (e.g. an interaction between a resident doctor and an intern during a session of skill evaluation), it might not necessarily be of importance in another (e.g. during a football match that is held every weekend and in which managers as well as workers of a company take part).

2. Hypothesis

Given the fact that the subject of this study is face and power relationships and that the participants are native and non-native speakers, and bearing in mind that there is no significant difference between participants in terms of other overt status characteristics (race, sex, age, attire, etc.), it is assumed that the fact of being a native or a non-native speaker of English will emerge as a factor of great significance in terms of power potential and, consequently, in dominance and politeness strategies. Everything being apparently equal, being a native speaker of the language which is the medium of interaction is assumed to be a source of power. Both the native and non-native participants are expected to assume that the native party is one position up in the power ranking and is therefore entitled to relatively more self-image enhancement and to dominant conversational behaviour.

It follows that in the dyads object of study there will be a high-status party (the native speaker) and a low-status one (the non-native speaker) in interaction for the first time. The fact that this interaction is a first encounter between the two participants is likely to result in relatively more distance in the approach they adopt towards each other. Taken at face value this means that there will be a +D (distance) +P (the native speaker being more powerful) relationship and, as a consequence, a tendency to use negative politeness strategies by the non-native speaker and on-record or positive politeness strategies by the native speaker; hence an asymmetrical face relationship originating in the power asymmetry. This assumption is based on Brown and Levinson's (1978/1987) face theory. The authors claim that in a distanced relationship (+D because of the formality of the context or lack of previous contact or intimacy) the interactants tend to use politeness strategies which are aimed at showing respect for one's interlocutor's autonomy and desire not to be imposed or encroached upon. In an encounter between two unacquainted passengers, for example, it is not common to find positive politeness manifestations such as flat requests, teasing or joking. Rather, interactants are expected to take their social distance into account and avoid impositions, apologise for the least face-threatening act (e.g. dropping the newspaper on one's companion's shoes) and make polite preparative moves for the least imposing request (e.g. asking one's companion to draw the bus window curtain). In a power asymmetry relationship (+P), on the other hand, Brown and Levinson claim that the less powerful party will tend to use negative politeness strategies—because the higher one's interlocutor's status is, the more freedom of imposition they require—while the more powerful party could avail themselves of on-record or positive politeness strategies, as they assume their interlocutor's face deserves less attention and think they could impose on them or threaten their face without risks. This is the kind of relationship and, therefore, politeness strategy difference we can find, for instance, between an employer and their employee.

However, this assumption, applied to the present study of interaction between native and non-native speakers, might sound too simplistic. Indeed, besides the nativity element there might be more important factors, such as peer closeness and gender similarity, which are possible sources of a more solidarity-based interaction. That is to say, distance, which is the result of meeting one's interlocutor for the first time in this study, and power differential, which, we assume, is the result of nativity, might be reduced or even overridden by the sense of closeness and solidarity that two young people of the same sex are likely to feel towards each other. In sum, there are likely to be two opposite forces at work during the interaction; both solidarity and power.

It has been found that some individuals and groups are more prone to competition, conflict and, therefore, to power exercise, while others tend to place more importance on emotional support, harmony and the expression of solidarity and affection (e.g. men and women, respectively in Leet-Pellegrini, 1979, and in Tannen, 1993 and 1995). Similarly, it has been argued that the nature of the activity/task being performed and the context in which it is performed may determine whether and the extent to which power or cooperation is at issue, with formal task activities being more likely to give rise to competition and power struggle (James and Drakich, 1993).

Therefore, since there are two parts in every recorded conversation—one in which participants get to know each other and one in which they discuss a topic—it is anticipated that there will be at least a slight difference between the two parts in terms of solidarity and power manifestations. In the first part solidarity is expected to override power asymmetry because there should be no competitiveness. On the other hand, in the second part, especially if the participants have different opinions, there will probably be more attempts to enhance one's self-image and to exercise power because discussion in general or the specific topic itself may be suggestive of a competitive interaction. In the first case the relationship is expected to be symmetrical and reciprocal in terms of face-nourishing strategies and the participants are anticipated to have more or less equal opportunities to gain interactional status and enhance their self-image. In the second case, however, we expect there will be an imbalance/asymmetry in power relationships and, therefore, more power-exercising strategies or acts from the part of the native speaker. The latter, therefore, is expected to hold the floor longer, to table topics, to interrupt more often, to ask more questions, etc., as these aspects of interpersonal communication have been associated with power exercise in linguistic and sociological research.

Some researchers doubt the correlation between communicative strategies and phenomena such as interruption, volubility/taciturnity/silence, topic tabling and directness/indirectness on the one hand and power/subordination on the other (Tannen, 1993 and James and Clarke, 1993, among others), or at least distinguish between contexts and groups in which the correlation may hold and the ones in which it may not (Rogers and Jones (1975), as cited in James and Clarke (1993:244), for example, found a correlation between interruptions and dominance in male–male dyads but not in female–female ones). Nonetheless, many other researchers corroborate the above correlation. Watts (1991:156), for example, claims that successful topic tabling (raising a topic which is accepted by the other interlocutor(s)) enhances the speaker's status in what he elsewhere calls the "emergent network" in an interaction, and that it may be a sign of power exercise, especially if the tabled topic is initially not perceived as interesting by the other interlocutor(s) (1991:208). McCall and Cousins (1990:29,46) relate volubility, directives, decision making and even bodily relaxation with dominance and power, and so does Grimshaw (1990:211) for floor holding, topic control and interruptions. James and Drakich (1993:289-290), in their turn, provide an explanation for the finding that higher-status participants, at least in formal-task-oriented activities, tend to speak and interrupt more than their lower-status interlocutors do:

Higher-status individuals, then, since they feel more competent, will be more willing to contribute to the interaction than will lower-status individuals. They will also tend to be less tolerant of, and less willing to wait for, contributions from lower-status individuals, since they perceive those individuals as less competent at the task. Lower-status individuals, on the other hand, expect higher-status individuals to be more competent than they are themselves. Thus, they encourage the participation of the higher-status individuals, they tend to wait for them to make contributions, and they are less willing to contribute to the interaction themselves. The effect is, of course, that higher-status individuals make significantly more verbal contributions and consequently take up significantly more time talking.

Applied to native/non-native interaction, this explanation seems to support our assumption that native speakers will perceive themselves and will be perceived by their interlocutors as more competent in the interaction, especially at the topic discussion stage, because of their higher linguistic and communicative competence, which no non-native speaker is likely to reach, however high their competence in English might be.[1] Some researchers go further and claim that native speakers, when interacting with non-native people, assume "the right to dominate and control" (Roberts *et al.*, 1992:35) and may even underestimate non-native speakers' competence in English and, consequently, may make negative value judgement about their intelligence or motivation (Ibid:49). This is often the case in gate-keeping encounters where a native speaker holds an institutional or hierarchical position that gives them the right and power to decide whether a non-native speaker, or a member of a minority group in general, can have access to a job, promotion, scholarship, etc.

Nevertheless, it is not expected that all interactions between native and non-native speakers will be influenced by possible negative judgements or the native participant's assumption of a higher status. Such stereotypes as well as the assumption of the "right" to dominate may be active only in competitive or conflictive contexts. In friendly conversations between two persons who have no professional relationship and no obvious interests at stake, and who are close to each other in terms of age, gender, or another identity component, the native speaker's assumption of higher status, as has been mentioned above, may be overridden by solidarity-oriented drives. Thus, in addition to, or rather instead of, manifestations of power exercise, the interactions may reveal accommodation strategies such as tempo adaptation (the native speaker speaking more slowly for the non-native interlocutor to follow more easily), the use (by native speakers of English) of words and expressions in Spanish, the mother tongue of most of the non-native participants in this study and the language spoken in the geographical setting of the interactions, simplification of the language, or phatic questions (checking if the addressee understands before continuing). Such

---

1. This, it should be noted, is a questionable statement, as it is perfectly possible to find cases where a non-native speaker is more linguistically and communicatively competent than some native speakers and as even the concept or myth, as some authors would say, of nativity has been challenged and questioned (see Rajagopalan, 1997).

accommodation strategies are indeed commonly observed in second-language research and research into communication between second-language learners and native speakers or teachers (Ellis, 1985).

Furthermore, as power and status may be based on a variety of social, cultural, and interpersonal factors, and since the conversations analysed in this study took place in Spain, the home country of the majority of the non-native participants, these non-native speakers may have felt "more at home" than their native interlocutors. This means that they could find in the context or the setting of the interaction itself a legitimate source of status or, at least, a sufficient reason to feel at ease during the conversation and to neutralise the factor of nativity. In fact, in a quite different field, namely team sports, it is common for the home team to assume a more powerful position and, therefore, expect and be expected to win the match. It goes without saying that human interaction, unlike sports, is not a competition or a match to be won. Still, the fact of "playing a home game" should be taken into consideration as a potential source of power allowing the non-native speaker (the Spanish participants in this study) to assume a higher position.

3. Methodology

As has been pointed out above, the data on which this study is based consist of twenty audio-recorded face-to-face conversations, the parties to which were one native and one non-native speaker of English. Data collection was completed in Madrid in March 2001.

Being aware of the fact that participants in any interaction "carry with them" different aspects that have something to do with background and group membership, and seeing that the aim of this study is to examine the role and importance, if any, of the nativity/non-nativity dimension, an attempt was made from an early stage of the study, the participant-selection stage, to neutralise the role/influence of factors that are not of interest to this research (gender, age, educational level, etc.). Dyads were formed with one native speaker and one non-native speaker. The two were of approximately the same age (there was a small difference of five or six years) and of the same sex (all the dyads were either male–male or female–female, with no mixed-sex dyads). Both had a university education (some participants were still studying at university while others had graduated). As for their respective social status, it was assumed that neither of the two had a significantly higher social status than the other (most of the participants were still university students, and all of them completed or were completing their studies at public universities). It should be admitted, however, that for such complex and sometimes latent factors as social status or social class no technique was used to measure the differences between participants in a more or less objective manner. Social status equality was assumed first because the participants were complete strangers to one another, which meant they knew nothing about the social class of their interlocutors or of their families, and second because there were no apparent differences in clothing standards, nor were there any status-conveying items/belongings in sight, such as vehicles, fashionable handbags, expensive briefcases, etc.

It should also be conceded that the fact that there was no significant difference in age and that all the interactions were same-sex does not mean that age and gender as meaningful factors were totally neutralised. These factors, like other group-membership dimensions, may have either a differentiation or a solidarity effect: If A is the same age or the same sex as B and gender is a significant factor in the situation, A will probably feel close to B, will tend to approach him or her and will transmit the idea that the two are similar (they belong to the same group) (Brown and Levinson, 1987). However, if A is male and B female or if A and B observe a significant age difference between them, they will most probably be more reserved in their dealing with each other and their interaction will likely be more deferential, tactful and distanced than in the former case. This is, of course, an overgeneralisation in need of specification and distinction of different possible patterns that are likely to arise because of the interaction and combination of certain personal, social and cultural factors. But this over-generalisation is meant to draw attention to the fact that social identity traits can work in two different directions (positively or negatively) and that if one direction is suspended the other might not necessarily be suspended at the same time.

Twenty-one people were selected to participate in the conversations (ten females and eleven males, mostly of American, British and Spanish nationalities). Before commencing data collection, the participants were briefly informed of what participation would involve and their consent was sought for their interaction to be audio recorded. When they were contacted by telephone to arrange the recording, they were individually informed that they would meet a non-native speaker of English (in the case of native speaker participants) or an English native speaker (for non-native speaker participants) of the same sex and approximately the same age, that first they would get to know each other, just like in any normal situation, and then choose and discuss a topic from a list provided by the researcher. The list included the following questions:

1. Do you think we live in a society of human rights?
2. Is humanity changing for better or for worse?
3. "Most of what is called love is sexual desire." What do you think?
4. Is your society sexist?
5. Are you for or against abortion/euthanasia?
6. Do you think religion is the opiate of the people?
7. Do you think football is a modern "disease"? A kind of drug?
8. Do you think your national or regional diet is the best?
9. Which is the best: the American, British or Spanish educational system?
10. Do you think more and more people are becoming obsessed with fashion?
11. Which do you think will be the world language in the 21st century: English or Spanish?

No clues were given to any of the participants as to the subject, hypothesis or purpose of the study. They were merely asked, as volunteers, to take part in two conversations each for a linguistic study without specifying the linguistic field or the subject of the research. The participants would ask if the study was interested in accent differences or grammatical errors, and the answer would be that it was not, that it was an attempt to study communication between native and non-native speakers of English, that the two parties of each dyad were expected to meet each other, behave in a natural manner and speak without any restrictions of time or topics. Although they were provided with a list of topics, these were just suggestions and participants were encouraged to choose (an)other topic(s) if none of the ones included in the list were of interest to them. Some of the Spanish participants were self-consciously worried about their performance with native speakers of English. Possibly out of modesty, they would say that they had not spoken English for a long time, that their pronunciation was "horrible" or that they made a lot of mistakes, etc. They were assured that the purpose of the study had nothing to do with grammatical errors or with native or foreign accents, and that the interaction was going to be relaxed and informal, so there would be no need to worry.

Before the two participants in each interaction were introduced to one another, the researcher met with them individually and reminded them that they were expected to get to know each other, as they would do in a real-life situation (in fact, the encounter was an authentic first meeting, except that in this case it was initiated by a non-participant observer for the sake of a linguistic study), and then freely discuss a topic, without paying any attention to the researcher or to any event that might occur while they were speaking (e.g. knocking on the door, a phone call or the sound of the audiotape recorder when one side of the tape was finished). Six conversations were recorded in a lecturer's office at the University of Alcala (Madrid, Spain), four in two private school classrooms (but not in a classroom situation) and the rest in a translation office that was very similar to the lecturer's office. In the first office there was a desk and the two participants sat on one side of the desk (facing each other) and the researcher sat on the opposite side. In the second setting, in each classroom there was a large table surrounded with chairs and the participants were sitting either opposite each other or side by side. In the third setting (the translation office) there was a table and two chairs (one opposite the other) for the participants.

The researcher was not present during all the conversations and only attended the first six. During the conversations the researcher attended, the participants barely looked at him, except in one case in which a female native speaker was looking at her interlocutor most of the time but would look at the researcher from time to time, thus including him intentionally as one of the addressees. The participants did not talk to the researcher, except in one case when a non-native speaker asked him if it was time to choose a topic for discussion, to which the researcher replied: "Feel free." The researcher was silent throughout, and sometimes he looked at the participants to see if there were any nonverbal patterns or peculiar behaviour (but did not take notes, so as not to make the participants self-conscious or distract them). Sometimes the researcher looked at the audiotape recorder to check if it was running correctly. During the four conversations recorded in the private school classrooms, since two conversations were taking place simultaneously, the researcher kept moving from one classroom to another, sitting in one room for five or ten minutes to see how the conversation was proceeding and then leave to sit in the other for approximately the same duration, without doing anything that would draw the participants' attention or distract them. During the rest of the conversations (in the second office) the researcher did not sit with the participants but only entered to make sure that the recorder was working.

The conversations lasted from a quarter of an hour to slightly more than half an hour. However, no recording covered more than half an hour, as turning the sixty-minute tape would have caused the loss of part of the conversations and could have made the participants more aware of the tape recorder. In such cases part of the conversation, the ending, was not recorded. In one case the conversation continued for approximately a quarter of an hour after the recorder had stopped (i.e. after the tape had reached its end), and in two other cases, always after the recording had stopped, the researcher was asked about the situation in his country of origin or for his opinion (it is worth noting that in both cases it was the native speaker who asked these questions). The fact that the researcher was asked to give his opinion only after the recording was completed shows the extent to which the two participants acted upon the assumption that the researcher was not included in the interaction in spite of his physical presence: he was a silent, non-participating observer.

As has been pointed out above, an audiotape recorder was used in this study as a means of data collection. No microphones or lapel microphones were used and no multi-track audio recording was utilised. A small tape recorder was placed near the two participants; it was visible but did not dominate the scene.

It goes without saying that this choice, like any other, has its consequences: recording a conversation by means of a simple tape recorder instead of a simple video tape, or independent video cameras, or split-screen video-recording, etc. can make the observation less comprehensive and less accurate. This choice causes a loss of information which is necessary to have a clearer and more comprehensive understanding and, therefore, interpretation of what goes on in an interpersonal interaction. Kinesic signs such as nodding, shaking one's head, frowning, moving aside, coming closer, stepping forward or backward, and using hand gestures, eye contact and movement, etc., all of which may be essential to the way an interaction proceeds and the way it may be interpreted, are unfortunately lost. Thus, the researcher is left with only a partial record of what happened during the interaction. Furthermore, following transcription of the recorded data, we are left with a lifeless body of symbols that Rommetveit (1974:62, as cited in Markova, 1978:8) equates with a "cadaver of speech":

> ...what is preserved in typed transcripts of face-to-face dialogues is in fact only the "cadaver of speech".

However, knowing beforehand that even a cadaver can be and is usually studied and analysed, and being aware of the fact that

> however the data is collected and however negotiated the agendas may have been, when the researcher produces representations of the research for an outside audience, control of the data and its meanings shift very much towards the researcher. (Cameron, 1992 a:132),

the audiotape recorded data will be relied on and referred to as the unique source of objective information. Moreover, in spite of the shortcomings that audiotape recording inherently implies, at least there are some comforting arguments that researchers like Sacks (1984:26) provide in favour of this data elicitation technique:

> I started to work with tape-recorded conversations. Such materials had a single virtue, that I could replay them. I could transcribe them somewhat and study them extendedly—however long it might take. The tape-recorded materials constituted a "good enough" record of what happened. It was not from any large interest in language or from some theoretical formulation of what should be studied that I started with tape-recorded conversations, but simply because I would get my hands on it and I could study it again and again, and also, consequently, because others could look at what I had studied and make of it what they could, if, for example, they wanted to be able to disagree with me.

Turnbull (1995, as cited in Turnbull and Saxton, 1997), among others, recommends that research into social acts be carried out using spontaneous conversational data, data that occurs naturally, is not elicited by a third outside party (the researcher or observer) and is collected while the participants are unaware of being recorded or of being the object of research. This, however, contradicts ethical considerations that equate surreptitious recording with an unauthorised intrusion into the privacy of other people, which is likely to result in mistrust or even hostility towards future researchers who need to approach and study any group of participants (once a researcher is discovered using underhanded tactics, trust in them and, consequently, in other (innocent) researchers will be lost, and once trust is lost it could be lost forever). An observer cannot have access to authentic and spontaneous social and linguistic behaviour unless they use surreptitious elicitation techniques, and this can only be done to the detriment of ethics and trust. On the other hand, overt recording techniques might "inhibit or change spontaneous behaviour" (Roger, 1989:80), hence what researchers call the "observer's paradox".

In this study, before they began their interaction the participants were informed that they were going to be recorded and they were aware of the presence of the tape recorder (it was visible). However, they did not pay much attention to it. After the recording the participants were asked whether they preferred the tapes to be destroyed after the transcription and analysis and all of them replied that they did not mind.

As mentioned earlier, the participants were asked to get to know each other for some time and then choose a topic and discuss it. In a sense and to some extent this was a "task" assigned to them; however, it was not a formal one, at least judging from James and Drakich's (1993:287) definition:

> Formal task activities are defined in sociology as activities in which a pair or group of individuals come together to accomplish specific instrumental goals such as solving a problem together or making a joint decision. These tasks require participants to exchange ideas, to take each other's opinions into account as they work at the task, and to complete the task successfully by producing a single, collective outcome such as a committee decision.

The participants in this study were asked to "come together"; they were given instructions to do something, some activity, but they were not asked to come out with any results or to make any joint or individual reports or decisions. Therefore, the task assigned to and performed by them cannot be categorised as a formal task. However, nor can it be considered a "non-task-oriented activity", in James and Drakich's terms, because it was not "naturally occurring casual conversation" (1993:287). It is a kind of in-between situation/task: what James and Drakich call an "informal task activity". In fact, the two authors set the task of getting to know one another as an example of informal tasks. On the other hand, there might be a subtle difference in the degree of formality between the first task (getting to know each other) and the second one (topic discussion) in each recorded interaction: discussion, however relaxed and casual it might be, is likely to be slightly more formal than small talk or social talk. Indeed, people in their first encounters tend to avoid contentious discussions of whether their society is sexist, for example, or whether religion is the opiate of the people; rather, they tend to phatically or referentially speak about neutral and safe topics such as the weather (an example of an "ice breaker" often given in Anglo-Saxon linguistic literature). However, this does not deny the possibility, if not the fact, that many first encounters smoothly move from getting-to-know-each-other talk into speaking (not necessarily disagreeing) about social phenomena or political issues. A common example is the discussion of language learning and language differences among native and non-native speakers even in the first encounter.

The choice of these two tasks (one more casual than the other) was intended to make it possible to study the behaviour of native and non-native speakers of English in a situation so close to spontaneous, informal talk (the part of getting to know each other) and another that might give rise to competition, disagreement or conflict and, therefore, power exercise and struggle for power. The discussion of topics such as sexism, religion, national diets, the death penalty, abortion, etc. is likely to trigger the desire to enhance one's position in a dyad or group, especially for those participants who have a lower threshold of competitiveness, the ones who tend to see activities as involving conflict, competition and power interests more easily than others (e.g. men in comparison with women, according to Leet-Pellegrini, 1979). It was also intended to make it possible to compare two slightly different tasks and verify the extent to which the formality of the task and the conflict potential of the topic could make a difference in terms of face attention and power exercise and possible reactions to that exercise.

4. Transcription

It seems that it is no exaggeration to affirm that, once transcribed, a recorded conversation is but the "cadaver of speech" (Rommetveit, 1974:62, as cited in Markova, 1978:8). Indeed, in addition to gestures, body movements and facial expressions that are omitted when we choose to audiotape record, the very transcription (the transformation of a spoken message into a written one) implies the loss, if not distortion and manipulation, of a considerable amount of information. Different conventions and techniques have been devised to render the spoken text into a written transcript as faithfully and accurately as possible. However, they are and will always be insufficient and lacking in accuracy and detail. This is because the spoken utterance in context is easier to understand and interpret, as it is normally preceded, accompanied and followed by other signs, the variation of which may give rise to a variety of meanings. The word "Hello!", for example, if transcribed as above, will mean nothing but a greeting in a language called English. However, the mere transcription of the word leads to the loss of many contextual and kinesic signs that would assist in obtaining more meanings out of it or, at least, decide which of the potential meanings is more likely to be the intended message:

> A wide span in pitch, as where speaker A meets speaker B and says 'Hello' in a way which starts high in the normal speaking range or even in the 'squeak' range, indicates an attitude. If said with a smile or a breathy quality, this might be interpreted as happy or excited. If, in addition, eyebrows are raised and eyes are wide open, it might be excitedly surprised. If instead of the breathy voice and the smile we replace it with turned-down corners of the mouth, it might be disagreeably surprised. If, on the other hand, A meets B and if it is accompanied by friendly gestures such as a smile and a warm tone of voice, the expectation is a warm response. If it is uttered on a low fall the speaker is declining to expose any positive attitude. (McCall and Cousins, 1990:41-42)

This long list of ifs, which can readily be added to, is but an example of the long list of possible personal, interpersonal, social and cultural meanings that the act of transcribing omits because, unfortunately, there is no efficient way to represent tone of voice, pitch, facial expressions and other verbal and nonverbal signs without affecting readability. What is more, if a single word like "hello" can be loaded with such a variety of meanings, we can only imagine the amount of information which is lost when a longer stretch of speech or an entire conversation is transcribed. If prosodic features and contextual explanations are included in the transcribed body for every utterance or intervention (that is, if every speech turn is accompanied by extra information about tone, intonation, facial expressions, body movement, etc.), the result will most probably be a grain of transcribed conversation buried in an overflowing sea of marginal specifications and descriptions of how things are said. What is worse is that some researchers, instead of explanations written in plain language, opt for complicated technical symbols to account for prosody, simultaneous speech, pauses, etc., which render it practically impossible to read, let alone understand, the text (as readers tend to read and immediately forget about the transcription conventions, or find it difficult to incorporate the code symbols into the meaningful linguistic items):

> Given CA's [Conversation Analysis] openness to new detail, certain readability problems may arise in the presentation of CA transcriptions to readers of written research. Phonetic renderings also bring readability problems; and any transcription system may face trade-offs between specification sufficient for professionals and readability by laypersons. (Hopper, 1989:55)

Besides the information loss to which transcription leads and the problems of readability that are posed by transcription conventions that are excessively technical and specific, there are other problems that are related to understanding what is recorded and interpreting it in the "right" way before transcribing it. In the present study, since one participant in every dyad was a native speaker of English and the other non-native, there were points in conversations where the researcher/transcriber, a non-native speaker of English and Spanish, had difficulties making out what was said. This was the case for a range of different reasons, the most common being the following:

- Fast speech tempo or peculiar accent of the native participant,
- Non-native speaker's idiosyncratic pronunciation,
- Use of Spanish words with an anglicised pronunciation (mother tongue transfer),
- Proper names which are unknown to the researcher,
- Overlapping speech or a very low tone of voice.

To overcome these problems the researcher replayed the recordings many times, trying to understand the unintelligible utterances in light of the context and the limited knowledge about the participants, and when this failed, the assistance of other listeners was sought. Still, there are some unintelligible utterances that are indicated by question marks within parentheses. Another problem was related to the linear presentation of the conversation, and, more specifically, to speech turn beginning and ending. In some cases, because of the difficulty to define speech turns (Edelsky, 1993:210), a stretch of speech could either be represented as part of the same (interrupted) turn or as different, successive turns, as in the following example:

S1: And you take classes or...?

S2: No, not taking classes, I've just had a teacher but it was English in general, no?

S1: Uh huh

S2: because I don't think that I have enough level to::: to:::

S1: to (?)...

S2: learn about businesses. English only, no? } but I left it at the
S1:   Aha

moment because he couldn't ...give more English classes, no? }
S1:   Uh huh

<u>And I was very enthusiastic about working in an enterprise</u>, so I'm not ...just at the moment, I have not ...clear ideas about (????) in the future } at the moment } Waiting for
S1:   Aha   You're waiting for inspiration

inspiration, no? } I have no inspiration at the moment.
(laugh tog.)

The underlined text can be represented as different turns (other than S2's initial turn), especially "waiting for inspiration, no?" and "I have no inspiration at the moment" because they seem to be responses to the other participant's (S1's) utterances. However, they can still be reported as components of one discontinuous turn, especially as such turns are common when there is a cooperative sentence completion (Wardhaugh, 1985) and a joint topic construction (Watts, 1991:140). Nevertheless, in some cases the choice was arbitrary (relying on the researcher's intuition). Also arbitrary was the use of punctuation, especially full stops and commas, because the spoken conversation and the written text have different conventions and are hardly comparable. Still, full stops in the transcription indicate pauses which are relatively longer than the ones indicated with commas. The transcription conventions used are as follows:

<u>Transcription Conventions:</u>

- Numbers: They are landmarks (usually indicating turn shift) for later reference,
- *Italics*: Words in Spanish or with a Spanish-sounding pronunciation,
- **Bold type**: emphasis,
- } : Simultaneous speech (the upper utterance always occurring before the lower one),
- Uh huh/Uhum/Aha: back-channel responses ("simultaneous speech that is used by the listener to signal continued attendance to the speaker such as 'uh huh' or 'yeah'" (Roger, 1989:92)),
- Um/er/eh: Pause fillers,
- ::: : Long vowels (sometimes used as pause fillers),
- ? : Question mark (usually indicating a rising intonation),
- (???) : Unintelligible utterance,
- ... : Pause,

- (...)   : Ellipsis (left-out utterances),
- (Laugh): Laughter (one participant),
- (Laugh tog.): Both participants laughing.

5. Analysis

Once the data were transcribed, the conversations were analysed in terms of politeness strategies used by each participant and power relationships between the native and non-native speakers. First, a thorough quantitative and qualitative analysis of two whole conversations was conducted and subsequently a more general, quantitative analysis of the twenty dyadic interactions. The focus was on communicative strategies that enhance one's interlocutor's positive face (praise, attention to the interlocutor's interests, approval, agreement, etc.), communicative strategies that show deference (hedges, apologies, over-generalisations, etc.) and face-threatening acts (such as interruption, criticism, disapproval, etc.). Special attention was paid to the resultant interactional relationship, that is, the balance/imbalance between the two participants in terms of what Bayraktaroglu (1991:15) calls face-boosting acts, Brown and Levinson's (1987) face-threatening acts, and also House and Kasper's (1981) downgraders (devices that serve to reduce the face-threatening potential) and upgraders (devices that serve the opposite purpose). Such acts were classified and counted to see whose self-image is enhanced more and whose suffers damage, if any, or at least does not receive as much attention. This was expected to be related to power a/symmetry between the participants.

The most important type of face-threatening intervention, it is assumed, is interruption, because it is an "illicit" intervention into somebody's speech turn, which often prevents them from "setting up and/or supporting a position" (Watts, 1991:208). What is normally meant by interruption is simultaneous speech, although, as James and Clarke (1993:237) claim, there is the possibility of an utterance performing the function of interruption even without simultaneous speech. Researchers distinguish between simultaneous speech which is interruption (intentional) and that which is just overlap (unintentional) (Murata, 1994:386) and between marked interruptions, which occur unexpectedly at a clause boundary or before the end of an utterance, and unmarked ones, that is, natural, sometimes cooperative, turn switches (Ulijn and Li, 1995:592). Zimmerman and West (1975:114) also distinguish between overlaps and interruptions, albeit, it should be observed, in quite abstract terms:

> In our view, overlaps are instances of simultaneous speech where a speaker other than the current speaker begins to speak at or very close to a possible transition place in a current speaker's utterance (i.e., within the boundaries of the last word). It is this proximity to a legitimate point of speaker alternation that leads us to distinguish overlaps from interruptions... An interruption in this context, then is seen as penetrating the boundaries of a unit type prior to the last lexical constituent that could define a possible terminal boundary...

In this study what counts as an interruption is any turn-taking by the second speaker at a non-Transition Relevant Place other than back-channel utterances and supportive or cooperative interruptions. The distinction between rapport-oriented interruptions and power-oriented ones is essential because the first kind can show affection, concern and solidarity, while the latter are normally manifestations of power exercise and might be seen as tactless or impolite conversational behaviour (Ulijn and Li, 1995:598; Goldberg, 1990). This means that, although apparently both kinds are "blatant interventions" (in Watts', 1991, terms), when it comes to the solidarity/power axis, they take opposite directions: cooperative "interruptions" are focused on the addressee's face, while real power-oriented interruptions are focused on the interrupter's interests.

To determine which is which may be quite difficult at times, as the only certain way to find out whether an interruption is supportive or disruptive/competitive is by verifying the interrupter's intention and the interruptee's perception (Murata, 1994:390). What is more, apparently supportive interventions can be misleading as "one can agree with what is being said as a precursor to taking over the floor" (James and Clarke, 1993:242), and as completions of one's interlocutor's sentences may "indicate a desire to take over the conversation because they can be used quite easily to engineer [non-supportive] interruptions" (Wardhaugh, 1985:135).

In addition to interruptions, the study examines other presumed manifestations of power such as floor holding, topic control and length of speech turn. Turn length and amount of speech were measured by counting words, not by the time spent by every speaker holding the floor. This was not done because of any methodological preference but because of the lack of data-processing tools at the time the study was conducted.

However straightforward and simple it might seem, the method chosen is not free from difficulties. The first question that faces the researcher is what to consider a word and what not to consider a word; whether to count contractions as one or two words; whether to count unintelligible utterances or gap fillers, etc. A decision had to be made and that was to count words as they appear in the dictionary, counting contracted forms as one single word and not counting pause fillers such as "er", "um", etc. In addition to the difficulty that arises when deciding what to count and what not to count, at the time of comparing the number of words produced by each participant in a conversation, the decision not to count pause fillers and to count contracted forms as one word probably led to a "distorted" account of the conversation. That is to say, pause fillers are tokens that show that the current speaker is still holding the floor, but they are not reflected in the final number of words. Similarly, the speaker who often contracts their words (in this study, most often the native speaker) is "wronged", as some of their words are not taken into account.

Methodological difficulties in mind, both interruptions and amount of speech were reported in an interdependent manner. In addition to counting interruptions and comparing the numbers of such interventions produced by each participant in a dyad, the rate of interruption in relation to amount of speech was calculated. Not only the raw numbers of interruptions were compared, as some studies have done, but also their respective rates, calculated by dividing the raw number of interruptions by the interruptee's amount of speech, which is a more accurate method to report how often each interlocutor interrupted the other (James and Clarke, 1993:265).

Chapter 3
Analysis of two interactions

Before reporting the results of the entire study, in this chapter two of the recorded conversations are analysed in greater detail, for two main reasons. Firstly, the quantitative aggregate reporting of all the data (as in the following chapter) would not be sufficient by itself, as it would not give the reader a clear and faithful description of what took place in the interactions subject of study. Secondly, a kind of microanalysis like the following allows us to study some linguistic and communicative aspects in context, in other words, with the possibility for both the analyst and the reader to refer to the whole conversation transcript, to see what precedes and what follows the utterance under consideration, to trace the development of topics throughout the interaction, to follow the progress in the relationship between the two participants, etc.

The two interactions analysed below have been chosen randomly. The intention is to study them in detail independently of whether they turn out to be representative of, or divergent from, the rest of the interactions, in terms of politeness strategies and face and power relationships.

A. First interaction

The following conversation took place between a 24-year-old Spanish university student who will be referred to by the name of Susana and a 26-year-old American exchange student referred to by the name Annie.

1. Transcript

1. Annie: So, are you a doctorate student?
2. Susana: No.
3. A: No? With all these books (laugh)?
4. S: Yes, because I have to::: to make a::: a work and er er for English literature and⌉ I'm in the third year.
5. A: Ah, but ⌋
6. A: Ah, OK. And all these books are from the library?
7. S: Yes, because one of them is the::: er is the::: seminar is the::: work and these ones are the critical..⌉
8. A: Ah, OK, the primary work and the secondary works, and then you have another one.
9. S: No, no.
10. A: Oh, OK, OK.
11. S: (??)
12. A: Because in Spain you can only take three books out of the library.⌉ In the States you can take out many books.
    Yes ⌋
13. S: No, but for example, we have there two libraries, here one library and you can take three books from here, three books from there...⌉
14. A: Ah, I didn't know that. Well, that's good to know (laugh). OK, so you're in your third year of English here?
15. S: Yeah.
16. A: Yes. Aha, and what do you want to do afterwards? Do you want to teach or...?
17. S: Yes, to teach.
18. A: Aha in an *instituto* or...?
19. S: Yes in *instituto*.⌉
20. A: Ah (laugh tog.) ⌋ we would say high school I guess.
21. S: And you?
22. A: I'm here for one year er I have to leave at the end of May, but I'm studying Spanish, Spanish *filología*, um, it's it's a Master's program (??) the university and the United States. I don't know if you heard of (??)?
23. S: No.
24. A: OK, anyway, the first year is here and the second year is back in the United States. So we're taking all sorts of different classes.

25. S: So, you speak Spanish very good, very well.
26. A: Er, I'm learning, I'm trying to perfect it, I don't know ... how ... something more you live into a language it seems harder to really perfect, you know ⌉little... little things...little
　　　　　　　　　　　　　　　　Yeah ⌡
details ..., you know, but hopefully by the end of my stay (laugh) I'll have come to a good level, I don't know.
27. S: The same happened with me when I ⌉went to London,
　　　　　　　　　　　　　　　　　Ah ⌡
and I thought that people er::: didn't understand me because uh, I don't know, I think they they noticed my accent ⌉and they
　　　　　　　　　　　　　　　　　　　Aha ⌡
speak to you very:::fast ⌉ You say oh, please more slowly but ...
　　　　　　　Yeah ⌡
they don't ⌉
28. A: (laugh) ⌡ Exactly the same here. I think the Spanish, because I spent a semester in Ecuador, um six years ago, but the Spaniards here they speak so fast and even when you say slower please or whatever they, they, they stay the same but they might speak louder or something like that (laugh), so, I don't know. But... So do you live in Alcala?
29. S: No, ⌉no, I live near here⌉ not not in ⌉Alcala.
30. A: No ⌡ 　　　　　　　　　　Ah ⌡ Yeah, yeah. So you've to take the train in or the bus?
31. S: No, my father ...er...brings me in here ⌉ because he
　　　　Uhum uhum very good, very good. ⌡
works near, near here in San Fernando ⌉
32. A: U:::h, OK. Ah, San Fernando, it's ⌡ very close to Alcala?
33. S: Yes.
34. A: OK. All these small villages I need to...to know ⌉
35. S: Yes, he works in er the water park near here in ⌡ *carretera de Barcelona* ⌉
36. A: OK ⌡(laugh) OK, very good. So what is the name of the town you live in?
37. S: Er, *Nuevo Baztan*, it's like er::: a residential area?
38. A: Ah, OK. It's a suburb?
39. S: Yes.
40. A: Yeah?
41. S: Yes.
42. A: OK. All right. Very good. Are we ... oh, we have ... suggested topics, do you wanna pick one? (Long pause) Is this your first time?
43. S: No.
44. A: No, OK.
45. S: It's the second one.
46. A: I don't know what, whichever one is fine for me. (Pause). I'll let you pick... (laugh).
47. S: No.

48. A: OK, do you want me to (pause, sound of unzipping). You, you're far-sighted?
49. S: Um?
50. A: You're **far-sighted**? Do you need glasses?
51. S: No.
52. A: Oh, OK. Oh, tissues! (laugh) (pause).
53. S: I don't know.
54. A: OK, er::: (pause) Which, which haven't you talked about? Shall we talk about number 4 "Is your society sexist?"
55. S: OK.
56. A: Yeah? (laugh tog). All right, so do you want to start? What do you think, what do you think of the Spanish society?
57. S: It's er very sexist, I think.
58. A: Yeah?
59. S: Yes because er::: men are very traditional in ideas and ... they think that women have to::: stay at home and work at home and, in the kitchen and things like that ⌊and then, when they, when they go back from er
                         Uhum⌋
their job er they have to::: to have er to have the::: the dinner prepared and all these things, I think the ... er::: it's only men, I think, not women.
60. A: OK, so you think only men are sexist?
61. S: Yes.
62. A: And the way ...and for example, your father does he have this mentality too?
63. S: Yes.
64. A: Ah, so he expects dinner on the table?
65. S: Yes.
66. A: And you've brothers?
67. S: Yes
68. A: And are they..⌉
69. S: But I think ..⌊it's because, for example, my mother er ::: has been living with my father a lot of years, and then she has educated my, my brothers in the same way as er::: my father treated them ⌉ So
                                                                               Aha. ⌋
er ::: it's... they don't make their bed or they they leave all the::: clothes in the floor and things like that ⌉
70. A: Oh, my Gosh! Yeah. It's very irritating, I'm sure (laugh).⌊And, so when you have children, are you going to make sure if your boys or whatever that ...that you'll bring them up equally or or what?
71. S: Yes, I think so, I don't know but⌈I want to treat them the
                                            Yeah ⌋
same way.
72. A: But what about ... if your brothers, I, I assume your brothers are our generation, um, so men our generation, Spanish men are still in that mentality? Or some yes some no or?

73. S: I think some yes and some no, because I think it depends on the education that you: that you have in er at home, and and sometimes they try to::: to::: make us think that they are very modern in ideas and they have changed but then when you are at home with them,⎫ because
    Ah ⎭
    for example my brother when his girlfriend is at home he says "Oh, I'm going to do this, I'm going to do that" but then when..⎫ she's not at home
    Oh no! (laugh tog.) ⎭
74. A: So he's false (????). Yeah, but what about the women who tolerate this? They ... they're tolerating sexism, so in a way they're adding to it too, for example, the mothers who do everything for their children, or whatever...
75. S: Yes, I think it's the same , it's education and then when you ::: when you ::: are er tolerating this a lot of years, that then you don't mind about er::: you want to change things⎫
76. A: Uhum, yeah. My experience here, I live with⎭ a family and I was actually pleasantly surprised that that the men I've known er::: through the family aren't as sexist as I thought they might be. For example, the father, the parents are 38 years old, so um ⎫
    Yes ⎭
    they're pretty young, but the father, for example, he'll make dinner, or he'll cook, or whatever, and you know he'll help with the housework and things like that, and I guess, I guess the mother she's she's very demanding too (laugh). So, you know, she really ... you know, she doesn't tolerate ... um sexism, in that way I guess they're very liberal, maybe, maybe they're they're very uncommon for the typical Spanish family, but um, but then things like, I don't know, like ... men ... men at home, even ... men our age, they seem to anything that's feminine, no, they can't do, for example, things like um lip gloss, do you know what I mean? Not
    lipstick⎫ but just to to protect your
    Uhum ⎭
    lips, you know, I'll have some that smells like mandarin and my brothers at home in the United States and my friends they probably wouldn't put it on their lips but here, you know, it's it's normal, nobody thinks about it.⎫ Or I don't know, they're
    No ⎭
    very affectionate even with their fathers, not only their mothers (telephone rings) or sisters but also with the men in the family. And that's something at home (telephone rings) that couldn't be, because, you know, taboo, you know homosexuals or whatever it is (telephone rings) but...
77. S: Yeah, I think things er ::: are changing but there's a lot er :::
    to do ⎫ but, for example in my house it's really funny
    Yeah ⎭
    because my brothers are ... a mess. ⎫ Everything, yeah because
    (laugh) ⎭

my mother er::: my mother doesn't mind if there is er::: there is er::: dirty clothes er::: there, she doesn't mind, she just take them and she::: she doesn't say anything to them.

78. A: And to you she would say something?
79. S: Yes, but I'm not er::: like them (laugh)
80. A: Ah, you you're more responsible.
81. S: Yes.
82. A: Ah, and your brothers are they younger or are they older?
83. S: No, one is younger and one is older.
84. A: Ah, and even the older one does that (????) ⎤ because,
                                  (laugh) ⎦

    because I'm I'm the oldest in my family and I grew up with two brothers, I've got a little sister too, but she's 10 years old, so there's a big big difference, so I always had to::: you know, do the dishes or whatever and then I would help my father with things outside the house too like chopping the wood because we've a wood stove and whatever, I liked to work with my dad outside but um, so I would always get really irritated especially when I was about 10 that my brothers would go out and play and I would have to help my mother with the ki...in the kitchen or whatever. So, little by little...

85. S: In my home it's not the same because my grandmother is with us and er::: she is a very big help because er::: she's young and then ⎤ she can
                                                                                                       Ah ⎦

    help us and ...but, for example, one thing that was very funny when I was younger er::: for example, my my older brother er::: had to come at home for example a:::t eleven ⎤ and when I was er::: the same y... the same age, ⎤
                                  Aha ⎦   Yeah ⎦

    my father said, "No, you are a girl and you have to stay... home er...earlier and⎤
86. A: Ah you ⎦would have to come home early.
87. S: My father is very sexist.
88. A: Ah, yes.
89. S: And also, I think er my grandmother is er sexist. Yeah.
90. A: I'm sure, she ... is the mother of your father?
91. S: No.
92. A: Of your mother ⎤But still your mother still continues this
                       (???) ⎦

    this old idea of, you know, the boys don't have to do anything and so, I mean, that would make sense of it, that would pass down ..., but now ... I don't know I don't know why our generation will be more against all this sexism but somehow (???) I wanna say we're more enlightened, but we are...because people talk more nowadays, there's communication, (???) I don't know, but anyway (laugh).
93. S: But, I think it's because society is trying to change er things ⎤ but er
                                                                                                                Uhum ⎦

    I think er many people try to::: to::: make people think that they are they

are different but then they're they're not for example, what happens
                                    Uhum
in my house and in many houses
                        Yeah

94. A: Well, I've ... I have this experience with um this ...this guy ... whatever, that I met here in Alcala, we went out um I met him very early on in my stay here, and then, one point we would go, we would go out, we would go running and things like that, and then one day we went out and we had a d... a more profound, a deeper conversation and he told me that friendship doesn't exist between men and women and I was blown away because I'm like, "Well, I thought you're my friend!" But I think
                                                                (laugh)
he, he said, he meant... he has a really tight group of male friends but that women destroy the the friendship between men. So, they don't really have any any women friends who are not their girlfriends, who are not their romantic relationship. And I used to think, "Oh, no!" because he's really young, he's 23 I think, but um, I don't know, I was, I was very sad about that you know.
     Yes

95. S: I think so, because when, for example, you you try to go out with, with er, with er a man or something and then he thinks he wan... you want er something with with him, but perhaps it's only a friendship but er here
                                                     Right
they don't understand
           Yeah
(???)

96. A: That's a ...a very nice thing in the United States which I miss, it's my male friendships, because although there is always sexual tension, you know, I'm sure, but what's more important is friendship, very often, you know. So I like that a lot (laugh tog.) from ... at home. Although, of course, I think there is sexism in every society, you know, every society. The more traditional the society, I think, the more ... sexism exists.

97. S: Yeah, but for example in London was different   for
                                                      Ah
example, in the family er they were very liberal. The::: the
                 Yeah
woman didn't do anything because I (laugh) did it in the::: in
                                                Ah
the house but er, for example, when the husband came er he he did the dinner or something   He prepared things and it was, I
Ah
think, like your family here that er she was very dominant
                                                        Um
and... he was ...

98. A: Yeah Well, here in ... the family here is is more equal because, well because the father has to work and the mother is at home, now with

a little girl, so she, I mean, mostly she cooks, but when she can't cook the father will cook, you know, or when he's the day off, when he's not working, he helps ...you know, which I think is is right, you know ... I don't know but anyway ..⎱Shall we pick another topic? Do we have...?
⎰Uhum⎱
Researcher: Well, that's enough. Thank you.

2. Context and participants

"Whenever two speakers interact", Scollon and Scollon (1981:183) state, "they make sense of the interaction on the basis of assumptions they carried into the situation, which are then sometimes reconsidered as the interaction continues." These assumptions may include the immediate physical environment, cultural assumptions and stereotypes, beliefs about the mental state and social status of one's interlocutor (Sperber and Wilson, 1986:15-16), previous interactions if any, relevant aspects of the interlocutors' lives, general rules of behaviour the participants abide by, etc. (Wardhaugh, 1985:101). However, this does not mean that all such assumptions are relevant to all contexts (Markova, 1978:11): the situation itself renders some aspects more relevant or salient than others (Rhodewatt, 1986, as cited in Tracy, 1990:218).

For the above conversation various contextual aspects may be relevant. First of all, the encounter is a first meeting between two complete strangers: no previous interaction had taken place between the two, not even on the telephone or by ordinary or electronic mail, except for the two-minute encounter in the corridor before entering the office where the conversation was recorded. Second, the two were asked to take part in this conversation for research purposes, which means that the meeting was arranged (not casual) to serve the goals of a third party (the researcher), which in turn means that spontaneity could be affected, as recording "turns private discourse public" (Lakoff, 1990:43). Third, it is an interaction that takes place between two young white women, one aged twenty-six and the other twenty-four, who did not know each other's exact age beforehand, as all the participants were informed they would interact with a partner of the same sex and approximately the same age but were not given further details. Fourth, the situation and the task are somewhat informal and the roles are the same for the native and non-native speakers: there were no formal tasks to perform, no institutional or game role differences, such as student/teacher, parent/child, tourist/information desk employee, etc., and no rules of interaction were set beforehand. Lastly, the conversation is conducted in English, a language which is not spoken as a mother tongue or a second language in Spain, the country where the conversation was recorded, and which is the mother tongue of only one participant, Annie, as Susana's mother tongue is Spanish.

At least the first four assumptions make the interaction look like a reciprocal conversation in which "participants have equal access to all possibilities of action and interpretation" (Lakoff, 1990:42). If it is a first encounter, it is so for both; if speech was recorded, it was the speech of both, if the researcher was present, he was sitting opposite the two; if the researcher was a stranger, that was the case for both; if the Spanish participant could think American people are standoffish, for example, the American one could think of another national or cultural stereotype, and so on and so forth. That is to say, since this is a first encounter for both participants, both are young and female and both take part in a linguistic experiment, it is expected that they would be equally free to contribute to the conversation and exchange information, that they would have equal "discoursal and pragmatic rights and obligations" (Fairclough, 1995:47), they would make assumptions about their partner and act upon them, and have similar intercultural or interpersonal communicative problems, if any.

However, reciprocity and equality are no longer assumed when the fifth factor, nativity, comes into play. One participant speaks the medium of interaction as a native speaker while the other does not or, to use Marriott's (1991:88) words, one is using the "base norm", the English communicative system, while the other is just aiming to "apply these target norms" as she is still going through the learning process or still at a certain interlingual stage[1]. Therefore, the first can use a range of lexical items, idiomatic expressions, slang, grammatical structures, etc. that the other cannot; the first can correct the other (or be referred to as a language authority) but the other "cannot"[2]; the first may be inhibited or self-conscious for psychological reasons, while the other may be inhibited or self-conscious because of her psychological nature and because she is speaking a foreign language with a native speaker, thus exposing her knowledge and putting her competence to the test.

This may mean that status, once the native/non-native dimension is in play, is no longer equal, for native competence is a kind of knowledge and, as Dant (1991:198) asserts, "...knowledge need not be knowledge about how to satisfy material needs in order that it may be powerful. Indeed, just about any knowledge can be powerful provided that it is recognised within a social context as knowledge." Therefore, in the conversation above Annie and Susana, presumably like all native and non-native speakers in this research,

---

1. "Interlanguage" or "interlingual stage" refers to the "structural system which the learner [of a foreign language] constructs at any given stage in his development", a structural (and we may add communicative) system that is always distinct from the actual system of the language in question (Ellis, 1985:47).

2. This, of course, is relative: it depends on the level of grammatical and communicative competence of both parties. Being a native speaker does not mean, per se, having an extensive range of linguistic and communicative resources. Likewise, being a non-native speaker of a language is not incompatible with having a profound knowledge of the language in question and being highly competent in different communicative situations.

end up having unequal status and are consequently likely to perform differently and not have the same "discoursal and pragmatic rights and obligations—for instance, the same turn-taking rights and the same obligations to avoid silences and interruptions, the rights to utter 'obligating' illocutionary acts (such as requests and questions), and the same obligation to respond to them" (Fairclough, 1995:47).

3. Topics and conversation structure

It has been pointed out above that every pair of participants was asked to do two tasks: to get to know each other and to discuss a topic from the list provided. Accordingly, all of the recorded conversations have two distinct parts[3] : in the first the two participants speak about themselves, about their studies, jobs, families, favourite football teams, etc., while in the second they speak about the topic of their choice. The two parts are easily identifiable, as when the two participants felt that they had "had enough" of getting to know each other, one of them said something like "Shall we pick a subject?", the other would accept, and the two would stay silent for some time, reading what was on the list, then they would ask each other about their preferences and finally decide to talk about a given topic.

The above conversation is no exception: it opens with a question about work or studies, it goes on with questions and answers about studies, future plans, languages and later embarks upon a discussion of sexism in society. A demarcation point can easily be drawn between the get-to-know-each-other stage and the topic discussion stage. The point in question is turn 42, when Annie says:

> "OK. All right. Very good. Are we ... oh, we have ... suggested topics, do you wanna pick one?"

This does not mean, however, that the two participants stop speaking about themselves at this point and only discuss the chosen topic formally and objectively. Rather, self-disclosure continues throughout the discussion, as both participants talk about sexism and the relationship between men and women through their own experience.

One of the outstanding differences between the first part of the conversation and the second one is turn length. The turns in the first part are, generally speaking, much shorter than the ones in the second one (compare, for

---

3. There are a few exceptions in which the two interlocutors shift smoothly from the get-to-know-each-other stage to the topic discussion. In these conversations there is no clearly identifiable borderline between "purely personal" questions and "objective" discussion: the participants speak, for instance, about each other's studies, and smoothly move on to speak about universities in their respective countries, the educational system, the ideology of teachers, capitalism, etc. All this was done without very long pauses, without any references to topic change, and always respecting coherence rules (subjects were conceptually interrelated and one of them triggered the other). Furthermore, what makes the distinction between the two parts difficult is that sometimes topics are discussed in association with personal experience and there is constant movement from Self towards Topic and the other way round.

example, the turns from 1 to 41 with the ones from 76 to 98). This is possibly typical of first encounters, in which the participants do not have the necessary background information to act upon and, consequently, tend to be cautious and tentative, first in order not to make social or interpersonal gaffes and, second, in order to obtain the necessary information from the addressee and, therefore, be able to incorporate it into the subsequent part of the interaction. In fact, we do not normally start a conversation with a stranger talking effusively and extensively about our lives, achievements, beliefs or opinions. Rather, we tend to sound out our interlocutor, getting information about them, and gradually interchanging little bits of personal information before moving on, if we ever do, to talk in more detail about possible topics of conversation[4].

This is exactly what Annie and Susana do in the conversation above: Annie takes the initiative to ask Susana if she is a doctorate student, to which the latter gives a minimal response ("No"). At this opening point in the interaction Annie seems to follow the normal procedure in a conversation between strangers, namely getting to know one's partner first. She starts with the question "Are you a doctorate student?" rather than something more general like "What do you do?" because the encounter takes place, as was mentioned earlier, inside a university building and she already knows that her partner is a university student. Susana's minimal response seems consistent with Grice's Cooperative Principle (more precisely the quantity maxim) to the letter, nothing more and nothing less: she answers her partner's question with one of the two possible answers (yes or no) but does not elaborate, which might be judged as an insufficient reply (interpersonally speaking) or as reluctance to speak or to self-reveal. To remedy this, Annie asks more questions to make Susana say more, a move which apparently succeeds, as turns 4, 7 and 13 show. However, this does not prevent Susana from falling back into her one-word or minimal responses, as turns 15, 17 and 19, for example, show.

In terms of structure and adjacency pairs, the first part of the conversation proceeds as follows:

1. Question.
2. Reply.
3. Exclamation/Question.
4. Reply.
5. Question.
6. Reply.
7. Repetition and implied question.

---

4. Schein (1981), quoted by McCall and Cousins (1990:28), neatly puts it as follows: "One way in which a relationship becomes more intimate is through successive minimal self-revelations which constitute interpersonal tests of acceptance. 'If you accept this much of me, then perhaps I can risk revealing a bit more about myself'. Total openness may be safe and creatively productive when acceptance is guaranteed."

8. Reply.
9. Acceptance/back channel response – New statement.
10. Response to the statement/new information.
11. Response to the new information – Question.
12. Reply.
13. Question.
14. Reply.
15. Question.
16. Reply.
17. Question (Susana's).
18. Reply.
19. Statement/question.
20. Reply.
21. Statement.
22. Statement – Question.
23. Reply.
24. Question.
25. Reply.
26. Question.
27. Reply.
28. Statement.
29. More explanation/reply.
30. Question.
31. Reply.
32. Question.
33. Reply.
34. Approval – Suggestion – Question.
35. Reply.

It is evident that most adjacency pairs are questions and answers, and at the same time it is worth noting that the participant who asks the most questions is Annie. She asks her interlocutor about her studies, the library system in Spanish universities, future job plans, place of residence, means of transport to university, and finally about whether it is the first time she has participated in an interaction for the present study. As for Susana, all she does in the first part of the conversation is answer Annie's questions. The only time she clearly asks a question is when she uses the reciprocity sendback question "and you?", while the other instance in turn 25 above does not constitute a clear question but something between a statement/supposition and a question.

As for the second part of the interaction, the topic discussion, it starts after the negotiation interval (from turn 42 to turn 56) and, significantly, it starts with Annie's question in turn 56: "What do you think, what do you think of the Spanish society?". What calls attention at this point, in addition to the fact that it is Annie who does the questioning, is that the two female participants choose sexism as their topic of conversation. As is the case in the opening of the interaction, when they talk about their studies and especially between turns 25 and 28, when they talk about their respective experiences with foreign languages and countries, in this (main) part of the conversation they also choose a common ground to "play in". That is to say, from all the topics suggested in the list, sexism is the most salient for two women and very likely to be chosen by them, not because some topics are the speciality of some social or gender groups rather than others, but simply because sexism is a common ground *par excellence* for the two participants and, therefore, a handy means to establishing a relationship, in this case a solidarity or rapport-oriented one.

4. Politeness strategies

When circumstances allow two unacquainted people to be at the same place, such as a bus stop or a waiting room, there can be different expectations and relational outcomes according to the cultural context and the individual idiosyncrasies. The two people may sit or stand side by side without interchanging a word, they may greet each other and keep silent or initiate a casual conversation that may or may not develop into a closer relationship, etc. In the case above, however, although Annie and Susana were not acquainted, it was unlikely that they would just sit side by side or greet each other without proceeding further. This is because their encounter was arranged, not casual: they were invited in and introduced to each other by a third party for a given purpose and their interaction per se was the main focus. Therefore, silence was not expected and if it had been the case it would have been a sheer failure or, worse, a flagrant offence for one or more of the three parties[5]. Thus, once placed in the situation, the two participants started interacting (Annie asked Susana: "So, are you a doctorate student?" to which the latter replied "No"), which means that, at least, they noticed each other (socially and interpersonally speaking) and showed the necessary or expected face attention. In other words, they mutually perceived and recognised each other as a "face owner".

What follows in the next twenty turns (and if we take away turns 26-28 we can even include the rest of the turns up to turn 41) is almost exclusively a series of questions (asked mainly by Annie) and short replies. The questions, as was said above, are about studies, the library system in Spanish universities, future job plans, place of residence, etc. That is to say, they are intended to get information from and about one's interlocutor. Nevertheless, not only is information exchange at issue here: by asking these questions, Annie (and later, and to a lesser degree, Susana) seems to tell her partner: "I'm not asking you this just to get information about you but also because I'm interested in you, I accept you, I'm pleased to meet and get to know you." What

---

5. "It seems that one cannot agree to participate in free verbal interaction and then not participate without losing respect from the others and endangering one's self-esteem" (Watts, 1991:175).

the two are doing at the beginning of the conversation, therefore, is nothing but applying Brown and Levinson's (1987) positive politeness strategy 1: notice, attend to the hearer (his interests, wants, needs, goods) as a means to claim common ground.

However, seeing that the enquiries about one's partner are a means to getting to know her and finding common ground with her, it seems curious that Susana does not contribute to this activity, for she does not use this strategy until the conversation reaches turn 21 (when she uses her right of reciprocity and asks back: "And you?"). This does not necessarily mean that she does not show as much interest in her partner as the latter does, as, firstly, answering one's partner's questions is one of the ways one can show them interest and attend to their face needs[6] and, secondly, Susana's question seems to have been delayed by the emergence of the topic of library systems in the United States and Spain.

Still, this last explanation seems to be easily overridden by the subsequent development of the conversation. Indeed, not only in the following twenty turns (i.e. up to the topic-selection point) does Annie continue asking questions, but also throughout the second part of the interaction (topic discussion), thus giving rise to a situation in which only one party is "made" to disclose information about herself (Annie also reveals personal information but mainly through her own initiative, not as replies to questions/stimuli). In this way Annie's questions allow her/us to know about Susana's studies, future plans, place of residence, means of transport, family, etc., while the information she reveals about her own studies, family and life experiences comes out spontaneously most of the time.

This leads us to pose the following questions: Why is this the case? Is it because Susana is too shy to ask? Is it because Annie is so fast in her speech tempo and in her asking questions that she does not give her partner enough time to take over and ask her back? Is it because the two are abiding by different norms or have different cultural attitudes towards asking personal and not so personal questions, different concepts of imposition/intrusiveness/politeness?

Actually, neither during the recording of the conversation nor later, at the transcription stage, did the researcher notice any obvious signs of shyness in Susana, which means that the first hypothesis is to be discarded. Similarly, it is true that Annie's speech tempo is faster than Susana's, which is understandable as the former is native and the latter

---

6. Answering one's interlocutor's questions is a manifestation of Grice's (1975) Cooperative Principle because it shows that the person who replies abides by the information-exchange purpose of communication. However, the reasons why people answer other people's questions are not only rationality and cooperation but also face considerations: one answers another's questions as long as one has some consideration for one's interlocutor's face (and of course, as long as the fact of answering the questions does not affect one's interests).

non-native[7], but the conversation features many instances in which Susana could have seized the opportunity but failed to do so. What is meant by such instances are points in the interaction where Annie seems ready to release the floor and indicates this with laughter (as in turn 14 above), laughter and expressions like, "I don't know" (as in turn 28) and expressions like, "OK. All right. Very good" (as in turn 42), all of which are uttered with a falling intonation and a tailing-off volume. The fact that Susana does not seize the opportunity to take over the floor and ask Annie questions at such points shows that tempo is probably not the reason. As for the third possibility, it seems that the literature on intercultural communication provides a clue: Wierzbicka (1991:63), for example, claims that "information is seen in Anglo-Saxon culture as a free and public good" and, therefore, "the restrictions on the use of the imperative seem to be compensated by a tremendous expansion of interrogative devices." However, instead of rushing into conclusions, suffice it to say at this stage that there may be cultural or simply personal differences between the two participants' perceptions of question asking and, just as likely as this, there may be another reason, probably power asymmetry, which is considered below.

At the negotiation interlude (from turn 42 to turn 56) Annie seems to be very attentive to Susana's face needs. She lets her partner choose the topic by saying:

- Do you wanna pick one?
- Whichever is fine for me.
- I'll let you pick.
- Which haven't you talked about?

Not only once but at least four times (and in different manners) does she give Susana priority to select a topic for discussion, thus placing her interlocutor's preferences and interests before hers and, in technical terms, using Brown and Levinson's (1987) positive politeness Strategy 1: notice, attend to H as a means to claim common ground.

Indeed, many societies consider it polite to let one's companion or interlocutor do something before oneself. "Ladies first", for example, is said and applied in many societies as a sign of gentlemanly (polite) behaviour towards women. Table etiquette, in formal settings and in some societies at least, requires that men sit after women, and men in their turn abide by this social rule as such and also as a sign of showing face consideration towards women. Similarly, the French "*Après vous*" (said when letting another person enter,

---

7. This should not be understood as a general rule but rather as a matter of likelihood and degree: not all native speakers have a fast tempo, neither do all non-native ones have a slow tempo. However, it is a common, and perhaps logical, observation that non-native speakers, especially those with a low level of competence or fluency, tend to speak more slowly, with more hesitation, repetition, self-correction, etc. This is because the language system they are using was learnt consciously and, therefore, consciousness interferes in the process of utterance construction, that is, language production.

exit or do something else first) fulfils the same politeness function. Giving way to pedestrians or to other drivers (when there are no traffic signs that induce the action) is another example. Giving way to the other (also when two speakers start speaking at the same time and everyone shows their willingness to release the floor to the other) means that one gives more importance to one's partner's face and needs than to one's own. In the above topic negotiation passage, however, it seems that Susana does not make as much effort as Annie to show that she wants to give her partner priority. In turn 47 she simply replies with a one-word utterance ("no"), which means that she declines to choose the topic herself (in other words, she seems to give way to her partner). In turn 53 she still hedges and avoids choosing first (by saying: "I don't know"), thus declining once again to be given priority and sending the ball back to Annie. In turn 55, after Annie suggests a topic (sexism), Susana readily answers "OK", thus accepting her partner's first suggestion. This *per se* can be interpreted as a gesture of face attention, as it gives priority to one's partner's (topic of) interest, seeks agreement, and avoids disagreement, disapproval and the potential face threat thereof.

In this way, though Susana apparently pays less attention to her partner's face because she fails to take the initiative and let her choose the topic, and because her utterances in this sense are not as clear and abundant as Annie's (hence probably an instance of imbalance), she turns out to be abiding by the same face principles, more or less. For, although in a somewhat passive manner, she does use Brown and Levinson's positive politeness strategies 1 (as above), 6 (avoiding disagreement in topic choice) and 15 (giving gifts, in this case cooperation, to the hearer). Still, there seems to remain an imbalance between the way Annie and Susana try to show they care about each other's face, interests and preferences. While Susana passively declines Annie's offer, reluctantly shows that she does not know what topic to choose and immediately welcomes Annie's suggested topic, the latter actively, plainly and repeatedly shows interest in her partner's point of view and her willingness to give her priority. She even shows what sounds like motherly concern when she asks her in turns 48 and 50, "You're far-sighted? Do you need glasses?"

In the rest of the interaction between Annie and Susana (the discussion of the topic of sexism in society) the dominant tendency is towards agreement and conflict avoidance (Brown and Levinson's, 1987, positive politeness strategies 5 and 6). To begin with, the chosen topic, as mentioned above, is likely to be a safe one for two women and may even constitute a common ground based on gender solidarity. In addition, Annie follows a strategy of sounding out before expressing her own opinion (asking her partner about her opinion, her intentions as far as child education is concerned, the situation and gender relationships in her family). Indeed, especially at the beginning of the topic discussion she almost adopts what looks like an interviewer role rather than participating in the discussion as an equal opinion provider. Consider the questions she asks Susana from turn 56 to turn 74 (reproduced below):

A. FIRST INTERACTION

- What do you think, what do you think of the Spanish society?
- OK, so you think only men are sexist?
- And the way ...and for example, your father does he have this mentality too?
- And you've brothers?
- And are they...?
- (...) so men our generation, Spanish men are still in that mentality?
- Yeah, but what about the women who tolerate this?

These questions can be interpreted as an act of "sitting on the fence", a strategy to avoid possible disagreement which may be face threatening and disruptive.

Susana, on the other hand, expresses her opinion openly while answering her interlocutor's questions. At the same time she shows tokens of agreement (using words and expressions like "Yes, I think it's the same" in turn 75 above, "Yeah" in turn 77 and "I think so" in turn 95). As for her recurrent use of "but", which in other contexts would sound like a challenger or a disagreement initiator, it turns out to be a mere tool to claim and take over the floor (when it is used at the beginning of the intervention) or a misused conjunction. For example, in turn 69 the word "but" is used by Susana not to contradict anything Annie said (what the latter actually utters is a question about whether the former has got brothers and an unfinished other question which is understood to be about Susana's brothers' attitude towards sexism), but just to add something about her mother's tolerance of sexist role division and later indirectly answer the unfinished question. In turn 93 she opens her intervention with "but" again, but not to disagree with her interlocutor. On the contrary, she agrees with her about the fact that society is changing. In turn 97 she starts with "yeah" and follows it with "but", but once again not to contradict anything said by Annie (even when she says "in London [it] was different" because the example of the London liberal family does not run counter to Annie's preceding statement, nor does it contradict the example of male–female friendship given earlier).

The same tendency to seek agreement and avoid disagreement may be said to be reinforced by the use of supportive minimal listener responses or back-channel utterances like "aha", "uh huh", "ok", etc. This kind of utterance is normally used to "signal continued attendance to the speaker" (Roger, 1989:92). That is to say, the listener uses these utterances to indicate that they are listening, following, paying attention to what the present speaker is saying and have no intention to compete for or take over the floor. Together with this purely conversational use, back-channel utterances can be said to pay attention to the speaker's positive face: speakers, as persons, need acceptance, approval and signs of interest. Indeed, failing to pay attention to a speaker (at least in situations in which speaker and listener(s) are present and within each other's sight range, thus excluding broadcast political speeches or mass meetings, for example) is generally considered impolite, a lack of respect and, in other words, a face-threatening act. By using back-channel utterances the listener avoids such a face-threatening act and satisfies the above face needs by indicating that they are interested in and paying attention to what the speaker is saying and, by implication, that they are sensitive to the speaker's face. In the conversation analysed here, Annie produces 30 instances of such utterances, while her partner, Susana, only uses them 6 times. This gives rise to a clear imbalance in the use of supportive utterances, which will be dealt with below.

In addition to the above, there are other manifestations of face concern throughout Annie and Susana's interaction. Following the same tendency towards claiming common ground, the two participants make use of in-group identity markers (Brown and Levinson's Strategy 4), especially solidarity pronouns like "we", "us" and "our" to indicate that they belong to the same group and, therefore, they are alike, they have common interests and are "friends" (co-operators) not "enemies" (competitors). In turn 72, for example, Annie says: "your brothers are **our** generation" and in turn 76 she says "men at home, even ... men **our** age" (the emphasis is the author's), thus using age as a common-ground reference to draw attention to and establish a relationship of sameness and group membership. Curiously enough, it is immediately after Annie's first instance of using the solidarity pronoun "our" that Susana makes use of a variant of the same pronoun "us" (in turn 73): "...they [men] try to: to: make **us** think that **they** are very modern in ideas and **they** have changed but then...", thus corroborating the fact that they (Annie and Susana) are indeed members of the same group. It is worth noting that in the latter case the use of the solidarity pronoun is highlighted by the contrast with "they" ("we" against "others").

It is worth noting also that the use of "we", "our" and "us" above is inclusive not exclusive (see Lakoff, 1990:190–191 for a distinction between the two uses of "we"). This is because these pronouns are meant to include the two participants in the same age or gender group, not to exclude one of them as would have been the case if Annie, for example, had said something like, "We don't do that in the United States," thus differentiating herself from her interlocutor and excluding the latter. Therefore, seeing that the instances of solidarity pronouns are used to convey the idea that the two interlocutors belong to one age and gender group which stands in contrast to another (older generations or men), it can be affirmed that this use of identity markers "is a powerful emotional force, bringing speaker and hearer together as one, united and sharing common interests" (Lakoff, 1990:190). It is a strategy that conveys a "warm, friendly and egalitarian" feeling (Lakoff, 1990:191).

Another strategy, this time used exclusively by the native speaker in the dyad, is explanation and accommodation. In turn 48, for example, Annie asks Susana: "You're far-sighted?", to which the latter replies "Um?", which indicates that she either did not understand the question (especially the term "far-sighted") or she did not hear it clearly. Subsequently, Annie adopts two alternative strategies at the same time: she repeats the same question with a clearer and louder pronunciation (stressing the word "far-sighted") and explains the question or the word by asking her "Do you need glasses?", thus solving the problem (whether it was a problem of mishearing or a non-native person's lack of knowledge of a new word). In turn 76 Annie is speaking about lip gloss and, anticipating possible comprehension difficulties, she asks Susana: "Do you know what I mean?" and immediately goes on to explain: "Not lipstick, but just to ... to protect your lips." Similarly, in turn 98 Annie says: "...when he's the day off, when he's not working, he helps...", thus explaining an expression (day off) that her non-native addressee might have found difficult to understand. These instances show that the native speaker keeps in mind the existing difference between her and her partner's linguistic competence and accordingly tries first to anticipate communicative problems and second to adapt her language to her addressee, which can also be considered a sign of face concern.

Indeed, this is something common in interactions between native and non-fluent speakers. Giles and Smith (1979) "...have suggested in their theory of accommodation that all speakers continually adjust their speech to their conversational partner in order to make it more comprehensible and congenial, with accommodation to non-fluent speakers serving as one example" (Smith *et al*, 1991:173). Similarly, accommodation research (for example, Freed 1978 and 1981; Long, 1981 and 1983; Perdue, 1984; Snow, Eeden and Muysken, 1981; and Gass and Varonis, 1985) has found that native speakers make some changes in their speech rhythm, vocabulary, constructions, etc. when they are interacting with non-native interlocutors. They even "take the responsibility for anticipating and repairing communicative problems, using strategies such as rephrasing, elaboration and confirmation checks" (Smith *et al.*, 1991:174).

Such instances of explanation, accommodation and comprehension monitoring may, of course, be simply and solely attributed to the rationality of (referential) communication. That is to say, communication cannot proceed smoothly and efficiently if one's interlocutor does not understand a keyword or expression or does not follow one's point. This is why it is common to check comprehension and "wave length" as a conversation proceeds, using expressions and questions like, "Do you see what I mean?", "Do you follow me?", "You know what this means, don't you?", etc. because if one's addressee misses the point or does not understand something, the conversation may break down. Thus, it can be said that Annie's explanations and comprehension checks are nothing but tools to maintain a coherent discourse, avoid communication breakdowns and, therefore, ensure the observance of Grice's (1975) Cooperative Principle. For, if Susana did not understand what "far-sighted" means, she would not be able to answer the question (appropriately and relevantly), and if she did not understand the meaning of "lip gloss", she would not be able to make out Annie's point (the relationship between lip gloss and sexism).

Notwithstanding, Annie's above utterances go beyond the strict application of the Cooperative Principle, conversation analysts' concept of coherence or Sperber and Wilson's (1986) relevance. By explaining "far-sighted" to Susana in turn 50 above, she does not only bridge a comprehension gap, which is a necessary action for the adjacency pair to be completed and for the conversation to continue, but also shows face concern to her partner. As pointed out above, Susana's utterance "um?" could be interpreted as a request for repetition (an equivalent of "Pardon!") or a request for explanation (an equivalent of "I don't understand what you mean"), but Annie does not only repeat her previous utterance/question, she also follows it with an instance of rephrasing. Thus, she avoids a potential situation in which Susana would hear what she said clearly but not understand the term and, therefore, be exposed as lacking in lexical competence. What Annie does is save her partner's face. Similarly, in turn 76, although she asks her partner if she understands what she means by "lip gloss", she does not wait for an answer, which makes her utterance sound more like a gap filler than a real question and, therefore, avoids putting her interlocutor in an "embarrassing" situation by testing her knowledge of English (vocabulary). The same can be said about the third instance of explanation in turn 98. In other words, what Annie seems to tell Susana is, "I always bear in mind that you speak English as a second or foreign language, so I will save you effort or embarrassment (face loss) by making things easy for you, simplifying my own language and anticipating any communication difficulties that might result from our different repertoires."

It has been found so far that the two participants in the interaction above use, among others, the following linguistic and communicative tools to show face concern and their interest in each other:

1. Silence avoidance.
2. Questions and answers.
3. Safe topics.
4. Giving way.
5. Agreement.
6. Solidarity pronouns.
7. Accommodation.
8. Back-channel utterances.

Silence avoidance, questions, answers, giving way, accommodation and back-channel utterances can all be subsumed under Brown and Levinson's (1978)[8] strategy 1: notice, attend to H (interests, wants, needs, goods). Safe topics and agreement can be subsumed under strategy 5 of the same theoretical framework: seek agreement. Finally, solidarity pronouns can fall under strategy 4: in-group identity markers.

---

8. Brown and Levinson's theoretical framework was formulated with the concept of speech act in mind; therefore, it may be asserted that it is not applicable to conversational acts such as back-channel utterances, accommodation, etc. However, the classification of such conversation behaviours under Brown and Levinson's politeness strategies takes into consideration the spirit of the theoretical framework and the communicative purposes served by those behaviours. If accommodation is an act of adapting one's language to the repertoire of one's interlocutor, it is legitimate to consider it an act of noticing or attending to H's face.

These politeness strategies and their realisations are reflected in statistical terms below (Table 3):

Table 3: Some of the politeness strategies in Annie and Susana's interaction

Politeness Strategy	Manifestation	Annie	Susana
Strategy 1: Notice, attend to H (his interests, wants, needs, goods).	Silence avoidance	4	0
	Questions	25	1
	Answers	1	25
	Giving way	4	1
	Accommodation	3	0
	Back-channel	30	6
	Total	67	33
Strategy 4: in-group identity markers	Solidarity pronouns	3	1
Strategy 5: Seek agreement	Safe topics	6	3
	Agreement	1	1
	Total	7	4

It must be noted that the above statistics are nothing but an approximate manner of approaching the manifestations of politeness strategies. It is quite difficult to render a conversation—with all its complex workings, slippery nature, and openness to different interpretations—into exact figures. Concepts like silence avoidance, safe topics and agreement are not easy to define as clearly as to make it possible to identify the utterances that embody instances of such concepts. What is even more difficult is to determine the boundaries of every instance (whether a topic is a new topic or just a subtopic is but one example).

Keeping in mind theoretical and practical difficulties, the above table reflects clear instances of the categories of politeness strategies used in the conversation under analysis. To begin with, as far as silence avoidance is concerned, any utterance is, of course, an act of silence avoidance, as the mere action of speaking puts an end to silence. However, the above table includes only the instances that occur initially (thus the participant who starts the conversation, Annie, scores one point) or after a relatively long pause (in this conversation when the two participants were thinking about which topic to choose). With just these instances, Annie turns out to have avoided silence more than her partner. This is supported by the number of questions she asks and words she utters (see below). The difference in the number of questions is quite significant (25 to 1) and so is the difference between Annie's and Susana's instances of supportive minimal responses (30 and 6, respectively). These two conversational aspects alone make a considerable difference between Annie's and Susana's manifestations of politeness strategy 1: a total of 67 to 33, which would amount to 66 to 8 if the number of answers were subtracted (answers are not actions in themselves but mere triggered reactions).

The fact that Annie's instances of positive politeness strategies outnumber Susana's might convey the idea that the two participants have different assumptions about the situation and interaction or that Annie is the least powerful party in the dyad. However, as is demonstrated below, a close consideration of the above, especially in light of other conversational aspects, shows this is not the case.

5. Power manifestations

5.1. Amount of speech

The whole conversation takes approximately 18 minutes and contains 2331 words (counting the contracted forms but not back-channel utterances or pause fillers), 1482 of which are spoken by Annie while only 849 are produced by Susana. There are 103 speech turns in the conversation (53 are Annie's and 50 Susana's). If the number of words is divided by the number of turns, the average turn length amounts to 28.1 words for Annie and 16.9 for Susana. The two participants have almost the same number of turns, which is reflected in the above list of contributions and adjacency pairs (every question is followed by an answer and every contribution is responded to, which gives rise to a speaker 1 – speaker 2 – speaker 1 – speaker 2 pattern).

The above statistics are visually reflected in the following table:

Table 4: Amount of speech in Annie and Susana's conversation

	Annie	Susana
A. Number of words	1482	849
B. Number of turns	53	50
C. Speech rate (C = A÷B)	28.1	16.9

In any conversation between two people, if no specific contextual rules imply or require the contrary, each participant is entitled to 50% of the floor and can therefore make contributions that amount to half the total speech produced. However, this is not always the case: there are talkative and taciturn participants, participants who have a lot of things to say and others who have very little, speakers who are more interested in a topic/task than others, etc. In the above conversation, far from having a fifty–fifty distribution of talk between the native and non-native speakers, it is observed that Annie speaks almost twice as much as Susana. This is not because the latter does not have enough opportunities to take the floor but because she sometimes fails to take over when there is a long pause or when her interlocutor seems to reach the end of her point or turn. For example, in turn 92 Annie seems to indicate that she wants to relinquish the floor, first with a falling intonation, a tailing-off voice volume and a long pause, and later by saying "but now", also with a falling intonation and a long pause, but Susana does not take over the floor. Furthermore, when she does occupy the floor she (willingly or unwillingly) does not hold it for as long as her interlocutor does. This means either that she has a preference for short interventions or that her interlocutor does not allow her to proceed, probably because she mistakenly perceives Transition Relevant Places where they do not exist, or because she is eager to speak herself.

Generally speaking, when one party monopolises speech in a spontaneous conversation, this may be due to a number of reasons. This party may be relatively more talkative by nature, relatively more powerful, an expert/authority in the subject(s) of conversation, or may be suffering from/enjoying a psychological state that induces them to speak more than usual, etc. In this conversation expertise as a factor can easily be discarded, as the topics discussed in the above conversation do not require any special expertise. Getting to know each other is a task that anybody can perform and sexism is a common subject about which any participant can talk, with the help of a little life experience and observation of social behaviour. Indeed both participants talk about this topic in light of their own experience, not any specialised (expert) knowledge. The factor of possible emotional excitement can also be discarded, as the two participants were apparently calm and neither of them showed any signs of a particular psychological state before or during the recording.

Accordingly, there remain two possible explanations: taciturnity/talkativeness and power relationship. As for the first, no background information is available about how talkative the two participants are in real life and the only clue apart from the conversation above is the other interaction Susana and Annie had with their respective second partners in the present research. Susana's conversation with the other partner confirms the observation that she speaks less than her native counterpart (slightly less than half her partner's amount of speech in the second conversation). Similarly, Annie's second participation in this research confirms that she speaks more than her non-native interlocutor does (more than twice as much as Catalina, her Spanish counterpart in the second interaction). However, this does not constitute decisive evidence on their respective talkativeness or taciturnity: it only reveals their respective amount of speech in relation to two different (but similar as far as the dimensions of nativity/non-nativity, gender and age are concerned) interlocutors. Taciturnity and talkativeness, after all, are a matter of degree, context and relationship.

As for power differential, it seems to be a plausible explanation for the imbalance in the amount of speech, especially in light of what researchers like James and Drakich (1993:289–290) claim regarding this conversational aspect: higher-status participants (in this case, presumably, the native speaker) assume a higher competence than their counterparts (at least in task-oriented interactions) and are therefore more willing to speak and hold the floor. Similarly, lower-status participants (in this case, presumably, the non-native speaker) assume and accept that their interlocutors are more competent than they are and, therefore, expect and encourage them to contribute more to the interaction.

However, although there seems to be some evidence in relevant literature that the party who monopolises the floor is normally more dominant or powerful (see Collins and Guetzkow, 1964:155–157 for a summary), no definitive conclusions can be reached, at least for the time being, because amount of speech is not necessarily and not always associated with power. As Tannen (1993:176) asserts, "[s]ilence alone ... is not a self-evident sign of powerlessness, nor volubility a self-evident sign of domination". In another publication, the author adds:

> ...the association of volubility with dominance does not hold for all people, all settings, and all cultures. Silence can also be the privilege of a higher-ranking person, and even an instrument of power (Tannen, 1995:234).

Rather, a relatively larger amount of speech may only be correlated with power if the context endorses such a correlation and if other linguistic and communicative aspects support the power-differential hypothesis.

5.2. Simultaneous speech

The instances of simultaneous speech in the conversation amount to 40 (see Table 5 below). These fall into two groups: back-channel utterances (36, 30 of which are produced by Annie and 6 by Susana) and interruptions (4, 3 of which are Annie's and 1 Susana's). If each participant's raw number of back-channel utterances is divided by her interlocutor's amount of speech (number of words), the result is a rate of 0.035 for Annie, who provides an assent term every 28.3 words of Susana's (1/28.3) and 0.004 for the latter, who provides one every 247 words of Annie's (1/247). And dividing Annie's 3 interruptions by Susana's 849 words, the result is 0.003, which means that Annie interrupts every 283 words of Susana's (1/283), while Susana interrupts her interlocutor only once in 1482 words (1/1482).

Table 5: Distribution of simultaneous speech (back-channel utterances and interruptions) between Susana and Annie

	Annie (native speaker)	Susana (non-native speaker)	Total or average
Simultaneous speech (raw numbers)	33	7	40
Back-channel utterances (raw numbers)	30	6	36
Back-channel utterances (rates)	1/28.3	1/247	1/64.75
Interruptions (raw numbers)	3	1	4
Interruptions (rates)	1/283	1/1482	1/582.75

Back-channel utterances, as pointed out above, normally serve the purpose of conveying to the current speaker that the addressee is following them.

They therefore have a supportive function, as they seem to encourage the current speaker to extend their floor-holding (Meltzer, Morris and Hayes, 1971:395; Schegloff, 1972:379; Duncan, 1973; and Roger, 1989:92). However, a distinction was made in this study between two groups of back-channel utterances, "uh huh" and "aha", on the one hand, and "yes/yeah/no/right" on the other. This is because there seems to be some evidence that "uh huh" is normally a sign of "passive recipiency" while words like "yes" usually foreshadow a topic-shift or topic-curtailing (Jefferson, 1981, 1983 and 1984) or even an interruption/turn-shift. According to this distinction, Annie's instances of back-channel utterances divide practically evenly (out of the 30 instances 14 are of the first type: "uh huh" and "aha", while 16 are of the second type: "yes", "yeah", "right"). Susana's back-channel utterances, on the other hand, are predominantly of the second type (5 out of 6).

While support utterances are, generally speaking, associated with subordinate or less powerful groups or parties, in the dyad under analysis here the case is apparently the other way round: Annie, as a native speaker and, therefore, as the supposedly more powerful party in the dyad, uses far more supportive back-channel utterances than Susana does. Rather than draw a hasty conclusion that the relationship of power is reversed or contrary to the main hypothesis of this study, it is worth recalling research findings that show that women have a different approach to power and tend to focus more on support and nurturance (Leet-Pellegrini, 1979 and 1980; Tannen, 1995). Still, if women have their own style and tend to be sensitive, cooperative and supportive, why should one of the women in the dyad utter so many assent terms while the other produces so few in return (the difference between raw numbers is obviously significant: 30 to 6, which means that one party produces five times more assent terms than the other, but more significant are the rates: 1/28.3 to 1/247)? A possible explanation is that Annie, the native speaker, feels so confident about her higher position in relation to her interlocutor, at least because of the mere fact of being a native speaker, that she does not mind supporting and encouraging Susana. In addition, because of her assumption of a higher status she feels she is responsible for the development of the interaction. As Givón (1989:166) states, "knowledge is power, but power is responsibility" and in the field of native–non-native communication, in particular, native speakers tend to assume the responsibility for leading the interaction, anticipating communicative breakdowns and repairing them, without damaging the face of their non-native interlocutor while they do so (Gass and Varonis, 1985 and Harding, 1986).

This is probably an instance of interaction between face and power, how to keep a balance between the need to maintain and express one's power and at the same time pay attention to the face needs of the other. If one's position in the power scale is invulnerable, there is no harm in nurturing one's interlocutor's image by, among other things, using support or back-channel utterances. Besides, if seen in light of the dependence dimension, a dimension which constitutes one of the three points of Scollon and Scollon's (1981) triangle of relationship, the fact that Annie produces so many supportive utterances may be considered an act of care-giving similar to the parental care shown towards children, which in itself is related to dominance and power, at least in some cultures (Scollon and Scollon, 1981:18).

As for simultaneous speech considered as instances of interruption, it must be noted that they have been identified partly by intuition and partly according to some of the criteria known in this field of research. It was pointed out in Chapter 2 that the concept of Transition Relevant Place would be used to identify cases of interruption, taking into consideration the difference between supportive and interruptive instances. It was also said that the distinction between the two types is quite difficult. Indeed, in the conversation analysed here it was difficult from the outset to distinguish simultaneous speech from successive turns. After all, different criteria have been suggested in the literature (pause length, point completion, topic shift, etc.), but their operationalisation is not straightforward. It has not been proved whether it is more accurate to adopt one of these criteria or a combination thereof. In addition, demarcation points between turns, points and topics are not always clear-cut in conversation. To take pause length as an example, it would be arbitrary to determine that a one-second or a two-second pause constitutes a TRP, as the perception of pause in speech varies from culture to culture and from one person to another.

Taking into consideration only pause length and completion of a turn unit (sentence, clause, phrase), that is to say, what constitutes a potential Transition Relevant Place in Sacks, Schegloff and Jefferson's (1974) opinion, the following instances of interruption can be identified:

- Turn 7 : S: Yes, because one of them is the ::: er is the ::: seminar is the::: work and these ones are the critical ...
A: Ah, OK, the primary work and the secondary works, and then you have another one.

- Turn 27: S: I think they they noticed my accent and they
  Aha
  speak to you very:::fast   You say oh, please more slowly but
  Yeah
  ...they don't
  A: (laugh) Exactly the same here. I think the Spanish, because I spent a semester in Ecuador, um six years ago, but the Spaniards here they speak so fast and even when you say slower please or whatever they, they, they stay the same but they might speak louder or something like that (laugh), so, I don't know.

- Turn 68: A: And are they ...
  S: But I think...it's because, for example, my mother er::: has been living with my father a lot of years, and then she has educated my, my brothers in the same way as er:::

- Turn 97: S: When the husband came er he he did the dinner or something ⎱He prepared things and it was, I think,
  Ah ⎰
  like your family here that er she was very dominant⎱ and...
                                              Um ⎰
  he was...⎱
  A: Yeah, well here in ... the family here is is more equal because, well because the father has to work and the mother is at home.

In turn 7 above, although there is a pause at the point of interruption, it can be easily seen that Annie takes over before Susana finishes her sentence, even before she finishes her noun phrase. Syntactically speaking, Susana's string of words "the critical..." is but a headless noun phrase. Taking into consideration that one of the possible structures of a noun phrase, according to transformational grammarians like Radford (1988), is the following:

NP = Det + AP + N

(where NP stands for a noun phrase, Det for a determiner, AP for an adjectival phrase and N for a noun), it turns out that the main component of the noun phrase is missing. "The" is a definite article (determiner), "critical" is a pre-modifying adjective or adjectival phrase and the two alone cannot constitute a noun phrase. Therefore, any listener who shares this knowledge about sentence and phrase construction would expect a noun to close the syntactic structure and complete the semantic content of the phrase. Similarly, in turn 27 Susana's "they don't" cannot be said to be a complete sentence, for if a sentence can consist of a noun phrase (subject) and a verb phrase (with or without a complement) and if a pronoun like "they" can form a noun phrase on its own while an auxiliary verb like "don't" cannot, except if the sentence is elliptic (Radford, 1988), the above string of words only constitutes an unfinished sentence with a headless verb phrase. The same can be said about the unfinished question in turn 68 and the unfinished statement in turn 97: both "are they...?" and "he was...", although the order of components is different because one is interrogative and the other affirmative, are unfinished sentences consisting of a subject (noun phrase realised by a pronoun) and an auxiliary verb, which leaves the hearer expecting another component (e.g. noun phrase, adjective phrase, prepositional phrase, or a present or past participle to complete the verb phrase and, therefore, the sentence). In addition to the syntactical explanation, prosody also provides a clue that there is still something to come. The fact that, except in the second instance, all the simultaneous speech above occurred when the previous speaker was using a rising intonation (in non-interrogative utterances) is a signal that she did not want to release the floor and, therefore, any encroachment upon her turn could be considered an interruption.

However, if analysis is not restricted to the syntactic and prosodic levels but goes beyond them to take into consideration other aspects such us the following:

1. The amount of time the interruptee has been speaking when the interruption occurs,
2. The content of the interruption (Murray, 1985),
3. Whether the interruptee loses the floor or not (Beattie, 1981),
4. Whether the interruption is supportive or competitive,
5. Whether the interruptee has made her point or not,

the above presumed instances of interruption may turn out not to be so. Indeed, in the first instance, judging from the amount of time Susana has been speaking before Annie interrupts her, especially if we take into consideration that turns at this stage of the conversation are relatively short, we can see that Annie, at least, does not try to snatch the floor too early. In addition, her interruption provides her interlocutor with words to express or complete her point ("primary work and the secondary works"), which means that her intervention is cooperative and supportive, not competitive or face threatening. However, this lexical assistance or sentence completion, as is the case for agreement and questions for clarification (James and Clarke, 1993:242), can be used as a resource/opportunity to take over the floor, although in this case Annie does not seize the floor for a long time, nor does she take it over in order to make a point. She simply provides her interlocutor with words, either to assist her or to show she understands, and moves on to ask another question or to make another comment about another book to keep the conversation going. Therefore, even if the first instance is counted as an interruption, it cannot be considered a blatant one.

In the second instance (turn 27), even if the sentence is not elliptic and although the intonation is not falling, it can easily be seen that the missing part (verb and adjunct) can be understood ("speak more slowly"). In addition, at the point where Susana is presumably interrupted, she has already spoken for some time, she has made her point clear and, what is more, Annie intervenes to support her (by relating her similar experience as a foreigner who finds it difficult to follow a native speaker speaking with a fast tempo). In the third interruption (turn 68) Susana's intervention occurs after a series of Annie's questions about sexist men, about Susana's father and a pave-the-way question about her brothers (Annie asks her if she has any brothers as a preparatory step for the subsequent question). Accordingly, when Annie says "And are they...?" it is easy for Susana and any analyst to guess what her question is about (whether Susana's brothers are as sexist as her father), which means that her intervention is not a blatant interruption, especially that this intervention is but an answer to the unfinished (but perfectly intelligible) question Annie was unable to complete. Similarly and finally, interruption number 4 (turn 97) occurs at a point where Susana seems to have finished her point (speaking about a family in London where there was no sexist work distribution) and both her interlocutor and any other audience or analyst can understand what would come at the end of her unfinished sentence (something like "submissive" or any word that has the opposite meaning of "dominant"). In addition, although her interlocutor (Annie) takes over the floor, she does so not to contradict anything

Susana said, but just to support her previous intervention with a similar case (another family in which the husband does not believe that housework is exclusively women's duty).

It can be seen, therefore, that there are relatively few instances of interruption, and even these are not of the blatant type. Rather, they seem to be of the "unmarked" kind, to use Ulijn and Li's (1995) term: a kind of interruption that "gives the impression of a normal, natural, even cooperative, turn switch" (Ulijn and Li's, 1995:592). Still, the fact that most of the interruptions are performed by the native speaker is significant, especially if we take into consideration not only the raw numbers but the interruption rates. If there were many interruptions from both sides, it could be interpreted as a sign of a high degree of involvement (Edelsky, 1993), but since it is Annie, the native speaker, who interrupts more (raw number) and more often (proportional rate), this may have a correlation with power. It is true that some researchers (e.g. Rogers and Jones, 1975) found that interruptions were not linked to dominance or power in female dyads. It is true that there are rapport-oriented interruptions that express solidarity and affection (Ulijn and Li, 1995:598; Goldberg, 1990). It is arguably true that blatant interruptions are more likely to be perceived as face threatening or to reveal power differentials than unmarked ones (Watts, 1991:143). However, the fact that the native speaker interrupts the non-native participant more often can legitimately be interpreted as a power manifestation. Because she assumes a higher status than her partner, Annie assumes the right to "encroach" upon Susana's "territory". Conversely, because Susana assumes that she is less powerful than her native interlocutor, she does not violate her territory as often as Annie does hers and when the latter interrupts, Susana offers no resistance (in Harris's, 1989, terms).

To conclude, most of the simultaneous speech found in the above conversation has been used in a supportive/accompanying manner. Contrary to Edelsky's (1993) claim that in non-task-oriented and collaboratively developed floors simultaneous talk is quite common, relatively very few interruptions have taken place in the interaction above. This scarcity of interruptive interventions may be due to face considerations and the non-competitive/non-conflictive nature of the topics discussed by the two participants. However, what is apparently confusing and contradictory is that the native speaker in the dyad is the participant who produces the largest share of both supportive back-channel utterances and interruptions. While the difference in proportion in the participants' respective interruptions seems to prove the hypothesis that native speakers would interrupt more because of their higher status in the interaction, the fact that the native speaker showed far more support than the non-native one appears to run counter to the hypothesis. Still, this can be accounted for by taking into consideration the conversational responsibility the powerful party, the native speaker, assumes and the caring and attentive forms power can take.

5.3 Topic control

Before embarking upon topic control in Annie and Susana's conversation, it is worth reiterating that the concept of "topic" is difficult to define. It is generally taken for granted that it is something people talk about, but "it is almost impossible to provide a narrow, technical definition" for it (Wardhaugh, 1985:139). It is therefore not a straightforward task to decide when a topic starts and another finishes. As is the case for many linguistic and communication concepts, there are many grey areas in the concept of "topic". In addition, "[a] conversational topic is a consensual outcome, not a private programme or agenda" (Wardhaugh, 1985:140), which means that when two or more people interact, it is their interaction that determines what is talked about, how and for how long. To say "consensual outcome", however, does not always mean that the interests of both or all participants converge. Rather, it means that decisions about topic are interactively taken, with the implication that one party may "impose" their interests on the other(s). It follows that when one party takes relatively more conversational decisions throughout the interaction, they project an image of someone in control and, at the same time, achieve their conversational and/or real-life goals.

To determine which of the two participants takes more decisions, tables more topics and exercises more control over the conversation above, let us start with a rough diagram of the topics talked about:

1. Annie → Topic: studies;
    Annie → Subtopic: Books and libraries;
    Annie → Subtopic: future (employment) plans;
2. Susana → Topic: language;
3. Annie → Topic: place of residence;
4. Annie → Topic: sexism in society;
    Annie → Subtopic: sexism in one's family;
    Annie → Subtopic: sexism in one's personal experience.

Roughly speaking, it is evident from the above diagram that the two interlocutors talk about four topics (studies, language, place of residence and sexism), which are further elaborated on in four subtopics (books and library systems in their respective countries, future employment, sexism in one's family and sexism in one's personal experience). The first three topics are part of the get-to-know-each-other stage of the interaction, while the last one is the discussion subject chosen for the second part of the interaction.

All the topics and subtopics but one are initiated or tabled by Annie, the native speaker, which indicates that she takes the initiative more than her partner does, that her attempts to introduce topics for conversation are (more) successful and, therefore, that she controls the development of the conversation. Taking into consideration that she starts the conversation, Scollon and Scollon's (1981) claim that the participant who speaks first controls the topic is proved true. This topic and conversation control, especially if viewed in light of the other manifestations of power outlined above, indicates that the native speaker in the dyad is more dominant or, at least, gains more status throughout the conversation because she not only practically exclusively tables successful topics but also contributes to their elaboration, thus gaining status in the dyad she interacts within. As Watts (1992b) affirms, tabling topics, especially if they are successful, is closely related to the status score.

5.4. Questions

When dealing with politeness strategies and manifestations in Annie and Susana's interaction above, questions were treated as a possible manifestation of face concern, that is to say, as a sign to show that one cares about one's interlocutor and wants to know something about them and, therefore, get closer to them. However, this is not the only possible function or interpretation of questions. The interpretation depends on the respective status and role of the participants, their relationship, the situational and cultural context, etc. For example, if the questions are asked by an examiner, it is obvious that they are intended to test the student or candidate who is being asked and not to obtain information or come closer to them. Similarly, if the questions are part of a police or court procedure, in addition to serving as a means to obtaining information, they usually reflect the power asymmetry existing between a police officer or a judge on the one hand and a detainee or defendant on the other (Wiemann, 1985; Harris, 1989). If they are asked by someone who is lost or who needs information about something, it is usually the case that the person asked is seen as an expert or information provider who has the power to give or withhold information (unless other factors or relationship variables force them to provide it). In sum, depending on whether one of the participants holds an institutional position of power and also on the nature of the question, this can be interpreted as a manifestation of power, just as counter questions or silence can be used as a means of resistance (see Harris, 1989, on strategies of resistance and Kurzon, 1998, on the discourse of silence).

In the above interaction neither of the two participants holds an institutional position of power. Both of them are female students, of approximately the same age, interacting as such and not playing the role of, say, a gatekeeper or interviewer. Also, neither of them is an expert as far as the topic of conversation (sexism) is concerned. The only aspect in which one of them, Annie, can be said to be an expert is the English language, in the sense of competence, not necessarily knowledge about or meta-language. Therefore, questions as such cannot automatically be interpreted as signs of power asymmetry. Still, it should be pointed out that asymmetry in linguistic and conversational surface manifestations can by itself be a sign of power asymmetry, independently of whether these manifestations "inherently" carry power connotations. This is why the analysis of the content of

Annie's and Susana's questions and the role they play in the whole interaction (who they favour and who they place in a one-down position) may reveal a given power relationship.

As was pointed out above, Annie asks 25 questions while her partner asks only one. Annie's questions can be roughly classified into three groups: 16 personal questions, 5 opinion questions and 4 requests for information. Personal questions include those questions about studies, future plans, family, place of residence, etc.; opinion questions include questions asked by Annie to elicit Susana's opinion about sexism in Spanish society and sexism in general; and finally requests for information include those questions about the location of a town or similar matters.

Naturally, since the above personal questions are not asked by an institutionally powerful agent, they remain just that: personal questions meant to acquaint oneself with one's interlocutor with a view to construct an image of her that would make communication smoother and safer (in terms of face risk). The same can be said about opinion questions. As for the other questions intended to obtain general information, the connotation of power can easily be discarded as Annie asks these questions to obtain information she does not really need. Susana has no power resources in this case, as the main condition for information to be a source of power is that the requester needs it.

However, all these questions affect the structure and content of the conversation somehow and, therefore, reveal the kind of interpersonal (power) relationship existing between the two participants. Bearing in mind that this is a conversation between equals and that Annie does not need the information she seeks, the fact that she produces so many questions while Susana produces only one send-back question leads to a conversation the largest part of which is a pattern of question–answer, that is initiator-responder or even agent–object or leader–follower. In other words, Annie, like an institutional interrogator, prescribes Susana's next actions because, by asking questions, she "narrowly constrains what will count as appropriate responses" (Wiemann, 1985:86) and, by doing so, she projects an image of "actor/agent". Susana, on the other hand, does not act but just reacts to her partner's questions or stimuli and, consequently, what is spoken about is what Annie wants her partner to talk about. Annie, the native speaker, controls the strings of the conversation and, therefore, exercises power over her interlocutor. Questions, after all, reinforce topic control, which itself is a manifestation of dominance and power.

Conclusion

As explained above, it was hypothesised in this study that the factor of nativity would play an important role in power distribution and exercise, that the native participant in each dyad would, therefore, have more possibilities to enhance their self-image and dominate the interaction (holding the floor longer, controlling the development of the conversation, interrupting more and asking more questions). It was also hypothesised that the fact that dyads were formed by two people of the same sex and approximately the same age would affect the interaction in a contrary direction: peer closeness and gender solidarity would lead the two participants towards solidarity-based and symmetrical communication and would lead the native participant to accommodate their language to their interlocutor.

In the above sample analysis, bearing in mind that:

- the interaction is a first encounter,
- the encounter is prompted, not spontaneous,
- the meeting is informal,
- the participants are of the same sex, age (approximately) and role,
- English is the medium of communication and the mother tongue of only one party,

it was found that the two participants did exactly what they were asked to do, namely, get to know each other and choose a subject for discussion. They showed interest in each other and in the topic, especially that the latter was sexism, a topic that is likely to draw two women closer to each other. As was hypothesised, it was found that two opposing forces were at work: solidarity and power.

As for solidarity or politeness strategies in general, the participants asked personal questions to show interest, gave priority to each other in topic choice (thus showing that they had the other's interests as the centre of their attention), tended towards safe topics and agreement (thus showing there was "no bone to fight over"), used in-group identity markers (thus conveying a warm and egalitarian feeling to each other) and the native speaker accommodated to her interlocutor. However, it was found that all this was not done by the two participants on an equal basis: the native speaker asked the non-native speaker more questions, she gave her priority more often and used more back-channel utterances to show support or agreement.

As for the power relationship between the two, it was found that the native speaker held the floor more than her partner (she spoke almost twice as much), that she controlled the topic and tabled topics successfully, she asked more questions and, although the instances of interruption were very few and not of a blatant type, she interrupted more.

The fact that the two forces, solidarity and dominance, were at work at the same time and that the native speaker made use of a larger number of power-related manifestations as well as (face) supportive strategies is explained by the notion of power as responsibility. Being a native speaker enabled Annie to assume a higher position in the dyad and, consequently, to contribute more to the conversation, to control it and somehow control her interlocutor, but at the same time and for the same reason (nativity power), she felt she had the responsibility to maintain the flow of the exchange between the two, nourish her interlocutor's face and show her support.

B. Second interaction

1. Transcript

What follows is the reproduction of the conversation which took place between a 24-year-old Spanish female participant referred to as Catalina and a 22-year-old American woman referred to as Tracy:

1. Catalina: So, you begin (laugh).
2. Tracy: OK, well, my name is [Tracy] and I'm American from New Jersey, but I studied in Washington DC. I finished my studies with a degree in Spanish and American studies and international relations and a certificate for teaching English. And I also studied some German (laugh). Ah, I'm here teaching English and I plan going back to the States, after being here on sabbatical, to::: to improve my Spanish to find a job and go back for my Master's degree in business. So, your turn (laugh).
3. Catalina: And did you study history or Spanish literature?
4. Tracy: Yes. Because that was kind of ... it's Spanish language and foreign studies not American studies, so I've read not the whole (??????) *Don Quijote,* a lot of old Spanish (????) ⎱ so
                  Uh huh ⎰
   as an American speaker of Spanish, *vosotros*... It was always difficult for me to catch on to::: I still don't do it very well (laughter) and what do you...what are you...you said you're looking for a job, what do you want to do?
5. C: U:::m, I don't really know what I want to do because I finished last year my studies of political science and my ideas and the things I want to do are different from... Well, when I began my studies I had the idea of being a politician⎱ and now
     Uh huh   ⎰
   I've realised I don't want to be this ⎱(??????) and I want to
            (laugh tog.) ⎰
   change. And the problem is that I don't really know what I want to do, I know what I don't want to do, and in order to find a job, that's a problem, because I don't really know er::: what I should do, what I could do, what I would like to do, so it's complicated for me. That's why I began to study the course of Cooperation because I think it's eh connected with politics, but from a different point of view⎱ Eh, I don't know, I'm
                                              Uh huh ⎰
   trying to find another thing, to change what I had thought before.
6. T: So, is the Cooperation type of non-profit work? I don't know if you have that here, in the States it's working with the public, but non-profit

B. SECOND INTERACTION

where ... you work doing type of voluntary work, for example, Green Peace is a non-profit organisation, Um the Red Cross is a non-profit, they bring in money but they don't make money. The business doesn't make money. Do you know what I mean?

7. C: Yes, it's true, I think it's non-profit, maybe I'll be a volunteer, er

8. T: No, you get paid but, for example, the cost...the cost of the business (????) so you still get paid but never make...tons of money (laugh). Yes

9. C: This is why I don't think I'll be professionally er dedicated to Cooperation, maybe I'll do it like...er...I don't know. I'll work I don't know where, which will be ⎤ my job but I want to know this world and maybe I
   Uh huh ⎦
want to work with trade unions or things like that. I have to know this new world,
ONG, ONGs ⎤ I don't know how you call it.

10. T: Ah! ONGs, NGOs: non-governmental organisations. ⎤
                                                Uh huh ⎦
Yeah and they're organisations that do not have contact with the government. ⎤ They're separate, they're non-profit. That's
   Yes ⎦
non-governmental organisations. ⎤ Um, we have in the States,
                            Uh huh ⎦
I studied in Washington DC and there's tons of non... NGOs, there's tons of them. I can't count them. And eh a lot of my friends have gone into non, NGOs, have gone to do that kind of work. It's...they say it's fulfilling, it's fulfilling as a job, but it's not well paid. You'll never be a millionaire. But you'll like your work. (????) ⎤ (laugh).
   C: Yeah ⎦

11. C: So, did you say before you wanted to work with an enterpri::se, to export, import, eh are you thinking of Latin America?

12. T: Yes. Well, I'll be working in Philadelphia, New York area um, you know where New York City is? ⎤ I live... an hour and

13. C: Ah, yes.   ⎦
a half from New York City and then half an hour from Philadelphia, two hours from Washington. (????????) the main centre of the States, the main heart, so there's a lot of, there's a lot of jobs, there's a lot of ... industries you can go into. When you study in the States you study a career, but it's not necessarily what you're going to do. Actually, it's almost never. Maybe five per cent of the people who study their first two years, who study certain career, go to the career, for example, we don't... if you study law you don't study law in the first four years, you study whatever and then you go to Law School afterwards. So, usually, the careers are very specific. If you want to study medicine, you study some medicine for the first four years and then you have three more or seven years more.

So, people, you can study medicine and then go to pharmacy or go into chemistry, it's basic sign to the first four (form?)

Uh huh

So, it's very general: you can study history and then go to politics, or study maths and go into er teaching, something, teaching maths or teaching...or going to business or going to politics, you never know. Then, supposedly the next ambassador to the States is a businessman, a businessman from Arizona and in Mexico, nothing to do with politics, but you find your way into something. While in Spain you study business go to business (laugh), you study history, politics, you go to politics. It's very direct but there it's not direct at all, so I don't know what I will do.

14. C: Do you think it's better or not?
15. T: It's different, because the studies are very different. Um when you study your career here in university you go right into your career. If you study law, your first day you study the history of law, but in the States you have almost two years, a year and a half of basic. For example, I studied Spanish language, I had two semesters of biology, a semester of maths er two semesters of history, general culture ...of...of writing, which is English, general things, I studied economics, so they're not... it helps preparing you to do more things, I came out with a ...degree in Arts, in languages but I understand the ideas of economics, supply and demand, I mean that you come out with a wider knowledge (???????)
16. C: I think it's better the American system (laugh)
17. T: I also had...I learned in the beginning (???) politics (???) I had an internship, working for a congressman, so it was volunteer but I worked in his office, I saw politics, I don't like it (laugh) I don't want to do this, so I knew my first year that, OK forget it, that's (????) So, you get introduced to a number of things and then you decide in your second year what you want to do, you enter and you have a general idea, you enter and say: "I want to study politics", they say: "OK, you study politics but you need to take these courses, these general courses, so...and you have one or two for your major, for your main studies, and er after two years you decide for sure what you want and you declare your study, so you get introduced to many different topics, you get introduced to er Cooperation and international Cooperation, I had a class called World Politics, they introduced me to it, er and another class called Human Geography. They introduced me to er not to countries but the NGOs that're working in countries and the politics that are involved. So I was introduced to these things. So I knew it was an opportunity, so you... you get introduced to more things and you know where you want to go...earlier. Some people finish, like me, in four years, and I said: "No (laugh) I still don't know, I'm not sure. So, I think...that's what's good about it and I also had the opportunity to ...be certified to teach English. You know, I did that, I did all this in four years, and my, my second study is international relations, which is associated with international cooperation, so I knew that kind of area, international area that I want to get into, more inter-

national business, so it gave me more information. Whereas here they say: "OK, what are you going to study?" And you can study for a year business, I hate this, but I don't know what else I want to do, because they don't show you anything. They don't introduce you to ... maybe law, or maybe English or ... international cooperation, you're hung up.

18. C: Yes, I think that's the problem. You have to decide, decide your future with a specific *puntuation*, because here you have to, to choose according to the *puntuation* that you have and well, in my case I was sure what I wanted to do without knowing what I wanted to do because I ...I said: "I want to study political science because I'm very interested", but when you get in touch with the university system you see that it's not the idea that you had ⎱ Um and that's why you see that you are
   Uh huh ⎰
lost. Um, I'm worried because here in Spain you will have to decide too soon what you want to do because the system was changed and even children have to decide if they want to take maths or language, and I think it's very negative, because I think to live with other people it's better to...to have a similar education, what you say, ⎱ that you're twenty and
   Right ⎰
you studied biology and history, for example, eh you get in touch with people, eh you have the same culture and then I think it's very positive because er you have more things in common, ⎱ I have friends who study
   Yeah ⎰
medicine, history, er psychology and I see that they're specialised. They have a special conversation with the colleagues, and then I see that I'm lost because I have my specific conversation, they have their specific conversation about medicine, for example, er and I think it's not positive, because you're so specialised that, that you lose things in common with other people. And I'm afraid of that (laugh tog.). I see my friends, they're different and I, I tend to stay with people who had studied the same as me⎱ and I think it's not positive, you find your friends er with
   Uh huh⎰
the same
um, um   ⎱ interests and it's good but I see that I lose
19. T : interests⎰
things in common with friends that I had before, and I think it's not good ⎱and I think the system of education you receive
20. T: No⎰
eh is connected with these things ⎱ so...
21. T : Yeah, the people stay in their⎰ school and in the university system, for example, just like here, you have my university, American university, and you have College of Business and the School of International Service and College of Arts and Sciences and you notice that the people usually stay in their, in their specialised group, ⎱ but they have other contacts,
   Yeah ⎰
because the classes, the course overlap...

2. Context and participants

There are no major differences between this conversation and the previous one: the conversation between Catalina and Tracy, like the one between Annie and Susana, was conducted in the framework of the following contextual variables:

- First encounter,
- Face to face,
- Interaction for research purposes,
- Participants: two young white women, with no significant age gap,
- Equal roles,
- Language of interaction: English,
- Status in relation to the language of interaction: Tracy is a native speaker and Catalina non-native.

3. Topics and conversation structure

The conversation opens with "So, you begin (laugh)", the non-native speaker asking the native speaker to contribute to the conversation first. This is responded to by the native speaker disclosing some information about herself (her name, nationality, city of origin, profession, studies, etc.). Instead of taking this option, Tracy could have "passed the buck" back to Catalina (saying, for example, "No, *you* first"), thus avoiding speaking first, or she could have accepted the turn assignment but chosen to ask a question (e.g. "What's your name?" or "Are you studying here?"). However, she obligingly (and probably self-confidently) responds to Catalina's suggestion (or request). When she finishes or thinks that she has provided sufficient information about herself for the time being, she selects her interlocutor as the next speaker by saying, "Your turn." Of course, since the interaction is dyadic, there are no other participants to select, but she could have continued self-selecting and, therefore, holding the floor. Once more, judging from the options that have been left out, Tracy could have said something like "Now you know more about me" in a falling intonation, thus giving Catalina a clue that she has finished and that her (Catalina's) turn can begin. She could also have asked a direct question like "And you?", "What about you?" or "Do you study here too?". Instead, she chose to "meta-communicate" about communication, like Catalina had done in the opening: "So, your turn."

Such overt references to beginning the conversation and shifting turns give the impression that the conversation (or at least the beginning) is not spontaneous. Normally, the rules and conventions of interaction are tacitly assumed and not overtly stated as they are above. When two individuals meet, they do not overtly decide who should speak first, for how long and about what subject. Rather, except for greetings and closings, which have some culturally set formulae and follow a certain conventional pattern, "what occurs in a conversation is *spontaneous* (unscripted and, by and large, uttered as it springs to the minds of participants)" (Lakoff, 1990:43). Of course, there are formal contexts where there might be a preset order of interventions and an agreed time limit for every speaker (e.g. conferences and law courts); however, this is not the case here. Catalina's "So, you begin" and Tracy's "So, your turn" remind us of the ballroom scene in Jane Austen's *Pride and Prejudice*, in which Elizabeth gives Mr. Darcy instruction-like comments about how their interaction should proceed, when they can be silent, and what each one of them can or should say at specific moments. In the context of the novel this can be interpreted as a satire upon the conventions of the high society Mr. Darcy represents.

In the context of the conversation under analysis, Catalina's "you begin" might be interpreted as reluctance to self-reveal first, as a cautious strategy to obtain more information about her interlocutor before starting "real" conversation. It might also mean something like "this is an artificial task, this is a kind of game, so you should lay your cards first". Tracy's "your turn" sounds like a payback: "you've selected me as the first speaker, so I'll select you as the next speaker". Judging from common assumptions about how a casual conversation should proceed (with contributions from both/all parties), Tracy's utterance can be understood as saying something like "this is a joint task, so it's high time you contributed to this ongoing conversation" or "self-disclosure in such a context should be reciprocal; I've revealed a bit about myself, I can't go on until you do the same about yourself". To Tracy's surprise (if she had this meaning in mind), Catalina responds with a question: "And did you study history or Spanish literature?", thus "forcing" Tracy to reveal more about herself (speak more) before she (Catalina) decides to talk about herself. This time Tracy chooses to ask a direct question: "And what do you...what are you...?", to which Catalina responds by disclosing something about herself (studies, unclear future...), thus balancing the self-disclosure relationship between herself and Tracy. At this point reciprocity can be said to be recovered.

Catalina's International Cooperation course leads Tracy to select cooperation/non-profit organisations as the next topic. She starts by asking if what Catalina refers to as cooperation is non-profit work, and (after listening to an explanation of what non-profit means) Catalina replies affirmatively. Tracy's cooperation/non-profit work as a topic can be seen as showing interest in what her interlocutor does (a positive politeness strategy: "What you are doing is worth speaking about, it's no insignificant activity that had better go unnoticed."). However, what Tracy also does is appear as the expert/authority on the topic of non-profit work and non-governmental organisations. First she asks whether cooperation is the same as non-profit work, but she does not wait for the answer. Rather, she gives a definition of the term and speaks about the existing non-profit organisations in the United States. In addition to this, when Catalina hesitates, repeats the acronym ONGs (the acronym in Spanish but with an English pronunciation of the letters) and seems to ask for assistance ("I don't know *how* you call it"), Tracy does not only provide the English equivalent (NGOs), but seizes the opportunity (and the floor) to explain what non-governmental organisations are, to speak about her friends who have joined NGOs, and to give her personal opinion about the kind of job NGO work is.

After this, Catalina changes the topic by asking Tracy about her future plans. The question seems like a payback to Tracy's question about Catalina's plans ("What do you want to do?"). Tracy replies with a long intervention (about 330 words) which answers the question and also goes on to speak about the American educational system and compare it with the Spanish one. This leads Catalina to ask her which is better in her opinion. Tracy, however, does not give a committed answer. Catalina's question, "Do you think it's better or not?" apparently leaves her with only two options: either "The American educational system is better" or "it is not". However, Tracy chooses a third one: "It is different", an option which might be induced by her avoidance of a "potential offence" ("comparisons are odious", and in this case they might offend the national feeling of the interlocutor or create conflict). After Tracy's explanation of the difference between the two educational systems, Catalina takes a speech turn just to say that she thinks the American system is better. Catalina, therefore, does compare the two systems; however, she does not create conflict, as her comparison favours the *other*. In fact, this might simply be a personal opinion based on her previous knowledge about the two systems or on Tracy's explanation/comparison, but it may also be a tactful gesture towards Tracy's positive face (downgrading oneself and one's talents/possessions/group and upgrading/praising one's interlocutor's is a common strategy to enhance one's interlocutor's self-image and to communicate one's perception of the interaction as cooperative and not competitive).

In this conversation, as is the case in a few others, the two research tasks were subtly joined. Instead of having two easily identifiable parts (getting-to-know-each-other and topic discussion, the two separated by a negotiation stage), in this case there is a smooth shift from one to the other, without any overt reference to or negotiation of the topic to discuss. In this conversation, however, what is a "purely" getting-to-know-each-other part is very short (actually, Catalina gives very little information about herself, maybe because of her reserved character), and what can be called the second part seems to begin when Tracy starts speaking about the American and Spanish educational systems, and more clearly when Catalina asks her, "Do you think it's better or not?" This apparent confusion/mixture of the two parts/tasks may have been a mere coincidence with one of the topics included in the list of suggestions, namely number 9: Which is the best: the American, British or Spanish educational system? For Tracy's move from speaking about her plans to speaking about jobs in the United States and the educational system is perfectly coherent and poses no relevance problems. It may also have risen as the main topic simply because one or both participants had a look at the list and tacitly chose it (without a negotiation stage). Nevertheless, it is difficult to guess which was the case, as both interpretations are plausible and the topic shift occurred very smoothly and subtly. One conclusion is almost certain, however: in the perception of (at least) these two participants, there was no significant difference between the nature/formality of the two tasks assigned by the researcher.

In terms of structure and adjacency pairs, the conversation proceeds as follows:

1. Suggestion (opening)
2. Acceptance
3. Question
4. Reply + question
5. Reply
6. Question + explanation
7. Reply
8. Correction + explanation
9. Response (new contribution)
10. Correction (word supply and explanation)
11. Question
12. Reply (with an imbedded question followed by Catalina's affirmative answer)
13. Question
14. Reply
15. Opinion (statement)
16. More reply (to 13)
17. Agreement + more explanation
18. Sentence completion (word supply)
19. Agreement + explanation.

4. Politeness strategies

Some possible psychological and situational interpretations have been proposed above for Catalina's opening with "you begin" (1). However, a question worth considering is whether this turn assignment can be understood as a politeness strategy. More precisely, Brown and Levinson's (1987) Strategy 1: notice, attend to H as a means to claim common ground. Indeed, by letting Tracy contribute to the conversation first, Catalina may be said to perform a positive politeness strategy. Moreover, by performing it in such a plain and straightforward manner as "you begin" she seems to presuppose familiarity in the S (speaker)–H (hearer) relationship, thus not only claiming but also presupposing common ground (Strategy 7 in Brown and Levinson, 1987). Similarly, Tracy's designation of Catalina as the next speaker after her first turn can be interpreted as including both S and H in the activity (Strategy 12 in Brown and Levinson, 1987) and assuming or asserting reciprocity (Strategy 14).

Catalina's question in (3) ("And did you study history or Spanish literature?") and Tracy's in (4) ("What do you want to do?") can be interpreted in the same terms. Both of them mean something like, "I'm not asking you this merely out of curiosity, but I'm really interested in what you've done/

you're going to do." In (6) we find something similar: "So... is the cooperation type of non-profit work?", which means that Tracy, immediately after Catalina mentions the cooperation course she is completing, shows interest in what her interlocutor is doing. Later in the conversation (10) Tracy performs more positive politeness strategies/face-boosting acts by praising the kind of job Catalina will be doing after graduating ("It's fulfilling as a job", "But you'll like your work"). To compensate her, Catalina asks her what she thinks about the American educational system and later shows her own preference for the way American students are prepared and oriented. In other words, she seems to tell her interlocutor: "Your opinion counts very much to me," and seeing that Tracy avoids a better-or-worse comparison of the Spanish and American educational systems (thus opting for Strategy 5: seek agreement choosing safe topics, and Strategy 6: hedging opinion), she herself seems to say, "Your (American) system is better, you should be proud of belonging to such a country and of having been educated in such a system." Strategy 5 is once again used by Catalina in (18) ("Yes, I think that's the problem"), which shows her agreement with what Tracy says before.

In sum, positive politeness strategies seem to be a dominant feature in the above conversation and they are centred around Strategies 1, 2, 5 and 6. These strategies show that each participant is concerned with the other's positive face (interests, future, group membership, etc.) and tries to convey the idea that both have enough things in common (difficulties with foreign languages, studies and worries about the future, etc.) as to seek agreement and avoid unsafe topics or discussions. Avoidance strategies, on the other hand, make the interaction look not as solidarity-based as strategies 1, 2, 5 and 6 would suggest (intimate topics and questions, for example, are avoided, and Tracy especially avoids asking Catalina personal questions when she notices that she does not respond to her own self-disclosure with a similar move). Therefore, the conversation includes a combination of avoidance strategies and positive politeness ones. The following table sums up the instances and kinds of positive politeness strategies used by each participant:

Table 6: Politeness strategies in Catalina and Tracy's interaction

Politeness strategy	Tracy	Catalina
Notice, attend to H	4	5
Exaggerate	3	2
In-group identity markers	2	1
Seek agreement	5	3
Avoid disagreement	4	1
Include both S and H in activity	1	1
Presuppose common ground	3	2

The above table shows that both participants use positive politeness strategies. What it does not show are the avoidance strategies because they are realised in the form of silence, that is to say, by not performing potential face-threatening acts, not asking about potentially unsafe personal topics, etc. Instances of noticing the other's interests and assuming common ground are more or less equally distributed between the two participants. On the other hand, the fact that Tracy avoids disagreement with hedges more than Catalina does not mean that the latter seeks disagreement. Rather, it is because she is not asked any risky questions requiring a diplomatic answer or an avoidance strategy.

5. Power manifestations

5.1. Topic control

The conversation between Tracy and Catalina covers four main topics, namely studies, employment prospects, non-profit work and educational systems. The third topic could be considered as a mere subtopic of the second one, especially in view of the fact that it is tackled at a point in the conversation which is engulfed by discussion of future employment plans. If it is considered as a topic on its own, however, the resulting topic structure will consist of five topics, three of which are tabled by the native speaker and two by the non-native participant. The native participant's topics are contributed to with eleven speech turns, while her interlocutor's receive nine turns only:

Catalina ➔ Initiator: "You begin."
1. Tracy ➔ Studies (3 speech turns)
2. Tracy ➔ Work plans (2 turns)
3. Tracy ➔ Non-profit work (6 turns)
4. Catalina ➔ Work plans (2 turns)
5. Catalina ➔ Educational systems (7 turns).

Obviously Catalina's initiator "you begin" does not table a topic; rather, it just opens the conversation or refers to its opening. The first topic is tabled by Tracy, the native speaker, when she introduces herself and starts speaking about her previous and present studies. The second topic is also tabled by Tracy and so is the third (sub)topic (non-profit work). The latter is first mentioned by the non-native speaker while she is talking about her studies and plans, but it is the native speaker who picks it up and tables it as a topic in turn 6 ("So, is the Cooperation type of non-profit work?") and develops it (with the help of her interlocutor) into a successful one (a topic that manages to get the attention and the contribution of the participants).

The fourth topic (or rather the resumption of the second one) starts in turn 11 ("So, did you say before you wanted to work with an enterprise, to export, import, eh are you thinking of Latin America?"). At this point Catalina goes back to talk about employment plans, in particular to ask her interlocutor what she intends to do in the future and, in this way, she completes the reciprocity adjacency pair (Tracy asked her earlier about her plans and now she returns the same question). This point does not clearly constitute a new topic, as it is the continuation of the previous one. Actually, in the turn immediately preceding turn 11, Tracy talks about work:

> And eh a lot of my friends have gone into non, NGOs, have gone to do that kind of work. It's...they say it's fulfilling, it's fulfilling as a job, but it's not well paid. You'll never be a millionaire. But you'll like your work.

In addition, Catalina's anaphoric reference in "Did you say **before** you wanted to work with an enterprise?" suggests the present point in conversation is closely linked to a previous point in the interaction, namely when Tracy started speaking about employment prospects.

As for the last topic of this conversation, namely educational systems, it has been pointed out that it was tabled by the non-native speaker, Catalina (turn 14). However, it is the native speaker, Tracy, who brings it up first (turn 13): While talking about employment plans, she tackles the topic of studies and the educational system in the United States and Spain:

> While in Spain you study business go to business (laugh), you study history, politics, you go to politics. It's very direct but there [in the United States] it's not direct at all, so I don't know what I will do.

Still, although Tracy is the first one to mention the topic of educational system and to make a comparison between the States and Spain, it is clear that she does so while she is talking about her employment plans, which is the main topic up to this point (turn 14). On the other hand, when Catalina asks her "Do you think it's [the American educational system] better or not?" (turn 14), it is clear that the topic shifts from employment plans to educational system and it is similarly clear that the non-native speaker is the agent of topic tabling at this point.

Accordingly, judging by the number of topics tabled by each participant and the number of speech turns each tabled topic receives, it can be said that Tracy, the native speaker, is in a slightly more advantageous position. She tables three topics out of five and her topics are contributed to with eleven turns out of twenty. When this is viewed in light of the amount of contribution to the development of topics (see the following section) and the degree of conversational, not real-life, expertise (see the discussion of co-operation and non-profit work above), it is verified that the asymmetry in topic development and control clearly favours Tracy, the native speaker.

5.2. Amount of speech

The length of the whole conversation is approximately 26 minutes; it consists of 1727 words (counting the contracted forms but not back-channel utterances or pause fillers), 1252 of which are spoken by Tracy, while only 475 are Catalina's. There are 21 speech turns in the conversation, 11 of which are Catalina's and 10 Tracy's. The average turn length is 125.2 words for Tracy and 43.18 for Catalina. The two participants have approximately the same number of turns (11 to 10), which is reflected in the above list of contributions and adjacency pairs (every question is followed by an answer and every contribution is responded to, which gives rise to a Catalina–Tracy–Catalina–Tracy pattern).

As is the case for Annie and Susana's conversation above, the interaction between Catalina and Tracy is far from a fifty–fifty distribution of talk between the participants. Tracy speaks almost three times as much as Catalina, whose speech turns do not occupy the floor for as long as her interlocutor's. The two potential explanations proposed above for the distribution of talk in the first interaction are applicable in this case too: either the non-native speaker idiosyncratically tends to speak in relatively short turns or her interlocutor does not allow her to hold the floor for long.

As has been pointed out above, while dealing with the amount of participation in the conversation, some factors, like expertise, status or power difference, emotional excitement, or psychological/personality traits (e.g. talkativeness/taciturnity) may be the reason why one participant contributes to the conversation more than the other(s). In this conversation, the role of expertise can easily be discarded, as it was Catalina who was the more knowledgeable participant in non-profit work and International Cooperation, as she was undertaking a postgraduate course in the subject when the conversation was recorded. In addition, she might know nothing about the American educational system but she certainly knows more than Tracy about the Spanish one, so if Tracy could speak about the American system Catalina could speak about the system in her own country too. The factor of possible emotional excitement can also be discarded, as the two participants were apparently calm and neither of them showed any signs of a particular psychological state before or during the recording.

The factors that could plausibly be behind the above asymmetry in contribution are taciturnity and power relationship. Actually, judging from the researcher's previous acquaintance with both Catalina and Tracy, but separately, it can be affirmed that the former is relatively more taciturn and introverted, although these attributes are not absolute but context-sensitive. As for power difference, and as the hypothesis of this study predicted, the fact that one of the parties is a native speaker and the other non-native may have led the participants to perceive their relationship and their respective status as asymmetrical. The native participant, therefore, assumed a higher position and contributed more to the conversation, while the non-native counterpart did just the opposite. This goes in harmony with James and Drakich's (1993) claim that higher-status participants perceive themselves as more competent and, as a consequence, tend to dominate the floor. However, and as was the case for the first conversation analysed above, tentativeness is required at this stage, as asymmetry in amount of speech cannot be correlated with status in absolute terms, especially in view of Tannen's (1993: 166 and 1995: 176) claim that a larger amount of speech is not always a sign of power.

5.3. Simultaneous speech

The instances of simultaneous speech in the conversation amount to 23. These fall into three groups: back-channel utterances (16, 10 of which are realised with "Uh huh", and 6 using yeah/yes/no/right), interruptions (5) and lexical assistance/sentence completion (2). Back-channel utterances are normally used to let the person who is speaking know that the addressee is paying attention. Therefore, these utterances have a supportive function as they give the current speaker signs to encourage them to continue holding the floor (Roger, 1989: 92). However, as was done in the analysis of Annie and Susana's conversation, these utterances have been classified into two groups, "Uh huh" on the one hand and yes/yeah/no/right on the other. This was done because "Uh huh" is normally a sign of "passive recipiency", while words like "yes" are often used to change or curtail the current topic (Jefferson, 1981, 1983 and 1984) or even to encroach upon the current speaker's speech turn. Indeed, three of the four interruptions in the conversation start with yes/yeah:

- 9: Yes, this is why I don't think I'll be professionally dedicated to cooperation.
- 18: Yes, I think that's the problem.
- 21: Yeah, the people stay...

Similarly, lexical assistance or sentence completion can be used as a resource/opportunity to take over the floor, and this is exactly what happens in (10): Tracy provides Catalina with the acronym NGO and continues speaking. Thus, as is the case for agreement and questions for clarification (James and Clarke, 1993: 242), providing one's interlocutor with the word they need can be used as a pretext to seize the floor.

Of the five interruptions, three are Tracy's and the rest, of course, are Catalina's. The difference is apparently insignificant. However, if the interruption rates, not the raw numbers, are compared, a significant difference emerges: the outcome is 0.006 for Tracy and only 0.001 for Catalina. In other words, while Tracy interrupts every 158 words of Catalina's speech, the latter interrupts every 626 words of Tracy's. Therefore, although the difference in instances of interruption is minimal, when the respective amounts of speech of the two participants are taken into account, Tracy turns out to interrupt more often than Catalina does. What is more, their respective interruptions vary in the circumstances of occurrence and the degree of blatancy as well: Catalina's two interruptions occur at points which can possibly be taken as Transition Relevant Places (after the laughter following the sentence "you still get paid but never make tons of money" and at the end of the sentence "you're hung up"). The only reason why they have been considered interruptions is that there are no pauses at all between Tracy's last utterance and Catalina's first one in either case. On the other hand, two of Tracy's interruptions occur after finished sentences but while Catalina is filling her pauses with "er" or "so", used as cues to signal that she has the intention to continue speaking, which makes the two interruptions more interruptive (it should be pointed out, however, that the interruption in (8) is urgently necessary because it is intended to avoid a misunderstanding, Catalina mistaking non-profit work for volunteer work). Tracy's other interruption occurs at Catalina's mid-turn, while she is looking for the right acronym in English (NGOs). As has been said earlier, Tracy does not only take her interlocutor "out of the woods" with her cooperative gesture, but seizes the opportunity to take over the floor—and for a long time. She seems to say, "Knowledge is power; I can share my knowledge with you, but my knowledgeable status as a native speaker gives me the right to interrupt you and get more conversational status."

To conclude, simultaneous speech is used in the above conversation in a supportive/accompanying manner most of the time. Relatively very few interruptions occur, although out of the few that take place the native speaker's sound more blatant. This scarcity of interruptive interventions may be the result of face considerations as well as the non-competitive/non-conflictive nature of the topics tackled. However, the difference in proportion and blatancy in the two participants' respective interruptions seems to prove the hypothesis that native speakers tend to interrupt more because of their relatively higher status in the interaction.

Conclusion

Unlike the conversation between Annie and Susana, the interaction between Catalina and Tracy opens with an explicit reference to turn-taking or turn assignment, that is, the conversational opening ritual. Unlike the first conversation too, the second one mixes the two conversational tasks assigned by the researcher, namely getting to know each other and topic discussion. However, as far as the main subject of this study (face and power relationships) is concerned, the two interactions show similar patterns in many aspects.

Like in the case of Susana and Annie, the interaction between Catalina and Tracy is smoothed over by the use of positive politeness strategies claiming common ground, showing interest, seeking agreement and avoiding disagreement. However, these strategies are used together with negative politeness (avoidance) strategies intended to respect the intimate sphere of one's interlocutor and to avoid impositions upon her. This mixture of both types of strategies is not contradictory; rather, it shows that the relationship is not totally solidarity-based but both the need to be approved of and the need to be free from imposition are at work and are being paid attention to (Brown and Levinson, 1987:230).

As for power manifestations, and as was predicted in the hypothesis of this study, the native speaker controls and dominates the interaction and, therefore, emerges as the most powerful party in the dyad. She tables slightly more topics than her interlocutor, she talks almost three times as much as the non-native speaker, her speech turns are longer on average and she interrupts more often (although the instances of interruption are very few, the proportion of the native speaker's interruptions in relation to her interlocutor's amount of speech shows an imbalance in her favour). What is more, she enhances this high status by appearing as the authority or the expert in the interaction: as a native speaker, her assistance is sought when lexical gaps or language matters emerge, and as a normal interlocutor she contributes effusively to the topics of conversation, including the one which is the field of expertise of the non-native speaker in this case, namely International Cooperation and non-profit work.

Chapter 4
Overall findings

I. Background

The total number of conversations, including the two analysed and discussed above, is twenty. Chronologically, six female dyads were recorded first, then four male ones, two months later, and finally six male and four female ones, three months later. The dyads were as follows (the names have been changed to de-identify the participants):

1. Susana (24, Spanish, student of English language and literature) and Ellen (22, American, exchange student).
2. Susana and Annie (26, American, exchange student).
3. Tracy (22, American, student and private language school teacher) and Catalina (24, Spanish, political sciences graduate).
4. Annie and Catalina.
5. Ellen and Rosa (20, Spanish, student of English language and literature).
6. Tracy and Rosa.
7. Brad (26, Irish, student and private language school teacher) and Juanito (20, Spanish, student of English language and literature).
8. Juanito and Bob (26, Irish, student and language school teacher).
9. Bob and Diego (27, Spanish graduate).
10. Diego and Sam (27, Irish, student and private language school teacher).
11. Camilia (32, Spanish, unemployed) and Rachel (28, American, student).

12. Camilia and Elizabeth (30, American, student).
13. Adriana (26, Spanish, NGO volunteer) and Rachel.
14. Adriana and Elizabeth.
15. Manolo (36, Spanish, lawyer) and Valentine (35, Irish, language teacher).
16. Manolo and Adam (38, Scottish, translator).
17. Adam and Petrovich (32, Serb, translator).
18. Petrovich and Valentine.
19. Moumen (29, Moroccan, translator) and Mitch (29, English, teacher).
20. Moumen and Adam.

Generally speaking, all the conversations seem relaxed, casual and positive-face centred. They are characterised by a tendency to opt for safe and impersonal topics such as football and travelling. However, there are certain intimacy traits (especially among women), for example, when the two participants in a dyad get to know each other by asking personal questions or by discussing general topics through their personal experiences.

The interactions began with openings in the form of introducing oneself, asking one's interlocutor about their place of residence or country of origin, noticing something they were carrying, etc. There are, however, a few conversations which began with an overt suggestion like "you begin" (e.g. Catalina and Tracy's interaction analysed above). The participants, then, became involved in what is identified in this study as a get-to-know-each-other stage. The interactions varied both in terms of the length of this stage and the way participants moved from one stage to another. Some of them talked effusively about themselves and about any topic that emerged on the way, without paying attention to the instructions of the researcher (asking them to choose a topic from a list for discussion after a five- or ten-minute personal introduction). Others started with a brief introduction and immediately negotiated or launched a topic (the topic discussion, thus, taking most of the time of the conversation), while a few others talked freely and for a long time about personal and non-personal matters, until they realised they had not chosen a topic from the list and proceeded to do so at the end of the conversation (the topic-discussion part, thus, occupying only an insignificant share of the interaction).

The conversations included a variety of topics, not only the ones suggested by the researcher but also others raised by the participants themselves. However, there was a tendency for male and female dyads to speak about different topics, men speaking about football and politics and women about sexism and their families. When, in one case, female participants did talk about football, they approached it from the angle of sexism. Football and politics were two recurrent topics among men, and they occupy a considerable share of speech time. In some cases the two participants spoke about football as a get-to-know-each-other topic and then went back to it after or within the other selected discussion topic. In one case, after the first part of the conversation, the participants considered that it was time to select a topic for discussion, thus starting the second part of their task. However, while they were thinking about which topic to choose, one of them wanted to resume football talk because he had not asked his interlocutor about his favourite team. The conversation about football continued for a considerable time before they decided to choose human rights as a discussion topic. As for the list of suggested topics for discussion, participants selected languages (five times: three female and two male dyads), sexism (twice, both female dyads), religion (three times: two female and one male), human rights (three times, all of them in male dyads), euthanasia and abortion (twice: one male and one female), football (twice as main topic, both times by male dyads) and education (once, by a female dyad).

When the participants felt there was nothing to add about their chosen topics, they showed their willingness or readiness to bring the discussion to an end through a falling intonation, repetition of each other's short utterances, closing cues such as "so...", "you know", "anyway", laughter, or looking silently at each other.

II. Phatic communion in openings

As pointed out above, the participants to this study were not acquainted with each other and did not have a pre-established role to play. They interacted with each other for the first time in an informal and apparently symmetrical encounter. The lack of previous contact and the fact that the situation did not have any institutionally or conventionally clear-cut role distribution leads us to expect the participants in each conversation to start by sounding out each other before getting involved in conversation. This sounding out is usually performed through what Malinowski calls "phatic communion", which is "a type of speech in which ties of union are created by a mere exchange of words" (Ogden and Richards, 1923:315). When the interactants do not know each other very well and do not already know the roles they are supposed to play, phatic communion provides them with a means to tentatively explore each other's social and cultural identity as well as mood or state of mind. It also allows them to define and assume a role or relational position for themselves and for their counterpart (Laver, 1975:219). This is why it is interesting to consider the "exchange of words" in the opening phase of the recorded conversations, as they will probably reveal the relational position of participants, especially knowing that the choice of one phatic communion token rather than another is likely to be determined by, and also convey, a status differential or a power relationship (Laver, 1975:224). What follows are the transcripts of the openings of the twenty conversations. It must be noted that a few turns were extracted from the beginning of each conversation without taking into consideration any objective criteria to determine whether those turns constitute the whole opening or just part of it:

1.
    N: (Laugh). This is (??)
    NN: Tell me something.
    N: (Laugh) Er, I guess I should explain where I'm from, what I'm doing here, er I'm from California, in the United States, I'm studying in Alcala this whole year in an exchange programme with other students from California, and I'm just studying, I have classes in the careers, majors of History and Humanities, and *Filologia, Filologia* (laugh) *Hispanica* and so that's, that's why I'm in Spain this year, and you?
    NN: I'm studying English philology here because I like English very much and languages and I don't know, I'm 24 years old and er, perhaps today I'm going to work as a teacher for the first time, an English teacher, and I went to London last year er for two months to study English and to attend a course and ... I don't know, nothing else.
    N: It's good. Did you grow up in Alcala? Are you from Alcala?
    NN: No, I live near here, 20 kilometres more or less ⌠It's
    N: Uh huh⌡
    difficult because there is no bus and my father has to bring me here and ⌠because he works
    N: Aah!⌡
    N: I see (laugh). Is it your third year?
    NN: Yes   ⌠yes one more and, and then er I
    N: Is this your third year? One more?
    hope to work as an English teacher.

2.
    N: So, are you a doctorate student?
    NN: No.
    N: No? With all these books (laugh)?
    NN: Yes, because I have to:::, to make a::: a work and er er for English literature and ⌠I'm in the third year.
    N: Ah, but ⌡
    N: Ah, OK. And all these books are from the library?
    NN: Yes, because one of them is the::: er is the::: seminar is the::: work and these ones are the critical..⌠
    N: Ah, OK, the primary work and the secondary works, and then you have another one.
    NN: No, no.
    N: Oh, OK, OK.
    NN: (??)
    N: Because in Spain you can only take three books out of the library. ⌠In the United States you can take out many books.
    NN: Yes ⌡
    NN: No, but for example, we have there two libraries, here one library and you can take three books from here, three books

from there ..⎱
N: Ah, I   didn't know that. Well, that's good to know (laugh). OK, so
you're in your third year of English here?
NN: Yeah.

3.

NN: So, you begin (laugh).
N: OK, well, my name is [......] and I'm American from New Jersey, but I
studied in Washington DC. I finished my studies with a degree in Spanish and American studies and international relations and a certificate for
teaching English. And I also studied some German (laugh). Ah, I'm here
teaching English and I plan going back to the States, after being here on
sabbatical, to::: to improve my Spanish to find a job and go back for my
Master's degree in business. So, your turn (laugh).
NN: And did you study history or Spanish literature?
N: Yes. Because that was kind of ... it's Spanish language and foreign
studies not American studies, so I've read not the whole (??????) *Don
Quijote,* a lot of old Spanish (????) ⎱ so as an American speaker of Spanish,
NN: Uhum   ⎰
vosotros... It was always difficult for me to catch on to::: I still don't do
it very well (laughter) and what do you...what are you...you said you're
looking for a job, what do you want to do?
NN: U:::m, I don't really know what I want to do because I finished last
year my studies of political science and my ideas and the things I want to
do are different from... Well, when I began my studies I had the idea of
being a politician ⎱ and now
Uhum   ⎰
I've realised I don't want to be this ⎱ (??????) and I want to
                   (laugh tog.)⎰
change. And the problem is that I don't really know what I want to do,
I know what I don't want to do, and in order to find a job, that's a problem, because I don't really know er::: what I should do, what I could do,
what I would like to do, so it's complicated for me. That's why I began to
study the course of Cooperation because I think it's eh connected with
politics, but from a different point of view⎱. Eh, I don't know, I'm
N: Uh huh   ⎰
trying to find another thing, to change what I had thought before.
N: So, is the cooperation type of non-profit work? I don't know if you
have that here, in the States it's working with the public, but non-profit
where ... you work doing type of voluntary work, for example, Green
Peace is a non-profit organisation, Um the Red Cross is a non-profit,
they bring in money but they don't make money. The business doesn't
make money. Do you know what I mean?
NN: Yes, it's true, I think it's non-profit, maybe I'll be a volunteer, er...

4.
N: So, what do you do? Do you study here?
NN: No, er yes, I mean I study but not not here in this university.
N: Ah, OK, in another one?
NN: No, not in in another er university, I'm studying international co-operation in an institute...in Madrid.
N: International cooperation! Great, interesting. And what subjects do you study? International politics, I guess? This kind of things? I don't know (laugh).
NN: Yes, international politics and relations, er economics, development, er environment, of everything a li...a little. And you?
N: I'm here in Alcala University studying Spanish language and literature, just for one year, a Master's program, you know.

5.
NN: Um, what's your name?
N: [Name]
NN: [Repeats name]?
N: [Repeats name], you're [name]
NN: Yeah.
N: Yes.
NN: You knew it?
N: Because he [the researcher]'s just introduced us.
NN: Oh, yeah. I've seen you in the::: in the classes.
N: Oh, you have!
NN: Yeah, I think you had last semester⌈Mexican Literature,
⌞Uh huh ⌟
no, Chicano⌉   yeah Chicano⌉
⌞Yeah ⌟   ⌞Yeah ⌟
N: Were you in the class?
NN: Yes, in the first room.

N: (Laugh tog.) I was always in the back⌉ and the professor⌉, I
⌞Yeah⌟   ⌞(laugh)⌟
hated that professor so bad.
NN: Very strange.

6.
N: Where do you live?
NN: In Guadalajara.
N: Guadalajara.
NN: You know that city?
N: I know where it is, anyway.
NN: Aha. Very near Madrid.
N: Yes.
NN: And you come from?

N: United States. My family is in New Jersey and I studied in Washington D.C.
NN: Uhum. And what are you studying?
N: I studied (I finished) ⎱ Yes ⎱ I studied Spanish
NN: Oh! You finished ⎰ Congratulations ⎰
language and international relations   Rela⎱tions
NN: And something about politics? International relations. ⎰
as far as dealing with other cultures⎱Politics, business and a bit
NN: Aha   ⎰
of everything.
NN: OK (laugh).

7.
N: Are you from Madrid?
NN: Yeah.
N: What part?
NN: Er...from Alcorcon, it's a village in the south of Madrid ⎱
                                                   Ah, OK. ⎰
but er very, it's very well communicated with the central part of Madrid.
N: OK, you take a bus? And ⎱   (??) I live in San Bernardo.
                    Yes⎰
NN: Sorry!
N: San Bernardo, you know where that is, in the centre.
NN: Oh no, no.
N: Yeah, right in the centre, between Bilbao and Plaza España ⎱
                                                        Yeah⎰
OK.
NN: Do you work here or ...?
N: Yeah, I work in Aximedia ⎱ but in Las Matas, so I take the
                     Ah⎰
train everyday to Las Matas and give classes there. So what do you do? Are you studying or?
NN: Yeah, I'm studying (??) in the University of Alcala and with... very far from here ⎱ you know, it's a travel everyday one
        Yeah⎰
hour and a half in train, you know.
N: So, return three hours?
NN: Three hours yes, and in the train I always arrive at home with this position.
N: Wow! You can study on the train, no?
NN: No, I want to sleep.

8.
NN: What do you like most of Madrid?
N: What I like most of Ma...about Madrid...er...er...I like the lifestyle, I like the Spanish lifestyle, you know...the...days you wake up, you have classes, I have classes, u:::m you can have lunch, you can eat well, I like the food...er...having siesta ⎱ Some days, when it's possible, I like the siesta,
NN: Parties? Very important.
er ... I like going out, I like the bars, I like the cafés, going for *tapas*, it's great!
NN: You know, er ... in Ireland there are no bars like these ones, with *tapas* and ..⎱
N: Er... not really, you have cafés and bars and then you can get food in the bars, of course, but not er ... not as much fresh food, not as much er selection, you know, so I think I like the food in Spain. Er...yeah, *tapas* (laugh)
NN: What about Ireland?
N: Ireland, you mean the food or lifestyle?
NN: The food, the nightlife...
N: OK, er food is ...is OK. (???)⎱
NN: It's, it's better than British?⎰
N: I don't know, I don't really know British food ... that much, I mean a lot of ... chips and⎱
NN: (??) I've been to London for a month and I didn't like British food. It's ... I think it is very horrible⎱ Well, compared
N: Uh huh   ⎰
to :: Spanish one I think that Spanish food and Italian and Greek food ⎱ are the best foods in the world. But I don't know ...
N: Uh huh ⎰
Irish food   ⎱ I've never been in an Irish restaurant.
N: Yeah ... OK. ⎰

9.
(???? Simultaneous speech)
NN: OK, I introducing myself⎱ So I'm [Name] (laugh)
           (Laugh) OK.⎰
N: I'm [Name].
NN: Where are you from?
N: From Ireland.
NN: From Ireland.
N: Yes.
NN: So, what are you ...you are teaching here? In this academy?
N: Yes, I teach in this academy also.
NN: So, it's the best way to survive in this country at the moment for foreign people, to give classes, no ?
N: I think so, it's a way to earn a living in Spain ⎱ teaching
(Laugh tog.)   ⎰

English (????) There are so many schools, a lot of people want to learn English.

10.
NN: I'm [Name]
N: I'm [Name]. Good to meet you.
NN: Nice to meet you. So ... I said I said Mustapha [the researcher] er my level of English is not a good one, no?
N: It sounds ⎫ it sounds nice.
NN: So ... ⎭
N: There's no rush, we'll take our time.
NN: OK, so what are you studying?
N: I'm teaching English.
NN: You're teaching?
N: Yes, I work for this academy here.
NN: Ah (laugh) (???)
N: Some fear, yeah, but don't fear, there are advantages in talking to English speakers. Yeah, I work in this academy and I teach English, mostly in business English, in er⎫
NN: Business English? OK. ⎭
N: Yeah, in companies and Repsol ⎫ and things like that. So ⎫
NN: Uh huh ⎭   But, sorry, ⎭ you teach English for people who is working for ...Repsol?
N: Aha.

11.
N: (Laugh tog.) Where are you from?
NN: Er, Madrid ⎫ Spanish. And you?
         OK ⎭
N: I'm from Boston, in the United States.
NN: All right, where is that?
N: Oh, it's (??) the East Coast (???) ... you know the United States?
NN: Yeah.
N: Well, (???)
NN: Ba:ston?
N: Boston, yeah.
NN: Ah, Boston!
N: Yeah.
NN: Boston, all right, I don't understand your accent.
N: Oh.
NN: I was in the United States er... last, last Autumn, I was in South Carolina ⎫ So I was used to a different accent.
Oh, South Carolina ⎭
N: Oh, why were you there?
NN: I was working at a ... Spanish-speaking (??) college.
N: Ah! OK, that's good.

12.
>   NN: (??) Are you American or?
>   N: Yes, from New York.
>   NN: Ah, From New York! Right.
>   N: (laugh) Where are you from? Are you from Madrid?
>   NN: Yeah.
>   N: And what do you do?
>   NN: Well, at the moment I'm unemployed, I'm looking for a job, I'm just back from the States.
>   N: Oh! What did you do?
>   NN: I was working as a Spanish teacher, I was working in South Carolina, in a (??) college (??) Bible there (??)(Laugh tog.).
>   N: And did you like it?
>   NN : Well, I liked the people, they are very warm and (??) but the religious things ⎤ They were Baptists. My students tried to
>   N: Keen on (??)   ⎦
>   convert me to Baptism.
>   N: No!

13.
>   N: So this is gonna be like the same conversation I had (laugh) very much.
>   NN: Do you want to have this ... the same one?
>   N: Oh, no.
>   NN: Sorry, but you should speak slowly.
>   N: Oh, OK.
>   NN: Because so...
>   N: OK.
>   NN: Yeah? If you want to:: to:: introduce ourself ⎤   first
>   N: OK Well, that's the
>   same thing in English, when speak really quickly in Spanish ⎤ I have no idea, I live with a family here and the
>   NN: Aha, you don't understand.
>   brother is always chattering away ⎤ And I always say *"Lo siento,*
>   Uh huh ⎦
>   *no te entiendo"*.
>   NN: Very difficult for you.
>   N: Uh huh.
>   NN: How long have you been studying Spanish?
>   N: Er, studying Spanish? Since eighth, since seventh grade, so seventh, eighth, ninth, tenth, eleventh, twelfth ...nine years, a long time.
>   NN: Nine years?
>   N: A long time, you know what, it's not the same as living in the country where they speak Spanish. In four months I could learn more than I did in five years. I mean it's totally different.

14.
   N: Er....(laugh).
   NN: So I ... I think you should start because you are the English one or American one.
                                                   OK
   N: So, ...(laugh) OK, how old are you?
   NN: Eh?
   N: How old are you?
   NN: I'm 26 years old.
   N: 26, and what do you do?
   NN: What?
   N: What do you do? What's your job? What are you studying?
   NN: I have studied Law and I'm a lawyer, yeah.
                         Law
   N: And were you born in Madrid?
   NN: I was born in San Sebastian, in the north ... of Spain. And how old are you?
   N: I'm thirty, I was born in New York, I went to school in (???) I have one more year left and I'm studying in Spain for 4 months.

15.
   N: Hello, good morning!
   NN: Good morning.
   N: How are you?
   NN: Fine.
   N: Uh huh, grand, nice weather we're having.
   NN: Yes, in Spain in this time is normal.
   N: Uh huh, a great advantage of this country is the weather.
   NN: Yes.
   N: Er, are you from Madrid?
   NN: Yes, I am from Madrid.
   N: You've always lived in Madrid?
   NN: I, I born in Madrid, I live in Madrid, but my fathers are from ...Extremadura.
   N: Ah, right, right.
   NN: My fathers was were immigrants.
   N: OK, what what, so you have a village...
   NN: Yes ...in Badajoz.
   N: Ah, right.
   NN: The town of my fathers is (??) Duque.
   N: Ah, great great, and do you go there often?
   NN: Only for weddings and some parties, two years ago, on holidays one week, and you? Where do you come from?

16.
N: So, where are you from?
NN: I am from Madrid.
N: Uh huh. What part of Madrid?
NN: What?
N: What er district of Madrid?
NN: Er in the south, in Usera.
N: Uh huh, I thought you were going to say you're from Vallecas.
NN: Yes, no, it's near but er it's not ... it's a place near of Casitas, what do you say? A worker district of Madrid. And you? Where do you come (???) from?
N: Um, my family from Scotland, well, my mother from Scotland and my father from South Africa and I was brought up in the Bahamas.
NN: In the ...Have you lived in the Bahamas?
N: Yes.
NN: Er, you didn't live in, in Scotland, never?

17.
N: (laugh) I'll start off just by asking you where you're from.
NN: Well, I'm from the er, they ask me "where are you from?" Well, I say (??) I'll let you guess, I'm from the worst country in the world and I belong to the worst people in the world, they say "you are from Serbia", I say (laugh) "yes, you're right". And...
N: Yes, I remember during the first Bosnia war, one of my er little boys (???) five and six, and one of them said to the other "you're a Serb" and the other one started crying.
NN: (laugh) Of course (??)
N: So, how do people from your country feel about that?
NN: Well, it's it's quite interesting er I mean they ...don't understand why is it so (...).

18.
N: Hello, good morning!
NN: Good morning (laugh).
N: How are you?
NN: Fine.
N: What is your name?
NN: My name is er, in English, I like to translate names, you know, [name]
N: Uh huh, [name] What's the origin of this name?
NN: It's a Greek name, I've heard it was a Greek historian, sixth sixth century er called [name], historian of Emperor Justino? He wrote *The Secret History of (??)* He was the person,
    Uh huh

the most famous person I know in history (??) ⎫I don't know,
                                   Uh huh   ⎭
there's also a restaurant in Paris called er the oldest, actual... they
say it's the oldest er café in the world, it's called Café
[name]⎫It's also (??), but it's not very, it's not very (??)⎫not in
Uh huh⎭, great, great   Uh huh   ⎭
my country. In Spain, well...
N: What do Spanish people call you?
NN: [name]
N: [name]
NN: It's Hispanised, but I like it.

19.
NN: Well (laugh)
N: Begin
NN: Me first?
N: Yeah.
NN: Where are you from?
N: I'm from er from London ⎫My mother is er my mother's Spanish.
                Uh huh   ⎭
NN: Uh huh, you were born in London?
N: Yeah, I was born in London. I lived there for about twenty years and
then moved to Spain.
NN: When did you come?
N: I'm sorry?
NN: When did you come?
N: When? Er ten years ago. Ten years ago.
NN: So, you've been living here for a long time.
N: Yeah.
NN: More than me.
N: Yeah.
NN: I, I've been here for only six years.
N: Uh huh.

20.
N: Nice to meet you.
NN: (laugh) Pleased to meet you (laugh tog.)
N: So, where are you from?
NN: I'm, I'm from Morocco, and you?
N: Er interesting story, my family er from Scotland, I was brought up in
the Bahamas and then I was sent to a boarding school in Scotland⎫ so
                                                       Uh huh   ⎭
I'm a bit of a traveller (???) in
NN: You were born in the Bahamas?
N: No, I was born in Scotland.
NN: Aha, and in Scotland where, where did you live?

N: First in Glasgow and then in Perth, which is north of Edinburgh, quite cold in winter ⌉
NN: Uh huh, The, the Scottish people speak differently from er English people?
N: Yes, thi: um the Scottish accent is (???) based on Gaelic.

As the conversation openings above illustrate, most of the interactants started off using common formulaic expressions such as, "Where are you from?" or "Nice to meet you." Still, a few others diverged from this conventional and predictable procedure and started with a general "request" (e.g. "tell me something" in the first conversation) or "meta-communication" utterances, such as "I think you should start because you are the English one" (in dyad 14 above), "So, you begin" (dyad 3) or "This is gonna be like the same conversation I had…" (dyad 13). While the formulaic greetings and questions about occupation or country of origin serve the purposes of "defusing the potential hostility of silence", feeling the way "towards the working consensus of [the] interaction" and initiating the conversation (Laver, 1975:220-221), the other opening moves referring to the conversation itself or overtly indicating who should speak first do serve (at least) the first and last functions, but in an uncommon fashion. Usually, when two people start an informal conversation, they do not say anything like "let's start a conversation" or "who should speak first?". That is to say, they do not explicitly meta-communicate, they just initiate their interaction following the tacit conventions at work in their speech community and applicable to the situation. So, the fact that some of the participants started their conversation with such explicit references reveals that the interaction, at least its beginning, was not natural or spontaneous. After all, it is known that it was arranged by a third party, in a specific physical context, for research purposes. However, saying that the interaction was not spontaneous in the beginning does not necessarily mean that it was not spontaneous at the later stages. Nor does it mean that the participants would not abide by the conversational conventions they learned and practised throughout their life experience. Rather, the very fact of starting with phatic communion is a sign of normality and constitutes evidence that conversational conventions were being applied.

Phatic communion at the opening stage, as Laver (1975:119) explains, includes several verbal and nonverbal stages, such as eye contact, greeting gestures, facial expressions of cordiality, proximity, and "stereotypical linguistic symbols". In the above conversations, however, some stages were skipped as a consequence of the very arrangement for the interaction to take place in a specific office or classroom. That is to say, because the researcher invited two participants to a specific closed place and asked them to sit in a certain arrangement, this made some phatic communion gestures such as movement towards one's interlocutor unnecessary, if not impossible, and also saved the participants the effort of making the necessary preparatory moves to start the conversation. However, if some of the phatic communion stages were skipped because of the situation itself, others (both verbal and nonverbal, such as eye contact, smiling, greeting, etc.) were still necessary and possible.

However, since only verbal interaction was recorded and only verbal tokens are reproduced above, the account below focuses only on verbal manifestations of phatic communion. According to Laver (1975:222), in phatic communion "all the tokens have deictic reference"; that is, except for formulaic greetings, phatic communion utterances refer to the situational context immediately relevant to the interaction. They can be of three types: neutral (referring to non-personal aspects such as the weather, a view, a party, etc.), self-oriented (referring to aspects which are narrowly specific to the speaker) or other-oriented (referring to objects, subjects or aspects which are personal to the addressee) (Laver, 1975:223).

In the above conversations what stands out is that there are no neutral phatic communion tokens, such as references to the weather, the physical surroundings or the recorder on the table. An exception is Valentine's "grand, nice weather we're having" in dyad 15, which comes after two speech turns for each participant, using formulaic greetings and responses ("Hello, good morning", "How are you?" and "Fine"). It should be pointed out, however, that this exception must be the result of Valentine's role-play acting, his obvious lack of spontaneity and attempt to simulate a typical opening. Indeed, in the beginning of his two conversations (dyads 15 and 18 above), it is clearly evident that he was acting in a manner that reminds the listener of classroom situational or functional role-play tasks, which require students to follow a given conversational model or script. This is corroborated first by the fact that he had already exchanged a few words with his partner before the recording started, so there was no need for his first moves and, second, by the high tone and rising intonation that obviously indicate affected role playing. It is curious that the rest of conversation openings do not include a neutral reference, while this one, which sounds like non-spontaneous role-play, does; when two or more language learners (in this case a teacher who is used to classroom tasks) are asked to perform a role-play task, what they are normally asked to perform is a prototypical conversation for the given situation or communicative function. It seems, then, that a prototypical phatic communion token, at least in some cultures, is reference to the weather and that since the conversations above were arranged rather than being casual or spontaneous, this token only appeared in one of them (precisely, the one that calls up the prototype because one of the interlocutors, Valentine, was acting without being asked to).

Most conversations opened with other-oriented questions, followed in number by formulaic expressions of introduction and, finally, greetings:

Other-oriented questions:

Annie (dyad 2)
Rosa (dyad 5)
Tracy (dyad 6)
Brad (dyad 7)

Juanito (dyad 8)
Rachel (dyad 11)
Camilia (dyad 12)
Adam (dyad 16)
Adam (dyad 17)

Introduction:
Diego (dyad 9)
Diego (dyad 10)
Adam (dyad 20)

Greeting:
Valentine (dyad 15)
Valentine (dyad 18)

As for the conversations that opened with references to the conversation itself (dyad 13) or with "negotiating" who had to start speaking first (dyads 3, 14, 19 and, to some extent, dyad 1), the participants later complied with the ritual of introducing oneself (dyad 1: "I guess I should explain where I'm from" and dyad 3: "Well, my name is...") or asking other-oriented questions (dyad 14: "How old are you?" and dyad 19: "Where are you from?").

The use of neutral tokens is normally available to everybody, independently of the social status or the relational position of the speaker and the addressee, and when speakers choose them, rather than the other two options (self-oriented and other-oriented tokens), they are on safe and uncontroversial ground (Laver, 1975:224). The choice of other-oriented tokens, on the other hand, may have a relational significance, since it means invading the psychological world of the addressee and, therefore, the interlocutor who makes use of it tends to be considered as higher in status than the addressee. However, if the user of other-oriented tokens is acknowledged as relationally inferior to their partner, the token tends to suggest that "the status differential between the two participants is irrelevant to the momentary relationship" (Laver, 1975:225).

Out of the twenty recorded conversations, nine opened with an other-oriented question. Classified according to the "nativity" criterion, most of these (6 out of 9, that is to say two-thirds) turn out to be asked by native speakers. Taking into consideration the hypothesis above that native speakers would be relationally more powerful, this disproportionate distribution could mean that native participants assumed a one-up position from the very start, allowing themselves to invade the psychological world or the personal territory of their interlocutors. If, on the other hand, there was no assumption of power or status differential, the same finding could be interpreted as a sign of solidarity. According to this reading, participants who chose other-oriented tokens would appear to convey that social status differential was not relevant in their interaction, and that their asking questions about the home town, country or job of their interlocutor was intended to show interest and to build up a picture or a working consensus, in order to pave the way for further interaction.

Indeed, the above openings can easily be seen as normal phatic communion openings in which the participants ask questions, first to break the ice, reduce distance and potential hostility and, second, to collect information about their counterpart which is necessary to know who they are interacting with. However, underlying this apparent normality there may be something else. It is because everyday conversation sounds so normal and common that we "tend to take it for granted and do not fully realize or acknowledge the extensive range of personal achievements and failures that are enacted in and through conversation" (Ng and Bradac, 1993:60). This means that in some contexts (e.g. court, classroom, consultation room, etc.) the relationship between interactants is clearly defined and institutionally known to confer a one-up position to one party over the other, while in everyday (apparently) equal encounters power relationships tend to go unperceived because the ritual and the commonality of the conversation make us take them for granted. Even for researchers, power differentials and exercise are harder to track in the non-hierarchical settings of everyday conversation (Ng and Bradac, 1993:61).

To avoid taking the above other-oriented questions for granted, a basic assumption should be pointed out which is associated with informal conversation, namely that "participants...share equal rights of speakership" (Drew, 1991:22). Everybody is free to start a conversation or to take a turn, while, of course, playing by the rules of social relationship and conversation itself. To this it should be added that speakership makes it possible for the floor holder to exercise control, because it "requires attentive listening to ongoing utterances" (Ng and Bradac, 1993:74), which means that when a participant speaks, the other *has* to listen and process what is said, because they may be "tested" about it later. Speakership also makes it possible for the speaker to increase their amount of talk and, therefore, to control the topic and emerge as a leader (Ng and Bradac, 1993:77–81). With these assumptions in mind, the facts of starting the conversation and asking other-oriented questions will probably turn out to have a function and an interpretation other than that of phatic communion.

Taking into account the participant who starts speaking and the number of other-oriented questions in every conversation opening above, regardless of whether one or both participants ask more questions later in the section of the conversation opening that is not transcribed above, the following account is intended to determine whether there is a significant pattern.

In dyad 1 the native speaker starts with an unintelligible utterance, to which the non-native participant replies, "Tell me something." This is followed by a sixty-nine-word self-introduction by the native speaker and a sixty-five-word self-introduction by the non-native one. The native speaker asks three other-oriented questions, while the non-native speaker does not ask any. In dyad 2 the native speaker starts with a question and asks four questions, while the non-native interlocutor does not ask any. In dyad 3 the non-native speaker starts with, "So, you begin," to which the native participant replies with an eighty-six-word self-introduction. The latter responds to the question and then asks another in return, to which the former replies with a hundred-and-sixty-four-word turn. The native participant still asks one more question, followed with an explanation of the term "non-profit" (seventy words). The latter then asks two other-oriented questions, while her partner asks only one. At the opening stage of dyad 4, the native speaker starts and asks three questions, while her interlocutor asks only one in return. In dyad 5 the non-native speaker opens the conversation by asking the name of her partner and the latter asks one question too. In dyad 6 the native participant speaks first, but she asks only one question, while her partner asks three. In dyad 7 the native speaker is the one who starts also; he asks six questions, not all of which are strictly other-oriented, while the non-native speaker asks only one. In dyad 8 it is the non-native participant who starts speaking, and he asks three questions, mainly about national lifestyle, while his addressee does not ask any. In the opening of conversation 9 there is simultaneous speech first, followed by a self-introduction by the Spanish participant, who asks three questions, while his partner asks none at this stage. In conversation 10 above, the non-native speaker starts by introducing himself and later asks two questions (it is worth noting that he also makes a self-oriented comment on his lack of competence in English). In dyad 11 the native speaker starts; she asks three questions and her partner only two. In dyad 12 the non-native participant starts with a question (the only one she asks at this stage), while the native speaker asks four. In conversation 13 the native speaker starts with a comment about the conversation and asks no questions, while her partner formulates two. In dyad 14 the native participant starts with a hesitation utterance or a gap filler ("er"), the non-native speaker yields the floor to her by saying, "I think you should start," and as for questions, only the native speaker asks them (four instances, two of which are repetitions). In dyad 15 the native participant starts; he asks three questions and his partner asks only one. In dyad 16 the native speaker starts also (with a question) and he and his partner ask three questions each. In conversation 17 the native speaker opens the conversation and asks two questions, while his partner formulates none. In dyad 18 the native participant starts speaking too and asks three questions. In 19 the non-native speaker starts with a hesitation or a floor claimer ("well..."), his native partner asks him to begin and he (non-native) later asks four questions, one of which is a repetition. Finally, in dyad 20 the native speaker starts with a formulaic expression ("Nice to meet you"); he asks one question and his non-native partner asks four.

Thus, out of the twenty conversations, twelve are clearly initiated by native speakers (2, 4, 6, 7, 9, 11, 13, 15, 16, 17, 18 and 20), while only five are clearly initiated by non-native participants (3, 5, 8, 10 and 12). As for questions in the opening stages above, and taking out the repeated instances, native speakers ask most of them, 41 to be exact, while their non-native co-participants ask only 31 (see Table 7 below for details).

The fact that more native speakers start the conversation may enable them to take hold of the floor, to table topics, to restrict the role of their co-participant, to serve their own purposes and to achieve their conversational goals. In other words, speakership may allow them to manifest their power to do things. Of course, it is not always true that speakership is equivalent to power or control, as in some situations, especially institutional ones, the spectator (the civil servant, the judge, etc. who speaks less and listens to others) is acknowledged as the one in control. In addition, it is not always true because in some other situations it is more advantageous to wait until one's interlocutor speaks first and reveals something about themselves, to let other people speak rather than be engaged in speaking oneself, in order not to go on record and not to reveal one's ignorance or shortcomings, etc. (Ng and Bradac, 1993:70). Still, speaking first and speakership in general give the speaker the opportunity to achieve their objectives, as keeping silent deprives one of the means to achieving these objectives (Ng and Bradac, 1993:70).

Table 7: Distribution of questions at the opening stage between native and non-native participants

Dyad	Native speaker	Non-native speaker
1	3	0
2	4	0
3	2	1
4	3	1
5	1	1
6	1	3
7	6	1
8	0	3
9	0	3
10	0	2
11	3	2
12	4	1
13	0	2
14	2	0
15	3	1
16	3	3
17	2	0
18	3	0
19	0	3
20	1	4
Total	41	31

One of the ways the first speaker may exercise control is through what Pearce (1976) and Ng and Bradac (1993) call "casting":

> An actor wanting to play a favourite part in a script must find a stage and a group of people to fill the other roles. The actor offers them particular roles and engages them to enact the assigned roles on his or her own terms. Likewise, speakers may cast, by direct or indirect means, their hearers into particular conversational roles. (Ng and Bradac, 1993: 63–64).

Thus, when the first speaker chooses to start with a question, the addressee's role is restricted to that of responder, and when the first speaker chooses an other-oriented question, the listener is "forced" to answer the question and reveal some information about themselves. It goes without saying that this addressee can dodge the question (by refusing to answer, being vague or replying with another question, for example), but normally, when the question is not seriously face threatening and the answer does not lead to disclosing confidential information (or anything that is not in the interest of the responder or the group or organisation they represent), the responder abides by Grice's (1975) Cooperative Principle and satisfies the expectations of adjacency pairs (question–answer, greeting–greeting reply, request–accepting/declining, etc.).

By providing the second part of the adjacency pair, the second speaker, at the surface level, does nothing but cooperate, be polite and play by the conversational rules. However, at a deeper level, they seem to play by the rules of the first speaker and, therefore, they may be under the first speaker's control. This is one of the possible interpretations of the relational function of the above 41 questions asked by native speakers. Indeed, in addition to invading the territory of the addressee and making them reveal personal information (in one instance, even age, which was not really necessary for the conversational purposes), these questions cast the non-native speaker to the role of responder and allow the native participant to choose the subject of conversation and direct its course (if the relationship allows them to, that is, if there is no resistance from the other party).

III. Topic negotiation and decision making

As is well known, the participants to this study were asked to select a topic from a list and talk about it once they finished the stage of socialising or getting to know each other. Obviously, this was a task to be performed, but this does not mean that all participants in all dyads proceeded as instructed. In fact, in some conversations, as will be seen below, the participants continued talking about themselves and a variety of topics, without paying attention to the list of suggested topics, or at least without overtly negotiating and deciding over a topic. Others, however, did negotiate, giving rise to a stage in the interaction which is easily identifiable as a topic-negotiation stage. Therefore, it is interesting to have a close look at this part of the conversation, to see how the negotiation works, how the decision is taken and

III. TOPIC NEGOTIATION AND DECISION MAKING

who takes it. Let us then start by reading through the transcripts of the negotiation stage of all the dyads:

1.
NN: (Addressing the researcher) OK, do we choose…a topic?
Researcher: Well, feel free. You can do it if you like.
N: They are, they are interesting, very much.
NN: Yes. I don't know. (Pause). Which one do you like?
N: Er, (pause) How about …(??) So many choices (laugh).
NN: Languages
N: Languages? OK (laugh tog.) It's typical. OK, when did you start learning English?

2.
N: OK. All right. Very good. Are we … oh, we have … suggested topics, do you wanna pick one? (long pause) Is this your first time?
NN: No.
N: No, OK.
NN: It's the second one.
N: I don't know what, whichever one is fine for me. (Pause). I'll let you pick… (laugh).
NN: No.
N: OK, do you want me to (pause, sound of unzipping). You, you're far-sighted?
NN: Um?
N: You're **far-sighted**? Do you need glasses?
NN: No.
N: Oh, OK. Oh, tissues! (laugh) (pause).
NN: I don't know.
N: OK, er::: (pause) Which, which haven't you talked about? Shall we talk about number 4 "Is your society sexist?"
NN: OK.
N: Yeah? (laugh tog.) All right, so do you want to start? What do you think, what do you think of the Spanish society?

3. Smooth move: no overt topic negotiation.

4.
N: OK, shall we pick a topic? Come on, choose one.
NN: Um (pause) I don't know.
N: We've been talking about sexism [name] and me. Would you like to talk about it?
NN: OK, why not?
N: Right, so do you think Spanish society is sexist?

5.
NN: Do you have any topic or something? (Pause)
N: (Laugh) These are interesting topics and questions (laugh)
             Yeah   (laugh)
What do you think?
NN: Er, you choose because I chose with the other (laugh)...
                                                  Oh
girl. I don't want to... You choose.
N: Let's see (pause) How about ...number 6?
NN: Number 6?
N: "Do you think religion is the opiate of the people?"
NN: OK, (laugh).

6.
N: They're touchy (laugh) touchy subjects (laugh) ...What are you most interested in?
NN: Um, I like, for example, number 11,   number 5. They're
                              OK
very interesting, all of them, and you?
N: Um, number, I like number 11 or ...9 or number 4 "Is society sexist?"
                                              Yeah
NN: Well, you choose.
N: No (laugh).
NN: OK, you don't want to choose?
N: (laugh) You choosing (laugh).
NN: Um, would you like number 11, for example, since you're
                                       Yeah
studying Spanish? You like it, OK?
N: I studied English and Spanish Linguistics because I'm certified as (....).

7.
NN: What do you want to talk about?
N: I don't know, I haven't got my glasses, one of the topics. "Do you think we live in a society of human rights?" (continues reading the suggested topics). I don't mind. What did you talk about last time?
NN: (???)
N: You spoke about football before, no?
NN: Yes, we spoke about everything but (???) of topics, we talked about movies, about football, but ...
N: We, we can talk about football about the football, about it
                     About what?
being a disease Do you have a strong opinion on this?
NN: OK.

NN: Yeah, I think (...).
Second topic:
N: Shall we talk about another topic? (Pause) Is your society sexist?
NN: Yeah.
N: Yeah?
NN: OK. (Pause) Do you think it's sexist?
N: In Spain? I don't know.

8. Smooth move.

9. Smooth move.

10.
NN: OK, we could choose to talk about one thing or...
N: Definitely, yeah, because I did (???)
NN: Because we have five minutes (laugh)
N: You pick one.
NN: But I haven't ... I asking you you're supporter of one team, or ...?
(They continue speaking about football for some time)
N: Right, pick pick a subject.
NN: I don't mind, the first one seems to me interesting but just a very, a big
N: What does it say?
NN: Do you think we live in a society of human rights, no?
N: Of human rights?
NN: This is the question (laugh) or you think we live in a society which is going to::: to:: make these human rights completely::: destroyed?
N: Er...
NN: This is the question.
N: I know, I know. Um...
NN: I know that for this year five years ago the first serious papers about human rights (...)

11.
NN: OK, shall we start with one of these? We're supposed to (??) ...
N: (muttering) Which is going to be the language of the 20th century? It's not gonna be Spanish, I'm sorry (laugh). I think it'll be English.
NN: It'll be English? Spanish will be
N: Spanish will be second.
NN: The second one.
N: Yeah. Yeah.

12.
N: Do you think we should talk about...?
NN: Yeah, we should start. What do you ...?
N: I don't know, you choose.
NN: Do you think football? (??) You're not very ...into that one, American football ⎱ soccer ...
          No ⎰
N: I'm not sure if he means soccer or football.
NN: Yeah, that's a good question to do. Er American football (??) er ... Are you for or against abortion?
N: Er, I don't know, I wouldn't do it personally but (...)

13.
NN: We didn't choose a ...subject.
N: OK, um what did... ⎱
NN: Yeah, but we need ⎰ to finish because we have been talking for a long time.
N: (Laugh) What did you talk about with [name]?
NN: We were talking about 6 is your society sexist.
N: Oh, is your society sexist.
NN: (??) Which, which ...one ... did you choose?
N: We did 6, we did 11 er... and we did a little of 8 ⎱ (pause)
                                         Uh huh ⎰
Yeah, very generic questions ... You kind of talked about one, do you think...
NN: Diet (laugh)
N: We talked about diet exactly.
NN: What do you think of American diet?

14.
N: Um, I don't know which one... (Pause) Which one do you pick? (Pause).
NN: Which one do you ... prefer?
N: Whatever, it doesn't matter (laugh) (pause). The easiest for you (laugh). For me, ...
NN: I don't mind. (Pause) So, do you want to talk about human rights? Religion?
N: About this one: "Is your society sexist?"
NN: Sexist? Yeah, if you want.
N: Is it OK?
NN: I don't know if I ...I can say much (laugh) much about that.
(Later)
NN: If you want to change the ... the top... the subject or the topic.
N: Do you want to?
NN: No, if you, if you want to go on with it, but I don't know if I can tell (??)

N: Well, I was going to ask you a question, I was going to say ... they have the running of the bulls.

(They continue speaking about the participation of Spanish women in bull running and other aspects of sexism).

15.
N: What subject would you like to talk about? Have you, have you read them?
NN: Um (pause)
N: Mr. Taibi has has chosen all those strange topics for discussion, no?
NN: "Are you ...for or against abortion⎰ euthanasia? (???) People's opi?
　　　　　For or Against abortion ⎱
N: Opiate.
NN: Ah, yes, yes (pause). Heheh, national diet, we agree, no?
N: Yeah, we agree a lot, there's no discussion there. "Do you think ...21st century: English or Spanish?"
NN: Very difficult.
N: Number 11?
NN: 11?
N: No, I ask, you think number 11 is very difficult?
NN: Very difficult to know er I think English could, because now (...) What do you prefer?
N: Well, possibly, possibly number 11 because we know something about it.

16.
NN: Er, we we choose er...any subject⎰ What do you prefer?
　　　　　　　　　　　　　　　　Yeah⎱
(Pause)
N: Whichever you want, I've talked about all of them (laugh) for years and years.
NN: Have you talked everything?
N: I've talked about all of these because I used to be an English teacher⎰　before I became a full-time translator, so (laugh) over
　Yes ⎱
years I discussed all these matters.
NN: Aha, OK. I don't know ...er ... about the ...abortion and euthanasia?
N: Sure, Why not?

17. Smooth move.

18. Smooth move.

19.
N: Do you wanna talk about one of these, or...?
NN: OK. (Pause) Whichever you like (Pause).
N: That's a good one.
NN: Sorry!
N: Number 6.
NN: Uh huh.
N: What do you think?
NN: Um, "Do you think religion is people's..."
N: How religious are you?

20.
N: So, would you like to discuss one of these subjects?
NN: OK, you can choose. (Pause)
N: All of them are very technical questions.
NN: (Laugh)
N: "Which will be the world language in the 21st century: English or Spanish?"
NN: Uh huh.
N: What do you think about that? (Laugh).

It can be seen that five of the conversations (3, 8, 9, 17 and 18) are not interrupted by an explicit topic negotiation, while fifteen are (1, 2, 4, 5, 6, 7, 10, 11, 12, 13, 14, 15, 16, 19 and 20) and three of the latter (dyads 7, 10 and 14) even include two negotiation stages. Generally speaking, during the selection or negotiation process, one participant asks the other which topic they are most interested in, or directly suggests one particular topic (saying, for example, "How about number 6?") and the other accepts. Also during the selection, many instances of giving-way tactics occur: every participant letting their interlocutor choose (saying, for example, "I'll let you pick " or "Well, you choose"). In one case (conversation number 5, between Rosa and Ellen) the non-native speaker starts by asking the native participant: "Do you have any topic or something?" Ellen answers that all the questions are interesting and "passes the buck" to Rosa: "What do you think?" The latter replies that she was the one who chose a topic in her previous conversation, so she has to let Ellen choose. The latter suggests number 6, religion, and Rosa immediately and readily accepts and starts answering her interlocutor's questions. This example shows that most topic choice is decided through a negotiation in which every participant strives to show that they put their interlocutor's preference higher in the priority scale, thus giving the impression that the interaction is guided by politeness rules.

However, it is important to verify who suggests selecting a topic first and who chooses one in the end. In dyad 1, the only one in which a participant addresses the researcher to ask if they should choose a topic, it is the non-native speaker who starts. She asks her partner which topic she likes, the latter suggests something unintelligible, the former suggests languages and the native speaker accepts and asks a question related to the chosen topic. Other dyads in which the non-native speaker initiates the negotiation are 5, 7 (the first negotiation), 10 (the first one), 11, 13, 14 (the second one) and 16. Thus, summing up the conversations in which there is a topic negotiation (15) and that of conversations which have two topic negotiations (3), we find that out of a total of 18, only 8 negotiations are initiated by non-native speakers.

This means that native speakers decide more than their non-native counterparts when to start the topic-selection stage, which is another sign that they are in control of the conversation. A clear example is dyad 15, in which there is an abrupt movement from the get-to-know-each-other stage to the topic-negotiation one. This abrupt shift takes place because Valentine, the native speaker, seems to want to avoid further personal questions from Manolo, who asks him if he has a Spanish girlfriend. Valentine answers the question as briefly as possible (using a one-word negative reply, "No") and, without pause or hesitation, he adds, "What subject would you like to talk about?" With this he achieves a personal objective, namely protecting his personal territory, and a conversational advantage, namely emerging as the participant in control, the one who decides what is talked about and when.

Regarding the question of which participant chooses the topic in the end, it can be verified from the above extracts that the native speakers do in dyads 1, 2, 4, 5, 7 (the first negotiation), 7 (the second one), 11, 14 (the first negotiation and, to some extent, the second one as well), 15, 19 and 20. The non-native speakers, on the other hand, choose the topic in dyads 6, 10 (the second negotiation), 12, 13 and 16. In the first negotiation of dyad 10 and the second of dyad 14 there is what might be called a negotiation failure, because no topic is chosen. In dyad 10 (1) the non-native speaker initiates the negotiation, but later interrupts it because he remembers he did not ask his partner about his favourite football team. In dyad 14 (2) the non-native speaker makes a move to change the topic and negotiate another, but she fails to achieve her objective as her partner asks her a question which is apparently new, but in reality it is relevant to the previous topic, sexism. Indeed, they continue speaking about sexism, although Adriana, the non-native speaker, has already said she does not have much to say about it. So, instead of considering these two cases (10–1 and 14–2) as failures, it is more accurate to consider the first one a successful strategy to be added to the non-native speaker's account (because he seems to be in control of the conversation at this stage) and the second one as a successful resistance strategy to be added to the native speaker's account (as she manages to maintain her topic of preference).

Taking into consideration these two instances together with topic choice, it can be seen that most of the topics are chosen by native speakers (twelve are suggested by native speakers and only five by non-native ones). It is true that, as mentioned above, both native and non-native speakers tend to give way and let their partner choose the topic they like, which shows their interpersonal skills and their observance of the rules of social tact. However, this does not deny that in the end most discussion topics are suggested by native speakers and accepted by non-native ones, and this, in addition to other conversational aspects, is significant. This is because the topic choice is a decision-making task and, since the native participants "have their own way", they emerge as leaders (participants in control) in their respective relationships. As Watts (1991:156) claims, "[i]f a topic is tabled and accepted, the topic presenter gains in status within the network". In addition, since the native speakers take the decision and choose a topic they like and about which they are likely to have some knowledge, they can be expected to contribute more to the development of the topic and thus probably control it. Furthermore, if they have information which is necessary for the development of the topic, while their partner does not, as is the case in dyad 14 above, they are likely to be in a position of power (Watts, 1991:156).

IV. Signs of power

It has been found so far that some conversational aspects reveal a possible power asymmetry between the native and the non-native participants. Starting from the early stages of their respective conversations, the native speakers used phatic communion tokens associated with a higher position (mainly other-oriented comments or questions) more often than their interlocutors did. Similarly, at the interval of topic negotiation the native speakers seemed to assume the role of the leader who takes decisions about when a topic should be chosen as well as what topic should be spoken about. These two stages of the interaction have been focused on specifically because they have special significance for the whole interaction (they are key stages). In what follows, other signs of power, some of which are related to the previous ones, are dealt with in order to verify whether or not the above tendency is confirmed.

1. Lexical assistance and error correction: knowledge asymmetry

It has been pointed out earlier that intercultural communication, in general, and communication between native and non-native speakers, in particular, are often likely to give rise to problems of encoding and decoding. One of these problems is the linguistic and communicative difficulty that the non-native speaker can experience, especially if they have a low competence in the language and communicative system being used. A close look at such difficulties and how the participants deal with them can provide more insight into the native-non-native relationship.

The first observation to be pointed out about all the conversations is that there is little correction by native speakers of errors made by their non-native partners. To take just one example, in dyad 16 there are at least 22 grammatical errors like the following:
- "...in the sixties area..." instead of "in the sixties" or "in the sixties era",
- "...don't say you anything" instead of "don't tell you anything",

- "When he don't want, she don't want and I want the...at the end decide the woman" instead of "doesn't want" and "in the end the woman decides",
- "In this case decide the women" instead of "women decide",
- "But the people er always go to the London to to make these things and the problem is ...I don't think that abortion have to be a way to don't have children. We have another er ways to *evit* this situation" (the use of the definite article with "London", the use of "make" instead of "do", "have" instead of the third person "has", "to don't" instead of "not to", "another ways" instead of "other ways" and, finally, the transfer of the Spanish verb "*evitar*", which means "avoid").

However, none of them is corrected by Adam, the native speaker. They go unacknowledged because they do not constitute a communicative problem, that is to say, they do not affect understanding. In another dyad (10), even though Diego's error or lack of knowledge does affect understanding, his native interlocutor does not comment on it:

Diego: I had, I had er er a friend working there and he was *expu:lsed*, no?
Sam: He was what?
Diego: He was *expu:lsed* for this company.
Sam: What's it?
Diego: Er... because they had to make er umm, they had to *expu:lse* people so ..⌈to have less costs⌉ and he was *expu:lsed*.
Sam: Uh huh   ⌊Less, yeah⌋

In this excerpt the non-native speaker uses "*expulsed*" to mean "fired" or "made redundant", so his interlocutor does not understand the message, hence his request for clarification: "He was what?" Diego repeats the word, Sam asks about the meaning, Diego tries to explain, but once again he uses the same word he needs to explain. It is clear from the recorded conversation that the native speaker does not manage to make out what his non-native partner means. However, he just lets him continue without drawing any further attention to the language difficulty (thus, as will be seen in politeness strategies, sacrificing understanding for the sake of saving his interlocutor's face).

In most cases, the few corrections found in the conversations are related to single words. For example, in dyad 13 Adriana says "birth language" and her native partner corrects her ("native language") and in conversation 15 Manolo uses "the camp" to refer to "the stadium" and Valentine corrects him. Indeed, it is lexical gaps that gave rise to most difficulties for the non-native speakers. The less proficient among them made a large number of errors in sentence construction and communicative function, but they managed to get their message through somehow. As for lexical items, they often sought the assistance of their native addressee as a knowledgeable authority, using expressions like the following (mainly in English, but once in Spanish):

- "Selectivism we can say?"
- "Do you call it faculty?"
- "How do you call *equilibrio*?"
- "*Voluntad*?"
- "Cómo se dice?" (How do you say it?)

The native speakers, as was expected, provided the word if they knew. In a few cases, in a collaborative gesture, they proactively provided the lexical item even before the non-native speaker asked for it, as can be seen from the following example (dyad 13):

Adriana: ...and you see a black woman with er

Rachel: braids.

Adriana: I don't know how you say *trenzas*.

Rachel: braids.

In this case the native speaker guesses what her non-native interlocutor wants to say (because of the conversational context, or maybe through a gesture indicating hair or braids) and she cooperatively provides the necessary word before Adriana asks for assistance by saying, "I don't know how you say *trenzas*."

In one conversation (dyad 5), however, it is the native speaker who asks for assistance, but in a jocular manner:

Ellen: My parents are very religious and my my myself? How do I say that in English⎱ I and my sister (laugh) How do you
⎵ (Laugh)⎰
say myse, I I am myself⎱...How weird ...My sister and I aren't religious.
In English⎰

Rosa: Do you want me to call a teacher?

In this case, which is the only one in all the data, the native speaker expresses her doubt about the use of the personal pronoun "I" or the reflexive pronoun "myself" in the subject position.

Just like making linguistic errors and exposing one's lexical gaps are likely to be seen as lack of competence, correcting errors and providing linguistic assistance are likely to be perceived as signs of higher status or power. This is the case because the situation that gives rise to this exposure of (lack of) knowledge brings to mind typical power relationships based on knowledge differential or asymmetry (e.g. teacher-student, doctor-patient, etc.). Therefore, since knowledge constitutes a source of power when it is recognised as such in a given social context (Dant, 1991:188) and one of the types of power is expert power, based on the belief that one participant has special expertise or knowledge in an area relevant to another's interests (French and Raven, 1959), it becomes clear that when non-native speakers in the present study made errors, needed assistance with vocabulary and overtly resorted to their native interlocutor as a resource person or expert, they were acknowledging the latter's higher status on the linguistic dimension. Furthermore, in addition to placing the native speakers in a one-up position, the asymmetry of linguistic and communicative competence provided them with advantageous opportunities to enhance their image and position in conversational terms. For, just like expressions of agreement and requests for clarification (James and Clarke, 1993:242), error correction and, more often, lexical assistance could be used as a legitimate resource to take over the floor, make a point and add scores to one's "conversational account".

As for the exception above (a native speaker exposing her "lack of competence" and asking for assistance), it will be seen in a later section that this kind of self-downgrading serves other solidarity purposes (joking, accommodation, showing the two participants are equal, have the same difficulties, etc.). Still, what is significant and in line with the power interpretation in the previous paragraph is the non-native speaker's reaction to this "incident". Unlike native speakers, who readily provided lexical items or linguistic assistance because they perceived themselves as holders of a legitimate right to "authoritative access to knowledge" (Drew, 1991:2), the non-native speaker in the above extract does not assume the role of expert and does not provide any linguistic assistance. Rather, she refers to another "legitimate" institutional authority ("Do you want me to call a teacher?"). She behaves thus not because she lacks competence (actually, she has an advanced level of English), but because, first, she takes the "incident" as a joke (as she cannot believe her partner does not know how to say what she wants to say) and, second, because she does not perceive herself as an expert.

2. Topic control

When dealing with topic control, the first difficulty one faces lies in the definition of the concept of "topic" (Wardhaugh, 1985:139) and the demarcation point to determine where one topic finishes and another starts. The vague idea people tend to have about "topic" is that it is "something talked about" (Wardhaugh, 1985:139), but what exactly that "thing" is escapes technical definition. Furthermore, "...it is very unusual in conversation ever to talk on a well defined topic in a highly systematic way; even well practised lecturers can experience that difficulty" (Wardhaugh, 1985:139). In fact, people can move from one "topic" to another very smoothly, without breaking the rules of coherence (Halliday and Hasan, 1976) or relevance (Sperber and Wilson, 1986). In casual conversation especially, as has been found in the conversations studied here, speakers can continually move from one subject to another, forming a chain of subjects where every subject is related to the one immediately preceding it but not necessarily to the rest. In dyad 7, for example, in one chain, participants start talking about football, then they move on to talk about sexism, then the media, nightlife, large and small cities and, finally, divorce. Every topic is related to the previous one with a coherence link but, at surface level, it is hard to find a connection between the media, for example, and divorce. The following transition extracts (from dyad 7) illustrate the point:

1. N: People were crazy, for example, in Italy 1990 people sold their houses and sold (???) mortgage to houses to get money to go to support Argentina, big problems, big financial problems, people running into Italian restaurants and hey hey hey, because we don't have a league, a professional league. (Pause) Shall we talk about another topic? (Pause) Is your society sexist?
    NN: Yeah.
    N: Yeah?
    NN: OK. (Pause) Do you think it's sexist?
    N: In Spain? I don't know, I'm not sure, I think there are defined roles for women and men in Spain, but it's changing.

2. NN: Women have the stereotype of cleaning the house ⎱
                                                          It's crazy ⎰
    watching TV programs about famous people ⎱
    N: Buying the *Hola* magazines, I can't understand this, people are so interested in other people's lives, it's very *morbo*, no?
    NN: The same happens in Ireland?

3. NN: There's a lot of people who read this kind of magazines.
    N: Another thing, talking about magazines, is the media in Spain, it's either black or white. I don't know, do you buy a newspaper?

4. NN : for example, two years ago when the other government was er powerful   ⎱ There er, a lot of things were
       Yeah, was in power ⎰
    different, good things and bad things, now there are a lot of good things but also bad things ⎱ for example, yesterday I went
                          Sure ⎰
    with my friends to have a drink and at two and half and three in the morning ⎱ the bars were closed.
    Uh huh ⎰
    N: Because of the new laws.

5. NN: Of course, things have changed because er perhaps er 20 years ago in Spain there was much respect for the elderly, even for priests   ⎱ Yeah, for establishment and nowadays
    Yeah, the establishment ⎰
    people doesn't care.
    N: Maybe it's a rebellion (??) and maybe it's taking time to
                                Perhaps ⎰
    readjust, no? Find the balance again ⎱ And do you think Madrid
                                Perhaps ⎰
    is er could be, I mean, is it is it the same in all Spain?

6. NN: They only worry about job, car, they don't care other things more. Other values are lost, like family.
    N: Yeah, I mean, abortion and things like this, divorce, a lot of divorce.

The above extracts show how one thing leads to another and how topics give rise to other topics through association or what de Beaugrande and Dressler (1981:89) call "spreading activation": "When some item of knowledge is activated, it appears that other items closely associated with it in mental storage also become active...". Thus, unlike in excerpt 1, in which transition from one topic to another is done explicitly and after a pause ("Shall we talk about another topic?"), in the rest of the excerpts transition is done subtly, making use of the association/conceptual relationship between the present topic, idea or word and the following one. In this way, sexism (in extract 2) triggers the stereotype of women as readers of gossip magazines, which itself leads to the "celebrity phenomenon". In excerpt 3, gossip magazines lead one of the participants to raise the topic, or subtopic, of the media in Spain. In transition passage 4, change of government and policy leads to talking about laws affecting nightlife (as an example of new measures) and, later, about civic behaviour among the youth. In excerpt 5, the conversation shifts from civic behaviour to comparing Madrid with other Spanish and international cities. Finally, in passage 6, talk about respect and politeness leads to talk about the loss of values and, because "spreading activation" permits it, divorce.

What this amounts to is that very often it is difficult to decide whether a chunk of conversation constitutes only one topic (with subtopics) or a series of different ones. The difficulty to decide is more obvious when there is a topic shift without pausing or explicit references, as is the case in the last five passages above. In fact, this is the case in most of the twenty conversations studied in this book. In some interactions, on the other hand, the participants speak about a topic and, when they have nothing else to say about it, they pause or keep silent until one of them raises a new topic. In a few others, just like in transition passage 1 above, participants overtly express their desire to change the topic (but not all of them are successful):

Adriana (dyad 14): "I don't know what more I can say, if you want to talk about..."

Adriana (dyad 14): "If you want to change the topic."

Adam (dyad 16): "I think we've done enough with this conversation."

Being aware of the slippery nature of "topic" and the methodological difficulties mentioned above, a rough list of topics tackled in the twenty conversations was intuitively and prototypically compiled in order to study topic choice and topic tabling as a way to gain status throughout the conversation (Watts, 1991:156). Indeed, it has already been found (in the analysis of the two samples in Chapter 3 and of the topic negotiation stage in the previous section) that there are signs of topic control and, therefore, conversation control by native participants. It has been seen that they tended to decide when a topic had to be chosen, what topic to choose and when it had to be dropped. To verify whether this conversational power of the native speaker is a general trend in the data, below is a detailed account of the number of topics and subtopics every party tables, how successful they are, the amount of attention (number of speech turns) they receive, and who conducts the conversation throughout the discussion of those topics. What follows is a rough list of topics and subtopics in each conversation, together with information about the participant who tables them (N standing for native speaker and NN for non-native) and the number of speech turns dedicated to each topic or subtopic raised.

Table 8: Topic and subtopic tabling

Dyad	Topic or subtopic	Tabled by	Turns
1	Studies	N	4
	Home town	N	4
	Studies	N	2
	Work plans	N	4
	Educational systems	NN	4
	Languages	NN	5
	Living abroad	NN	3
2	Studies and books	N	13
	Language learning	N	4
	Home town	N	10
	Sexism (main topic)	N	34
3	Studies	N	3
	Work plans	N	2
	Non-profit work	N	6
	Work plans	NN	2
	Educational systems	NN	7
4	Studies	N	12
	Sexism	N	36
5	Studies	NN	12
	Living abroad	NN	5
	Studies	N	3
	Living abroad	NN	12
	Religion (main topic)	N	17
6	Home town and country	N	10
	Studies	NN	5
	Town	NN	6
	Studies	NN	3
	Travelling	N	8
	Age	N	4
	21st century world language	NN	51

7	Town and job	N	10
	Irish beauty	NN	4
	Football (main topic)	N	20
	Sexism	N	12
	The media	N	11
	Nightlife and new laws	NN	11
	Madrid and other cities	N	7
	Divorce	N	2
	Exchange programmes	N	22
8	Lifestyle in Madrid	NN	17
	Music	N	7
	Girls	NN	5
	Films	NN	26
	Irish and Spanish humour	N	4
	Football	NN	18
9	Job	NN	8
	Life in Madrid and large cities	N	11
	Studies	N	4
	Clubs/societies	N	2
	Ways of thinking/ideology	NN	10
	World organisations	N	10
10	Job	NN	18
	Management and business	N	23
	Home town	N	16
	Football (main topic)	N	48
	Human rights	NN	11
	Racism	NN	18
	European Union	N	3
11	Home town/country	N	7
	The present research	N	6
	The U.S.A.	N	6
	Job/studies	NN	6
	People in the States	NN	7
	World language in 21st century	N	13
	Future plans	NN	4
	Places visited in Spain and the USA	NN	9
	Studies and research	NN	7
	Religion	N	9
	Living on one's own	N	16
12	Country of origin	NN	2
	Job experience	N	12
	American and Spanish people	NN	5
	Racism	N	6
	Places to see	NN	5
	Abortion and euthanasia (main topic)	NN	26

13	Language learning	N	14
	Cultural differences (main topic)	NN	38
	Prejudice	NN	6
	Diet	NN	9
14	Personal information (age, job, etc.)	N	10
	Immigration and cultural differences	NN	9
	Sexism (main topic)	N	56
	Grants and studies	NN	10
15	Weather	N	3
	Home town/origin	N	8
	Job	NN	2
	Girlfriend	NN	2
	Football (main topic)	N	23
16	Home town	N	12
	Abortion (main topic)	NN	20
	Legal English	N	7
17	Home town	N	2
	Serbia and the Balkan War	N	16
18	Name	N	8
	Hemingway	NN	2
	Bullfighting	N	5
	Tourism	N	9
	Gaelic	NN	18
19	Town/country of origin	NN	15
	Religion (main topic)	N	25
20	Country of origin	N	12
	World language in the 21st century	N	17
	Red herring	N	3

From the above it can be seen that both the native and non-native speakers contributed to the development of conversations, not only by tabling topics but also by participating in the discussion of tabled ones. However, a closer look at the number of topics and subtopics tabled by each group and the amount of attention received by the topics of each side reveals an asymmetrical contribution pattern. In fact, the native speakers tabled far more topics than their non-native counterparts. Out of a total of 103 topics, 60 were tabled by native speakers and 43 by non-natives. In addition, the native participants' topics received more attention, in terms of speech turns, than the ones tabled by their non-native interlocutors. In total, 679 turns were contributed to topics tabled by native speakers and 466 to the ones tabled by non-natives.

This asymmetry is a sign of power, as it shows the native participants as being more influential and exercising conversational control over their non-native interlocutors. They do so not only by tabling topics but sometimes also by overtly directing the course of the conversation, as the following examples show:

1. "I think we've done enough with this conversation." (Dyad 16)
2. "We're not talking about suicide, we're talking about euthanasia." (Dyad 16)
3. "That's a red herring." (Dyad 20).

In the first example, the native speaker puts an end to a topic (abortion) and, without pausing, starts another one (legal English), which is totally different. In the second and last examples, the native speaker controls the topic by reminding his interlocutor of what they are talking about or by judging their contribution as a digression, thus directing or redirecting the course of the conversation.

On the other hand, it is significant that the non-native speakers' attempts to change the topic are not so successful, as the following examples show:

1. I don't know what more I can say, if you want to talk about... (Dyad 14).
2. NN: If you want to change the subject the topic.
   N: Do you want to?
   NN: No, if you want to go on with it, but I don't know if I can say more.
   N: Well, I was going to ask you a question. I was going to say you know er they have the running of the bulls (...) the women are not allowed? (Dyad 14).

In this conversation the non-native speaker tries, at two different stages, to change the subject because she finds she cannot say much about it. However, the first attempt is not even noticed by her partner, while the second one is responded to with a question asking her to say if *she* wants to change the topic (as her suggestion is made in a polite and tentative manner rather than by stating explicitly that she wants to change the topic, as the native speaker did above). Along the same polite lines, she expresses her desire not to impose on her partner ("if you want to go on with it") and explains the reason behind her suggestion ("I don't know if I can say more"). At this point the native speaker interrupts to ask a question that she *was* going to ask (note the "*was*" in italics, which means that she continues her course of action, without any changes or attention to her partner's suggestion). Indeed, the question related to sexism in some Spanish traditions and, through it, conversation about the previous topic (sexism) continues for rather a long time, hence a failure of the non-native speaker's attempt.

The fact that native speakers chose most discussion topics (see the analysis of topic negotiation and choice above), that they tabled more topics (practically 60%), that their topics were slightly more successful than the non-native speakers', and that they received more attention (practically 60% of the speech turns), all this suggests that it is because of their relatively higher status in their respective dyads. It is true that the success of a tabled topic and the attention it receives depend on whether it is relevant to the context, whether it is interesting to the participants, whether it excludes one of the participants, whether it is embarrassing, etc. (Wardhaugh, 1985:141). Still, this does not totally deny that an accepted topic enhances the status of the person who tables it (Watts, 1991:156) and that the participant who controls the proceeding of topics and, therefore, of the whole conversation, emerges as the dominant party in the interaction. Therefore, if the above findings indicate that the native speakers emerge as the dominant party in most conversations, this is likely to be because they assume and they are assumed to be higher than their interlocutors in the status scale. As native speakers (high-status holders because of their higher competence in the language spoken), they were allowed to impose their choices, albeit subtly, and to have a relatively more salient role in the manner in which the conversations proceeded.

3. Amount of speech

As mentioned earlier, the recorded conversations varied in length (they took from 15 to 30 minutes) and, because of this (and other factors, such as speech tempo and the length of pauses), they also varied in the amount of speech. What is of interest here, however, is not the variation in the

Table 9: Distribution of amount of speech among native and non-native speakers

Dyad Number	Amount of speech (in words)		
	Native	Non-native	Total
1	1278	618	1896
2	1482	849	2331
3	1252	475	1727
4	1293	759	2152
5	583	538	1121
6	2751	1348	4099
7	877	842	1719
8	629	583	1212
9	720	1185	1905
10	1584	1960	3544
11	1005	910	1915
12	850	725	1575
13	1085	355	1440
14	795	520	1315
15	465	555	1020
16	345	470	815
17	285	540	825
18	570	335	905
19	485	330	815
20	445	380	825
Total	18779	14277	33056

amount of talk from one conversation to another, but the differential, if any, between the amount corresponding to native speakers and that corresponding to non-native ones. The distribution of talk (measured by number of words) is reflected in the table above.

As Table 9 shows, there is a significant difference in the amount of speech in half of the conversations (dyads 1, 2, 3, 4, 6, 9, 13, 14, 17 and 18), while others (especially, dyads 5, 7, 8, 11, 12 and 20) show a practically symmetrical distribution. In most of the dyads where asymmetry is noticeable, the native speaker is the party who speaks more (dyad 1: 67%, dyad 2: 63.5%, dyad 3: 72%, dyad 4: 60%, dyad 6: 67%, dyad 13: 75%, dyad 14: 60% and dyad 18: 63%). The rest, comprising only two dyads, goes to non-native participants (dyad 9: 63% and dyad 17: 65.5%).

These two exceptions to the dominant pattern can be explained with different factors: speech tempo, talkativeness and resource person (the person who provides information or expertise about the subject of conversation). In dyad 9 (and also dyad 10) Diego speaks more than his interlocutor does because of his exceptional fast tempo and his talkativeness. Indeed, he is famous among the people who know him for his fast speech and active participation in any kind of conversation, and his conversations in English, despite his relatively low competence, were no exception (see dyad 10 also). As for Petrovich (dyad 17), the fact of speaking more than his native co-participant is likely to be due, first, to his native-like linguistic and communicative competence and, second, to the fact that he was the resource person in his conversation with Adam. That is to say, since the whole conversation was about Serbia, the Balkan War and related historical subtopics, he was the expert, not only because of his nationality, but also because of his encyclopaedic knowledge. What probably confirms this is his second conversation (with Valentine in dyad 18), in which the main topic was Gaelic and Irish culture and, therefore, the resource person was his partner, not him. This is reflected in their respective amounts of speech: almost 63% for Valentine and 37% for Petrovich.

Processing all the conversations aggregately, it is found that out of a total of 33,056 words, the native speakers produced 18,779 words, while the non-native speakers uttered only 14,277, which shows a difference of 4502 words. To verify the significance of the difference in amount between the speech of all the native participants put together, on the one hand, and that of all the non-native speakers, on the other, it is worth converting the raw numbers into percentages. Out of 33,056 words, the 18,779 corresponding to the native speakers represent 56.8%, while the 14,277 words corresponding to the non-native ones represent 43.2 %.

This imbalance in contribution to conversation between the native and the non-native participants may be a mere coincidence, as no spontaneous conversation results in a fifty–fifty distribution of words produced. It may be the result of pace/tempo differences, the native speakers speaking faster and, therefore, saying much more words in the same span of time. Indeed, as mentioned above, this may be an explanation for Diego's greater amount of speech in comparison with his native interlocutor (in dyad 9). The imbalance in amount of speech may also be the outcome of a combination of linguistic and communicative competence, on the one hand, and status assumptions, on the other. It goes without saying that someone who speaks a language as their mother tongue finds it easier than a language learner to express themselves and, therefore, make more contributions to the ongoing conversation. This fact, if not affected by other factors such as expertise and personality traits, may lead the native and non-native parties to expect the native speaker to speak more.

4. Interruptions

At this stage, and before dealing with the instances of interruption found in the data, it is worth recalling some assumptions already mentioned in the theoretical background:

- Higher-status participants perceive themselves and are perceived by their interlocutors as more competent and, therefore, tend to contribute more to the interaction and are less willing to wait for contributions from their lower-status partners (James and Drakich, 1993:289–290).
- An interruption is any instance of turn-taking by the second speaker at a non-Transition Relevant Place, other than back-channel utterances and supportive or cooperative simultaneous speech.
- Interruption should not be unquestioningly correlated with dominance and power (Watts, 1991:75).
- Interruption is one of the most salient resources available for interactants to enhance their self-image or status and exercise power (Watts, 1991:75).

With these assumptions in mind, it can be said that a general observation about the recorded conversations is that instances of what can be called blatant interruption are very few (see Table 10 below). Indeed, most occurrences of simultaneous speech are either back-channel utterances (Uh huh, Ah hah, right, etc.) or supportive overlaps (instances of simultaneous speech which serve the purpose of supporting the current speaker by completing their utterance, providing a word, etc.). Interruptive interventions were relatively few because, in general, there was a tendency towards territory observance, each participant respecting the other's turn and waiting until they have finished to take over the floor. This is why the predominant pattern in the conversations is that of Speaker 1 – Speaker 2 – Speaker 1 – Speaker 2 and so on, with turns accompanied with back-channel utterances in some cases. On the other hand, in some conversations where there was a relatively higher degree of involvement and, presumably, an assumption of less distance (e.g. Dyad 2, Annie and Susana and Dyad 7, Juanito and Bob), supportive turns and sentence completion were very common. In such cases the personal territory (turn) was not shown much deference, but that was because the relationship was assumed to be intimate (intimacy reflected in jokes, short turns, and joint construction of sentences and arguments).

Because supportive overlaps are, as their name suggests, supportive, and, therefore, perform a function which is quite the opposite of that of interruption, they were not included. What are counted are instances of simultaneous speech (speech by the second participant while the first one is still holding the floor) occurring at non-Transition Relevant Places, and serving the purpose of taking over the floor, not to support the previous speaker, but to make one's own point, as is the case in the following passage from dyad 10:

1. Diego: But I haven't ...I asking you you're supporter of one team, or...?
2. Sam: Yeah, Manchester United.
3. Diego: Manchester United.
4. Sam: Yeah, because I was born in Manchester, I lived there for 3 years and I find the same as you that er ⎰
5. Diego: But I don't know what happens ⎱with Manchester because firstly in ... the first part of the year I heard that he::: they played very well⎰ and finally he::: he::
   Excellen⎱
6. Sam: His problem is he didn't buy anybody, he just kept the same squad of the last 3 years and (???) because they're almost all young players. And also, they're so used to winning that they::: when the pressure came (???) they could be beaten.

At this point in the conversation, Diego and Sam have already talked about Diego's favourite team, its problems and its president, and also about the enormous amounts of money footballers earn. In turn 1 Diego asks Sam about his favourite football team, to which the latter replies with turn 2. In turn 4 Sam starts explaining something which remains incomplete, as he is interrupted by his interlocutor with turn 5. He is interrupted immediately after the pause filler ("er") and before finishing his sentence (the relative pronoun "that" makes the hearer expect a whole clause including at least a noun phrase and a verb phrase). It is obvious therefore that Diego intervenes in a non-Transition Relevant Place and "snatches" the floor from his interlocutor to ask, to comment or to give his opinion about the performance of Manchester United. In turn 6, however, he himself is interrupted at the beginning of a sentence ("finally, he..." makes the listener or reader expect a verb phrase to complete the sentence). If Diego's intervention in turn 5 is meant to ask a question, as his opening utterance "I don't know what happens..." seems to suggest, it can be considered as practically complete, for the rest of the question can be deduced (something like "and finally they collapsed"). If, on the other hand, his intervention was meant to express an opinion or make a point, he must have felt frustrated, as Sam's interruption left his sentence unfinished.

Such clear instances of interruption are indeed very few in the data. However, it is worth considering whether the distribution of these few occurrences is balanced among the native and the non-native participants (see Table 10 below).

Table 10: Distribution of interruptions between native and non-native speakers

Dyad number	N. Interruptions	N-N. Interruptions
1	1	0
2	3	1
3	3	2
4	2	0
5	0	0
6	1	1
7	1	0
8	0	0
9	0	2
10	3	7
11	1	0
12	0	1
13	3	0
14	1	0
15	0	0
16	0	0
17	0	0
18	0	0
19	1	0
20	1	0
Total	**21**	**14**

First of all, it should be pointed out that six out of the twenty conversations do not contain any instances that could be labelled as interruptions, adopting as criteria the position of occurrence and function of simultaneous speech. The ones that do, on the other hand, show an asymmetry in favour of the native speaker, a pattern which is of importance for the present study. Except for three dyads in which the non-native speakers interrupt more (dyads 9, 10 and 12), and dyad 6, in which interruptions are evenly distributed, all the dyads that contain interruptions reveal a tendency for the native speaker to interrupt more. In other words, while native speakers interrupt more in ten conversations, non-native participants do so in only three interactions. What is more, when the numbers of interruptions are aggregately converted into percentages for each of the two groups, it is found that 60% of the interruptions are carried out by the native speakers and 40% by the other group. This by itself is a significant difference, in spite of the small number of interruptions. When the number of interruptions of each group is divided by the amount of speech of the other in order to calculate the rate of interruption, the imbalance looks more prominent: the result is that the native speakers interrupt the non-native participants every 679 words while the latter interrupt every 1341 words. This means that the native speakers interrupt more often and that their interruptions, in addition to being greater in number, are disproportionate (see Table 11 below).

Table 11: Rate of interruptions by native and non-native participants.

	Natives	Non-natives
Amount of speech (in words)	18779	14277
Interruptions	21	14
Rate	1/679	1/1341

This asymmetry in interruptive behaviour may be due to cultural differences, although the findings of the present study seem to contradict the findings of researchers like Graham (1993), who claims that people from Latin cultures tend to interrupt more than Anglo-Saxon people. It may be the result of "misreading of cultural cues for recognising a point, readiness to relinquish the floor" (Murray, 1987:105). Thus, for example, while the non-native speakers were looking for words or considering the structure or the vocabulary in their minds before speaking, which is common among second-language learners, the native speakers might have mistaken the pauses or the hesitations for cues to relinquish the floor. It may also be a manifestation of differences in personal styles (Murata, 1994:396) or differences in tempo (the native speakers speaking faster, thus making it more difficult for the non-native participants to find a transition place, and non-native speakers using a slower tempo and, therefore, allowing more turn shifts or interruptions). Another explanation is the ubiquitous power differential and power exercise: because the native speakers are assumed to be of a higher status in these interactions, they allow themselves and are allowed by their interlocutors to interrupt more.

In theory, this correlation between interruption and power should not be taken for granted, especially in informal conversations like the ones analysed here. As James and Clarke (1993:244) say,

> ... a significant percentage of interruptions in casual conversation may be non-dominance-related. The proportion of interruptions which are dominance-related may be higher in contexts involving formal tasks, and highest in interactions involving competition and conflict.

However, since interrupting behaviour is less legitimate in dyads than in groups, simply because two participants have more floor access available to them than members of a larger group (Kennedy and Camden, 1983:55), it becomes legitimate to interpret asymmetry in the distribution of interruption as a sign of power imbalance, especially if other power-sensitive conversational aspects support this interpretation. Indeed, it has been demonstrated above that other conversational aspects such as amount of speech, topic control and other-oriented questions do confirm the tendency of native speakers to control the interaction and emerge as the more powerful party.

5. Supportive minimal listener responses

Supportive minimal listener responses (SMLR) like "uh huh", "yeah" and "right", perform quite the opposite function to that of interruption: they show continued attendance to the current speaker (Roger, 1989:92) and have, as their name suggests, a supportive role (Leet-Pellegrini, 1979). As such, they are often considered as typical traits of powerless style, as they do not constitute action but passive reception and support for one's interlocutor, who makes a point, argues, takes the conversation towards the course they like or, in a word, serves their own communicative or other purposes. This does not mean, however, that they may be automatically correlated with lack of power, as this conversational behaviour does not depend only on the power relationship between participants, but also on personal style and gender. For example, as far as gender is concerned, Leet-Pellegrini (1979:106) observes that women tend to show support more than men do.

In the data of the study this book is based on, the native speakers produce most of the SMLRs (see table 12 below). Fifteen out of the twenty conversations show that the native speaker uses a larger number of SMLRs than their non-native interlocutor does. The only exceptions are dyads 5, 6, 13, 14 and 20. Furthermore, the difference in number is significant both in individual dyads (especially 9, 10, 11, and 15) and in the totals of the two participant groups. The native speakers produced 721 instances of SMLRs, while their non-native interlocutors uttered only 373. This means that the former were responsible for 65.9% of the instances, while the latter produced only 34.1%. Seen in light of their respective amounts of talk, on average, the native speakers provide an SMLR every 19.8 words uttered by their interlocutors, while the latter provide one every 50.8 words produced by native speakers.

Table 12: Distribution of Supportive Minimal Listener Responses between native and non-native participants

Dyad	SMLR by natives	SMLR by non-natives
1	13	7
2	30	6
3	9	7
4	35	15
5	20	23
6	19	66
7	26	3
8	36	17
9	88	15
10	98	15
11	66	12
12	25	13
13	14	42
14	20	33
15	92	9
16	27	8
17	26	4
18	42	21
19	32	16
20	3	41
Total	721	373

Taken at face value, this seems to contradict the finding that, judging by the conversational aspects dealt with so far, the native speakers emerge as the dominant party in most dyads. If SMLRs are considered a sign of relative powerlessness, the non-native participants, not the native speakers as is the case, would be expected to produce more instances of them. In addition to this, taking into account the assumption that this conversational feature (SMLR) is used to show that the listener is still following the speaker and paying attention to what they are saying, and bearing in mind that the native speakers spoke more than the non-native participants (see table 9 above), it would be logical for the non-native participants to produce more SMLRs. However, since the opposite is the case, an explanation is called for. The first one that could be proposed is cultural difference. However, it seems that the participants in the present study are all members of cultures (American, British, Spanish, Moroccan and Serb) in which supportive minimal responses are used to indicate attendance to the current speaker and understanding of what they say. Another explanation could be that the non-native speakers used nonverbal listener responses such as nodding and facial expressions, which are not reflected in the audio-taped data.

A more plausible explanation, which has already been put forward in Chapter 3 to explain a similar finding in Annie and Susana's conversation, is that the native speakers feel so confident about their higher conversational status in relation to their non-native interlocutors (at least because of linguistic and communicative competence) that they do not mind supporting and encouraging them. They support their non-native interlocutors not only because they do not perceive any risk of losing that advantageous position, but also because of the responsibility they assume in the interaction. As Givón (1989:166) states, "knowledge is power, but power is responsibility". This is why the native speakers seem to assume the responsibility to lead the interaction, anticipate communicative breakdowns, and encourage their non-native counterparts to speak or continue speaking, thus making frequent use of SMLRs.

6. Questions

Questions have often been associated with power exercise; not everybody can ask questions. At a consultation room, for example, a doctor can ask a patient about their private life and medical history, but not vice versa. During police interrogatories and court hearings it is taken for granted who has the institutionally established right to ask questions and who is expected to respond. In addition to being accessible only to agents holding a higher status in some institutional contexts, questions can also play a role in conversational dominance, even in casual conversation. This is because the questioner "casts" the questioned in a specific role (Ng and Bradac, 1993:64) and "constrains what will count as appropriate responses" (Wiemann, 1985:86). By so doing, the questioner "provides a definition of the relationship" that the person questioned accepts by responding in an appropriate manner (Wiemann, 1985:86). Conversationally speaking, therefore, questioning is an instance of making someone do something, a tool of power exercise.

On the other hand, there is a type of question which does not enhance the position of the questioner but, on the contrary, makes the responder appear as a knowledgeable resource person, someone who holds information or expertise that the questioner needs (expertise power). For example, when students ask their teacher questions or when journalists ask a politician, the teacher/politician is often the more powerful party, because the questions are requests for information or knowledge which the one who asks questions does not have. The function of questions, however, just like that of other linguistic and communicative tools, is complex indeed (Tannen, 1987b:6). Direct or indirect questions can be a sign of power in some contexts, but not necessarily in others.

In the present study, the native speakers asked more questions than their non-native partners did in half of the conversations, namely dyads 1, 2, 4, 7, 9, 10, 11, 16, 17 and 18, as Table 13 below shows:

Table 13: Distribution of questions between native and non-native speakers

Conversation number	Native speaker's questions	Non-native speaker's questions
1	7	3
2	25	1
3	3	3
4	15	6
5	8	10
6	5	11
7	19	2
8	9	9
9	9	4
10	13	5
11	10	8
12	4	8
13	4	8
14	7	7
15	4	6
16	8	5
17	3	0
18	6	1
19	4	4
20	4	5
Total	167	106

This does not mean that in the other half of conversations the non-native participants asked more questions. They did so in 6 dyads only (5, 6, 12, 13, 15 and 20), while the rest (dyads 3, 8, 14 and 19) show an even distribution between the native and the non-native participants. In total, the native speakers asked 167 questions, while their interlocutors asked only 106, which amounts to a percentage of 61.17% for the former and 38.82% for the latter.

These questions can be classified into five main categories:

1. Personal information questions,
2. Opinion questions,
3. Task-related questions,
4. Information requests addressed to a resource person,
5. Clarification questions.

In the first category the questioner asked about their interlocutor's name, place of residence, studies, travel experiences, favourite team, etc. (e.g. "What's your name?", "You're from Madrid?", "Did you grow up in Alcala?"). In the second group the question related to one's interlocutor's opinion about the phenomenon or topic being discussed (e.g. "Do you think this is a way for the government to control people?", "You think, from an American point of view, that Spanish is really a threat?"). The third group includes relatively fewer questions referring to the task the two participants were performing or wanted to start (e.g. "Shall we pick a subject?", "Do we have to choose another subject?"). In the fourth category, mainly the non-native participants would ask how something is said in English or whether what was said was correctly expressed (e.g. "How do you call *equilibrio*?", "Do you say opium?"; the native speakers also asked questions like, "What's the Spanish for 'management'?"). This group also includes questions about a specific subject which falls within one's interlocutor's field of expertise, as is the case in the following excerpt from dyad 20:

Adam: Er, I think in Algeria they have this music of Rai
　　　　　　　　　　　　　　　　　　　　　　　　　Uh huh

and they try to express new things er do you know if this affects the language, whether it's modernising the language to speak about new things which weren't expressible before?

Moumen: Um, I don't know, I don't think er the music itself would bring this change er but I think it's a change that comes out of the society itself, because, well, if you look at the language of er if you look at the lyrics of these songs, er they're not different from the language spoken in everyday life. So, it's just a reflection of what people already speak, it's a mixture of French and Arabic, colloquial Arabic, Algerian colloquial Arabic and if if you compare it with the colloquial language spoken in the street, there's practically no difference. I wouldn't say that they're initiating a change in the language, but they're just using a language that is already used in everyday life.

Finally, the fifth group includes questions about what one's interlocutor meant by their previous utterance or point, as is the case in the following example from dyad 10:

Diego: I had, I had er er a friend working there and he was *expu:lsed*, no?
Sam: He was what?
Diego: He was *expu:lsed* for this company.
Sam: What's it?
Diego: Er... because they had to make er umm, they had to *expu:lse* people so ... to have less costs and he was *expu:lsed*
Sam: Uh huh　　　　　　　　　　Less, yeah

The distribution of these types of questions is not equal between the native and the non-native speakers. Except for type 4 (questions addressed to a resource person), the native participants asked more questions than their non-native counterparts did (see the table below):

Table 14: Types and distribution of questions in the 20 conversations

Question type	Native	Non-native
Personal	76	50
Opinion	42	14
Task-oriented	11	5
Resource person	10	22
Clarification	28	15
Total	167	106

The fact that both the native and the non-native speakers asked each other personal questions (and "personal" should be understood in its broader sense here) suggests that they assumed a kind of solidarity relationship, in which each party perceived the other as an accessible equal and everybody felt equally free to ask their interlocutor questions about their family, hobbies, likes and dislikes, etc. Still, the fact that the native speakers asked slightly more questions of this type than their non-native co-participants suggests that the former perceived the latter's territory as more approachable, if not more "encroachable". The fact that they asked more opinion- and task-oriented questions supports the above conclusion that the native speakers seem to control topics and, therefore, the whole conversation. This is because when they ask an opinion question, they cast the addressee in a defined role, and when they ask questions about whether they should start the discussion task, it is not intended to elicit an answer to their questions but to suggest something which is, in most cases, accepted by the non-native participant. As for resource person questions, since most of these relate to words and expressions, it is not surprising that the non-native participants produced more of them than the natives did, as the conversations were conducted in English, and it was normal that the second-language learners asked for assistance with lexical items or expressions they needed to continue the conversation. It is not surprising but it confirms the hypothesis that native speakers appear more knowledgeable and, therefore, higher in status.

What is surprising, however, is that questions for clarification were mostly asked by native speakers. It is normal for the native speakers to ask for clarification if they do not make out what exactly their respective interlocutors mean. In fact, in native–non-native communication, misunderstandings and failures to understand are common because of different pronunciation, mispronunciation, misuse of words and expressions, etc. What is odd, however, is that the non-native speakers did not ask as many of this type of questions as their native partners. Furthermore, the few instances found in the data are produced mainly by one participant, namely Adriana in dyads 13 and 14. Bearing in mind the natives' larger amount of speech, relatively faster tempo and use of vocabulary and expressions which were unknown to the non-native addressees, the latter must have failed to understand quite a few utterances. Therefore, either they had no difficulty understanding what their native interlocutors said (indeed, it is common to find a higher comprehension competence than communicative competence among language learners) or they were too self-conscious and inhibited to ask for clarification because they did not want to expose their comprehension gaps, which might have been interpreted as lack of competence in the language they were speaking.

To conclude, the larger number of questions asked by the native speakers seems to confirm the findings above, that they emerge as more powerful and dominant in their interaction with non-native speakers of English. This is the case not only when the total numbers of questions are compared but also when these questions are classified into different categories or types. Asking more personal questions can be perceived as a sign of cordiality and social interest, but, at the same time, reveals that the questioner (the native speaker here) assumes a one-up position. Asking more opinion- and task-oriented questions, which do not seek assistance or convey uncertainty, leads to exercising control over the addressee. The fact that the non-native speakers asked more resource-person questions enhances the native speakers' status in the interaction, as their assistance is sought and they are perceived as sources of knowledge. Finally, the fact that the native speakers asked more clarification questions does not affect their status, as it does not convey a possible lack of comprehension or information-processing competence, but rather reveals their non-native interlocutors' lower communicative competence in English. Thus, when non-native speakers ask for clarification, it is because *they* do not understand, and when native speakers ask for clarification, it is because *their interlocutors* do not express themselves clearly and appropriately because of poor linguistic and communicative competence.

V. Face relationship

Introduction

Judging by the above account on amount of speech, topic control, questions and interruptions, the conversations analysed in this study might appear as a field of competition and power exercise. However, in addition to power manifestations, there are ubiquitous (positive) face strategies that create a sense of solidarity in most of the interactions. The two participants in every dyad strived to convey a sense of belonging to the same group (in spite of the clear native/non-native division and cultural differences), and of having similar problems, opinions and experiences. In other words, the two participants tended to come closer to each other rather than distance themselves or compete for something on the floor. To achieve this, they made use of a number of positive politeness strategies described by Brown and Levinson (1978/1987), such as claiming common ground, noticing and attending to one's addressee's wants and interests, agreeing, using in-group identity markers, joking and giving symbolic gifts (sympathy, understanding and cooperation).

1. Attention to one's interlocutor

As pointed out above, all the conversations started with some social or small talk. This phatic communion opening was foreseen and required by the researcher as a first stage in the interaction. However, independently of the instructions of the researcher, it would have been odd if the participants had not engaged in small talk, as this is almost an indispensable feature of the ritual of informal conversation. As mentioned above, this talk or phatic communion allows the participants to break the ice, to create a bond and to find out necessary information on which to build the rest of the interaction in a safe manner. From a face-focused point of view, the verbal exchange at the beginning of every conversation is a tribute paid to each other's desire to be approved of and socially accepted. By starting a conversation with a formulaic introduction or greeting or by asking a personal question, the initiator notices the addressee (socially speaking) and expects them to do the same (reciprocity). In addition to this, what talk at the opening stage (and also later on) does is show interest in one's interlocutor's person, experience, point of view, etc. In other words, it satisfies the need for approval and acceptance (positive face).

To pay tribute to one's interlocutor's positive face, the participants asked questions about interests, hobbies, family, studies, etc. Paying attention to one's interlocutor's desire to be noticed and for their interests to be cared for (positive face), every participant kept asking questions whenever an interesting aspect of the other's life was pointed out. Questions from both the native and the non-native side about studies, specialisation, future plans, likes and dislikes, etc. are recurrent, so much so that even when one participant fails or forgets to pay the expected attention at a specific point, they later redress this failure. In dyad 10, for example, Diego fails to ask Sam in return about his favourite football team. So, even when they have finished the get-to-know-each-other part of the conversation and are about to start choosing a topic for discussion, he interrupts this activity (topic choice) to ask Sam what team he supports, thus restoring the conversational and face-attention balance:

Diego: OK. We could choose to talk about one thing or...
Sam: Definitely, yeah (...) you pick one.
Diego: But I haven't...I asking you you're supporter of one team or...?
Sam: Yeah, Manchester United.

By doing this, Diego repairs a local face attention imbalance that arises because one participant shows interest in the other's favourite team, while the latter does not respond reciprocally (up to this point). It is not a serious face-threatening act of the kind that would have the status of an "incident" of "disequilibrium or disgrace" in Goffman's (1972:19) terms, that is to say, an instance of "a threat that deserves direct official attention—and to proceed to try to correct for its effects". Still, Diego manages to go back to the previous topic in order to comply with the reciprocity rule and pay the expected attention to his interlocutor's positive face.

2. In-group solidarity

The participants in most of the dyads tended to create a group of their own. That is to say, by highlighting what they have in common, they co-constructed a group conception which drew them closer to each other, sometimes at the expense of others. Personal, national and cultural differences were overridden by other shared aspects, thus creating an emergent sense of "us". This sense of belonging was based on gender, age, occupation, beliefs, experience, and other identity dimensions.

As far as age is concerned, although the participants were informed before the recording that their partner was going to be approximately the same age as them, and although age was obvious from physical appearance during the face-to-face interaction, there are explicit references to age like the following:

- "Men our age" and "your brothers are our generation?" (Dyad 2)
- "So, how old are you?"
- "Um, twenty-one."
- "Twenty-one. I'm twenty-two. Same age." (Dyad 6)

Such explicit references serve the purpose of creating a group bond based on the age variable. What is more, this common ground is sometimes reinforced through contrast with other age groups, as is the case, for example, in dyads 2 and 14:

- "But still, **your mother** still continues this this **old idea** of, you know, the boys don't have to do anything and so, I mean, that would make sense of it, that would pass down, but now...I don't know, I don't know why **our generation** will be more against this sexism (??) I wanna say **we're** more enlightened." (Author's emphasis)

- S1: For example, the woman that I live with, because for the programme here I live with a *señora*, an **old woman** (Author's emphasis)
  S2: Here in Spain, *Española*, Spanish?
  S1: Uh huh, she asked me and my roommate, we're both from the States, she asked us why are we going to college? Why not just find someone to marry and be a housewife (laugh).

This contrast of co-participants with older generations strengthens the in-group bond by setting a boundary between what "we", as young people, think and what "others" (older generations) think. In other words, the participants use the age variable to draw a circle including them and excluding other age groups.

As for gender, it is sometimes reflected in topic choice, with female and male participants choosing topics that highlight their sense of belonging to their respective gender groups. Football and women are two of the most common solidarity topics among the male participants. Indeed, in some of the conversations these two topics served the purpose of creating a gender bond between participants. Thus, Juanito and Brad (dyad 7) and Juanito and Bob (dyad 8), for example, spoke about girls, a topic that seems to unite male participants and make gender similarity override other differences. Similarly, football was chosen as a conversational topic at least in four male encounters, namely dyads 7, 8, 10 and 15. Female participants, on the other hand, did something similar, but in their case drawing on sexism (and in one case abortion) as a female solidarity topic. Annie and Susana (in dyad 2), Annie and Catalina (dyad 4) and Adriana and Elizabeth (dyad 14), for example, spoke mostly about sexism, and Camilia and Elizabeth (dyad 12) spoke about abortion, another topic which is closely related to women.

Some participants in the study, namely students, also created an in-group relationship through occupation, that is, the status of being a student and related experiences. Thus, in addition to talking about what they studied or were still studying, some of the students also set themselves as an "interest group" against teachers. Bob and Diego (dyad 9), for example, speak about lecturers and their biased approach to history and economics. Similarly, Ellen and Rosa (dyad 5) spontaneously use the case of a "weird" lecturer in order to establish an in-group bond. The following two excerpts are from the beginning of their interaction. They talk about the lecturer, change the topic and later go back to talk about the same lecturer again:

1. Ellen: And the professor, I hated that professor
   Rosa: (Laugh) He's very strange.
   Ellen: He's so bad, so bad. I couldn't believe we didn't read one book.
   Rosa: You didn't read...?
   Ellen: I read the papers but it's not like reading the whole book. ⌉ You get like 3 pages
   Yeah ⌋
   Rosa: And he sounds very strange.
   Ellen: Yeah.
   Rosa: But all of us know this teacher because he is in this faculty, you know, do you say faculty?
   Ellen: Faculty, yeah, he is in the faculty.
   Rosa: So, he he and we know him and that's the way he gives the classes, just dictating, it's very boring.
2. Ellen: (...) I don't know why I had the bad idea of taking [course name].
   Rosa: But he always gives the classes in that way. I had him last year and this one and it depends on the year, sometimes the *notes* [marks] are very good and last, like this year, the *notes* [marks] are very bad. It depends on his humour, but classes are very bad, yeah. But he is not going to give you any other subjects?

Ellen: No.
Rosa: That's the only one?
Ellen: That's the only one.

The topic of the lecturer arises because the two participants discover that both of them attended this lecturer's classes. Since the character, behaviour and teaching practices of this staff member are (negatively) salient, the two students find him an interesting topic of conversation. However, it is not only because this lecturer is salient that they talk about him, but also because he is an "Other". If one of the two interlocutors was a notoriously incompetent student in the class they refer to, or was involved in an embarrassing incident, the other participant would be unlikely to raise the subject or draw attention to the face-threatening incident, precisely because the person in question is present and because such an act would damage her face. However, since the threatened face in this case is that of an "Other", the participants allow themselves to create a group of their own at the expense of the lecturer. They do so first of all by defining themselves as members of the same group (students) who, as a consequence, have the same interests, and secondly by casting the teacher out as an outsider whose face does not count in the present situation and, what is more, whose damaged face serves the purpose of enhancing the common positive face of the interlocutors[1].

Similarly, the narration of similar experiences and the response to a personal problem with a similar experience serve the purpose of creating a bond of common ground and consolidating the temporary in-group. Indeed, in almost every conversation there is at least one instance of this. In some cases, the similarity is introduced with expressions such as "like you", "me too", "the same as you" or "the same thing happened to me", and in others it is straightforwardly pointed out or narrated, without a similarity-conveying expression. Susana and Ellen (dyad 1), for example, relate their similar experience with learning a foreign language. Annie and Susana (dyad 2) find in their respective experiences in the families they were living with as foreign students a common ground and another "excuse" to come closer to each other. In dyad 3 the participants speak about their experience in the field of international relations and cooperation. In dyad 4 the two female interlocutors relate similar experiences within sexist societies. In dyad 5 Ellen and Rosa talk about their upbringing in a religious family and their subse-

---

1. This is not to say that the face of absent people is always accessible and can be subjected to damage or threatening. Rather, it depends on the relationship between the participants in the interaction and the absent person(s) in question. It goes without saying that if the absent person is a dear member of one of the participants' family, peer group or professional network, their face would be as "sacred" as the participants'. In the case above, the lecturer's face was used and abused not only because he was absent from the scene of interaction, but also because he did not belong to the close social network of the interlocutors. He was an outsider for both of them and even his institutional power over these two students had come to an end, as their course with him had been completed.

quent ethical and ideological emancipation. In dyad 6 the participants' similar experiences are about regional stereotypes. In dyad 8 the interlocutors relate their respective attitudes when they cannot understand culture-specific references or humour in foreign films. In dyad 9 the similar experiences are related to studies and lecturers. In dyad 10 the participants describe how they feel as supporters of their respective football teams. In dyad 11 they relate their personal experiences in a foreign country, Spain and the United States, respectively. In dyad 12 they relate their experiences with bigoted religious groups and also their training in psychology and social work. Finally, in dyad 18 the interlocutors relate similar stories about their respective names.

To sum up, whether the common ground is age, gender, occupation or a similar life experience, the interactional objective the interlocutors achieve is the creation of a group in which both of them fit. By creating and, later, consolidating this in-group membership, they come closer to each other and mutually convey the social and interpersonal message of being similar and equal, thus giving rise to an environment and a relationship based on positive face.

3. Conversational joking

Jokes are also a manifestation of the solidarity/positive face nature of an interaction (Brown and Levinson, 1978/1987), as the very act of joking relies heavily on shared knowledge (otherwise, jokes would fall flat) and is a sign of a lesser distance. This does not mean that jokes are the exclusive prerogative of intimate friends and close relatives. Rather, conversational joking and word play are also used by strangers "to establish a momentary bond" (Boxer and Cortés-Conde, 1997:287) and, therefore, make the relationship friendlier and the interaction fluid and easy-going.

In the data of the present study, although there are many instances of laughter, there are not many instances of joking. However, the few occurrences do play a role in the creation of a solidarity-based interaction, as the following examples illustrate:

Dyad 5:

Ellen: My parents are very religious and my my myself? How do I say that in English⎱ I and my sister (laugh) How do you
(Laugh)⎰
say myse,   ⎱ I I am myself ...How weird...My sister and I
In English? ⎰
aren't religious.
Rosa: Do you want me to call a teacher?

Dyad 11:

Rachel: I was an intern.
Camilia: Oh, like Monica Lewinsky (laugh).

Dyad 12:

Camilia: Some people in in the East Coast think that people from California they are so crazy they move the earth, that is why they have earthquakes. Have you heard about that?
Elizabeth: No (laugh).
Camilia: They told me this joke (laugh).
Elizabeth: I never heard that.
Camilia: Yeah, people told me they are completely crazy (???)
Elizabeth: People from the East Coast think that people from the West Coast (???) the earth, that's why there are earthquakes?
Camilia: Yes they're so crazy.

In dyad 5, Ellen hesitates at the beginning of a sentence because she is not sure whether to say "I and..." or "Myself and..." and she later says, "I've forgotten English", which is a kind of self-degrading act or a "self-denigration irony", which Boxer and Cortés-Conde (1997:290) claim is common among women. This jocular act may be intended to bring her closer to her non-native interlocutor (i.e. sending a comforting message like, "Don't worry, even *I*, a native speaker, can make mistakes and can face difficulties speaking English"). Rosa responds to this act with a joke, another distance reducer or solidarity marker: "Do you want me to call a teacher?" In the second example (dyad 11) the native speaker is talking about her studies and professional experience when she utters the word "intern", which, because of the world-famous case of Bill Clinton and Monica Lewinsky, triggers the non-native speaker's joke. This may have the usual function of a joke, namely that of creating an environment of humour, shared knowledge and solidarity. Still, because of the negative (sexual) associations of Monica Lewinsky, the analogy between her and the native speaker could be perceived as an instance of "high-risk teasing" (Boxer and Cortés-Conde, 1997:286) or even a face-threatening act, seeing that the interlocutors were complete strangers before their interaction. However, taking into account Wolfson's (1988) "bulge" theory of social distance, claiming that "what strangers and intimates have in common is the relative certainty of their relationship", high-risk teasing may be expected to occur in either social distance extreme, that is to say, between intimates as well as between strangers (Boxer and Cortés-Conde, 1997:286). As for the joke in dyad 12, although it is about (some) American people and the native speaker is American, it is clear that it is about an "Other" that does not include her, as it is about a smaller group of American people (Californians) and she is a New Yorker. The function of this joke, in addition to what has been said above about common knowledge and humour, is to create an emergent group that includes the two participants, in spite of the fact that the other national, cultural and, to some extent, linguistic factors set them apart. What this amounts to is that through the previous talk about people from Madrid, Atlanta, New York and California and through the above joke, the interlocutors reciprocally convey the feeling that they are "normal, wise and nice people" set in contrast with other "crazy, rude and inconsiderate people".

The above are not the only dyads in which joking is present; similar joking instances can be found in other conversations as well. In dyad 7 Juanito mentions the Spanish film director Ricardo Franco and makes a joke about the Spanish former president, Francisco Franco. In dyad 9 Diego makes a joke about companies requiring, among other conditions, that new employees make no friends. Another example is the story the native speaker in dyad 20 relates about "red herring": an English lecturer was delivering a lecture in a South American country and after giving an outline of his presentation he said "there will be a lot of red herrings". So when he finished, a member of the audience, who had understood "red herring" literally, reminded him of the "red herring" slide he had forgotten.

All such jokes have as a function what Boxer and Cortés-Conde (1997) call "relational bonding". They seem to suggest that the context is friendly and casual, that the participants have the intention to come closer to each other and that the relationship between them is not of the deference or unequal type. However, the absence of more personal joking and teasing or high-risk teasing (or what Boxer and Cortés-Conde, 1997:286, call "biting") is a reminder that the interactants are still strangers. "With strangers", Boxer and Cortés-Conde (1997:287) claim, "the bonding is through joking and word play, not through teasing".

4. Complimenting/praising

In a study on compliments among British and Spanish university students, Lorenzo-Dus (2001) found some cultural differences between the two groups which are likely to give rise to misinterpretation and stereotyping. While there is a tendency in both cultures to abide by the modesty maxim and to avoid self-praise "on topics such as natural talent and intelligence" (114), there are some aspects that draw the two cultures apart. For example, the British participants, the author says, question the truth of the compliment more than the Spanish ones do (113), while the latter tend to request repetition or expansion of the compliment more than the former do. This request for repetition or explanation may lead the British interlocutors to perceive their Spanish counterparts as lacking self-esteem and needing reassurance (122). On the other hand, the Spanish participants in Lorenzo-Dus' (2001) study tended to use ironic upgrades more often than their British interlocutors, which is likely, the author claims, to make the British perceive the Spanish people as exceedingly self-confident or even boastful (122).

Unlike in Lorenzo-Dus' (2001) study, in the present research compliments were not focussed on specifically. The instances of complimenting that occurred in the recorded conversations emerged casually and, because the main part of each conversation was the discussion of a non-personal topic, and also because there was no specific skill-related task involved, there were very few instances of compliments. In fact, in the twenty conversations, only eight instances of compliments could be found. Among these, only half were personal compliments, and the other half were directed towards the addressee's nation, not themselves as individuals, and only in an indirect way (implication) could they be considered compliments (if one praises a given nation, country, culture, group, etc. and one's addressee is a citizen or member of that country, culture or group, the compliment includes this individual by implication).

The eight instances of complimenting/praising are the following:

1. Dyad 2: NN: So you speak Spanish very good, very well.
   N: I'm learning, I'm trying to perfect it.
2. Dyad 3: I think it's better the American [educational] system.
3. Dyad 6: N: (...) the grammar you learn, for example, you speak better grammar than my American friends, for example, er ... the grammar that the native speak is not always very good.
4. Dyad 6: N: What is your stereotype of an American?
   NN: Um, I ...for example, from my point of view, because we studied this in history and culture of the United States, um we think that the American person is a blond girl or boy um very er light skin, very white, um that, very intelligent people, that's our opinion because you are the leading country in the world, um you have very, you have a lot of power er in the world (...)
   N: Great.
5. Dyad 8: NN: One thing that I love of Ireland is ...Irish girls (laugh) I love Irish beauty.
6. Dyad 10: NN: (...) my level of English is not a good one, no?
   N: It sounds it sounds nice.
7. Dyad 15: NN: And did you decide to stay in Spain for forever?
   N: Yes.
   NN: Why?
   N: Spain is wonderful (...) good climate, good food, good wine, good girls, what more do you want?
8. Dyad 18: NN (Serb): You have an island.
   N (Irish): You know the island?
   NN: Who doesn't?
   N: Who doesn't! Spanish peop...I've never met a Spanish person who does.

It can be seen from the above excerpts that only four of the praising/complimenting instances are aimed at a specific skill or attribute the individual addressee possesses (1, 3 and 6: linguistic competence; 8: world/geographical knowledge). In addition, only two of these compliments are formulated after the skill or attribute is demonstrated (3 and 8), while the other two are given "for free". In instance number 1 the non-native speaker tells her American interlocutor, "So, you speak Spanish very good, very well", not because she heard her speaking Spanish but simply because she told her she was studying Spanish at university. Similarly, in number 6 the native speaker, referring to his interlocutor's English, says, "It sounds nice," just to reassure him, not because he is a witness to a high communicative competence in English (this adjacency pair of self-denigrating/reassurance takes place at the opening of the conversation).

As for the responses of the complimented parties, it can be said that most of them do not follow the expected compliment-thanks or compliment-downplaying patterns. The only ones that do are the non-native (Serb) participant in dyad 18 and the native speaker in dyad 2. In dyad 18 the native speaker praises his interlocutor's knowledge about something very few people outside Ireland or Britain know, to which the latter replies, "Who doesn't?", a response which is intended to downplay his knowledge and, therefore, comply with the modesty principle. Similarly, in dyad 2 the non-native speaker compliments her American interlocutor's competence in the Spanish language, to which the latter replies that she is still studying and improving her skills (also a downplaying and modesty-driven gesture). The rest of compliments go unacknowledged because, in most cases, they are not personal and they occur in the middle of discussion or as a reply to a question. In excerpt 2 above (dyad 3), for example, the "compliment" is aimed at the American educational system and it occurs in the middle of the discussion/comparison of the Spanish and American systems. Similarly, in excerpt 7 (dyad 15) the compliment is paid to the interlocutor's country (nice weather, good food, etc.) and it comes as a reply to the non-native speaker's question about the reason the native participant decided to stay in Spain.

Whether the compliment was aimed at one's interlocutor as an individual or at the group or country they belong to, it is clear that the purpose and effect of this speech act is to enhance one's addressee's self-image and, when the circumstances require it, to reassure them and help them recover self-confidence. However, since the complimenting instances are few, half of them are non-personal, and most of them are not responded to, it is not possible to draw generalisations such as the ones made by Lorenzo-Dus (2001).

The above and other solidarity/positive face strategies are included below in a quantitative account of face-boosting acts as opposed to face-threatening acts to verify whether there is any asymmetrical or imbalanced distribution among the native and the non-native participants. Bearing in mind that both face-boosting acts and face-threatening acts can be aimed at oneself or at the Other, four categories are included in the account: FBA of Self, FBA of Other, FTA of Self and FTA of Other.

5. Face-boosting and face-threatening acts

As their respective names suggest, FBAs and FTAs have opposite effects on a person's face. The verb "boost" is often applied to speed, profits, production, reputation, confidence, morale, etc. to mean "increase", "improve" or "enhance". A face-boosting act, therefore, enhances the self-image of its target and suggests reassurance, approval, or even admiration (in the case of other-FBA), and self-confidence and high self-esteem (in the case of self-FBA). On the other hand, the word "threatening" in FTA suffices to trigger in the listener's or reader's mind a set of negative meanings and connotations, such as aggression, danger, disruption, etc. The person who receives an FTA, therefore, is likely to suffer face damage, to feel offended, humiliated or denigrated. In other words, while an FBA is a plus sign for face, an FTA is a minus sign.

The following statistical report of face-boosting and face-threatening acts in the twenty conversations takes into account any communicative strategy or act intended or having the potential to enhance one's or the other's face (FBA) or to damage one's or the other's self-image (FTA). Instances of FBAs found in the conversations include (tacit) bragging (self-FBA: e.g. "The United States have a lot of power"), praise/compliment (other-FBA: e.g. "You speak better grammar than my mother"), approval, agreement or support terms (other-FBA: e.g. "That's the right thing to do", "You're right", "Exactly"), giving way (other-FBA: e.g. "You choose"), etc. Obviously, these speech acts and communicative features have been considered because they enhance the target's face. In the case of bragging or boasting, in spite of the possible negative connotations in some cultures, it is clear that the speaker adds to their score as far as self-image is concerned. In the case of complimenting it goes without saying that the receiver gains social likeability and approval. Finally, support, agreement and giving way may be mere expressions of the speaker's opinion or preference. Still, as has been argued earlier, agreeing with one's interlocutor enhances their face just as disagreement threatens it and threatens the relationship (it is a human tendency to mix and make friends with people who think like oneself). Similarly, giving way, as has also been explained above, means one cares about one's interlocutor and makes their likes and dislikes the top priority. Therefore, needless to say, the person who receives such a gesture is likely to feel appreciated and gain face.

On the other hand, instances of FTAs include interruptions and potential insults (other-FTA) and self-denigrating, making fun of oneself (self-FTA: e.g. "My level of English is not good", "I'm useless"), etc. It has been mentioned at the beginning of this book that interruption (one participant speaking before the other one finishes their turn) may take place because of a high involvement in the discussion or an assumption of "friendly talk". However, it has also been stated that what an interruption does is encroach upon the territory of the current speaker and, as such, causes them a face loss because it could be interpreted as "a lack of respect". As for the other kind of other-FTA, namely potential insults such as "...sometimes we hear (...) that you don't know where (...) Spain is. (...) that you're racist", it is clear that, although they are not directed at the addressee as an individual (the non-native speaker is talking here about a stereotype of American people), they could lower their self-image in comparison with the state of affairs preceding this utterance. It should be pointed out, however, that such instances are almost nonexistent in the interactions under analysis and that, accordingly, almost all other-FTAs below are interruptions:

Table 15: FBAs and FTAs performed by native and non-native participants

Act type	Native	Non-native
FBA of Self	6	2
FBA of Other	762	425
FTA of Self	10	18
FTA of Other	23	16

The above statistics indicate a tendency among the native as well as the non-native participants to comply with the modesty principle, for there are very few instances of self-face-boosting acts. In fact, the instances counted above are mostly boosting acts directed towards one's country or culture and no one is outright bragging about themselves; they have been intuitively considered FBAs because when one praises one's country or town they seem to enhance their sense of belonging, that is to say, an aspect of their face/identity. In comparison with self FBAs, FBAs directed at the other (one's interlocutor or their country, home town, etc.) are more numerous (762 were performed by native speakers and 425 by non-native ones). However, it should be pointed out that this large number is the result of including back-channel utterances (minimal listener responses) dealt with above (they have been included because they do enhance the addressee's self-image, although not to the same extent as praise, for example).

It is not surprising to find that FBAs directed towards the other are more numerous than self-FBAs, as praising the other or exaggerating interest in and approval of them is a common strategy to enhance one's interlocutor's face in cultures such as West European cultures, while other acts such as boasting or bragging are stigmatised (because they violate the modesty principle). In the particular case of the native and non-native participants in this study, it was found that the natives showed a considerable amount of interest and encouragement. This is why they appear in the table above as the group who produce more other-oriented FBAs. They might have done so to compensate for their interlocutors' relatively lower level of linguistic and communicative competence in English or, as has been said above, because they assumed responsibility for the development of the interaction.

As for FTAs, the above table shows that the non-native speakers "denigrated" themselves more than their native partners did. They produced more FTAs the target of which were themselves (18 versus 10), while the native speakers performed more other-FTAs (23 versus 16). The first finding may be due to a feeling of inferiority and powerlessness that some non-native speakers at least might have had because of their lack of native or native-like fluency. In fact, most of the self-FTAs performed by non-native participants are related to their competence in English. The second finding does not mean that the native speakers were more "impolite" or less respectful towards their non-native addressees. Rather, most of the above instances of other-FTAs (21 out of 23) are interruptions, not propositional content or speech acts that are usually considered face damaging, such as criticism, sarcasm and giving orders.

Conclusion

The study on which this book is based started with the assumption that relational variables are traceable in surface output, that is to say, interpersonal, hierarchical and social relationships are likely to be reflected in language form and linguistic and communicative strategies. More precisely, it began with the assumption that symmetry or asymmetry in face rituals and power relationship may be reflected in conversational phenomena such as (un)equally distributed speech turns, speech monopoly, interruption, and so on. With this assumption in mind, it was necessary to define or decide the type of relationship or interaction in which such a hypothesis would be tested. The interaction type chosen was interaction between native and non-native speakers of English as a representation of interaction between native and non-native speakers in general.

To do this, bearing in mind that native and non-native speakers have identity dimensions other than the nativity criterion, a sample of participants was selected and dyads were formed as homogeneously as possible. Apart from mother tongue, nationality and culture, the difference of which goes without saying (in most encounters between native and non-native speakers this difference is a corollary feature), homogeneity meant selecting participants as close to each other in terms of self-characteristics as possible (the same sex, approximately the same age, more or less equal educational level, material status equality). Then, twenty dyadic conversations were audio recorded, each of which occurred between one native and one non-native speaker of English, interacting in a seemingly casual and free encounter and performing two tasks: getting to know one's partner and discussing a topic from a list provided by the researcher.

Once the conversations were recorded and later transcribed, they were analysed, focusing on instances of face-boosting or face-threatening acts as well as manifestations of power exercise or dominance. As it was not possible to analyse such instances one by one in detail in all the recorded conversations, a decision was made to analyse only two specimen conversations in detail and to offer a quantitative report about the twenty interactions, which was intended to give the reader an overview of what occurred during the interactions. This option, like any other, has its consequences, one of which is that statistical reporting may distort the data by obscuring the details and the specificity of each dyad. However, the reflection of politeness and power strategies in comparable numbers made it easier to obtain an overall and more statistically valuable view of what happened in the interactions as a whole, and to see the a/symmetrical relationship between native and non-native speakers more clearly.

The interactions between American, British and Irish participants on the one hand and Spanish, Serb and Moroccan ones on the other tended towards casual, solidarity-oriented, equal-to-equal relationships. Nevertheless, there were some aspects in the interactions which reflected a kind of asymmetry like, for example, the instances of interruption, the amount of speech and topic control corresponding to native and non-native participants.

With respect to solidarity or positive-face-oriented behaviour, the twenty interactions seemed to confirm the expectation that participants would pay the necessary attention to each other's face. The participants in almost every conversation paid attention to their interlocutor's need for approval by using positive politeness strategies such as seeking agreement, creating an emergent in-group, giving way, joking, etc. Generally speaking, both the native and non-native participants performed a considerable number of strategies with the intention to encourage and enhance their respective addressees' self-image. However, in some cases, native speakers performed much more of these strategies because they assumed responsibility to conduct the interaction and make it successful and, therefore, encouraged their interlocutors by showing approval and support. In some other conversations, on the other hand, there was a tendency towards avoidance strategies, which shows that there was still some distance between the two parties. This distance made FTAs less frequent. In fact, except for interruptions, there were hardly any inherently or contextually face-threatening acts.

Concerning power-related conversational aspects, it was found that the native speakers initiated most discussion topics, that they tabled more topics than their non-native interlocutors, and that their tabled topics were more successful than those tabled by the non-native participants. At the beginning of the second part of the conversations, topic discussion, there was certain negotiation or, rather, polite giving way, with each participant showing their willingness to let the other take the decision according to their personal preference. Still, in spite of the cooperative and face-preserving nature of such negotiation, the native speakers turned out to "impose" their choices and to have their way somehow in most dyads. In addition, they took the initiative to table topics and subtopics more often than their partners, and these topics received more approval and willingness to speak about them (as reflected in the amount of speech and the number of turns dedicated to them) than the ones tabled by the non-native participants. Translated into power terms, this seems to confirm the assumption that native speakers would appear as the higher-status party and, therefore, be dominant through topic control.

It was also found that the native speakers, generally speaking, contributed to the conversations more than the non-native participants did. According to researchers who consider amount of speech as a manifestation of power, at least in contexts where no participant has institutional or role power, this imbalance in speech production is the result of status inequality. This means that in the case of the data of this study, the native speakers spoke more because they had a higher status and, accordingly, they were expected to be authorities who should be listened to more than challenged or competed with.

As for interruptive or intrusive behaviour, it was found that, in comparison with supportive and cooperative strategies (support terms, agreement, joint sentence construction, etc.), it was less frequent. That is to say, the conversations were centred on mutual help and cooperation rather than competitiveness or conflict. Nevertheless, the distribution of the few instances of interruption shows an asymmetrical tendency, with the native speakers interrupting more and more blatantly than their non-native interlocutors. Translated also into power relationship, this confirms the hypothesis that native speakers, because of their relatively higher power position, would allow themselves to intrude into their non-native interlocutors' turns more than the other way around. This, however, should be interpreted cautiously, as the interruption phenomenon is complex and may be the outcome of different factors (involvement and interest in the subject spoken about, misreading of prosodic clues, tempo differences between participants and differences in assumptions about the task or the frame of interaction).

Questions were also analysed as a possible surface manifestation of power exercise and it was found that, in total, the native participants asked far more questions than their non-native partners did, which proves right the hypothesis of this study concerning questions as a manifestation of power. When these questions were sorted out into types (personal, opinion, task-oriented, resource person and clarification), the native participants still emerged as the source of a higher number of questions of all types but one (resource person). This asymmetry seems to convey a power differential, as the native speakers produce more questions in all power-conveying types and fewer in the subordination-conveying one (resource person). The exception is their higher number of questions for clarification, which can easily be accounted for and discarded as a possible source of status loss. On the one hand, it can easily be explained by their interlocutor's lesser degree of linguistic and communicative competence in English (especially pronunciation and syntactic constructions), which made it difficult for them to understand them at some points of the interaction. On the other hand, their powerful position is not in danger, as their questions for clarification do not indicate a lack of competence. Rather, this lack of competence is already associated with non-native speakers, and if the latter had not been shy or self-conscious about their performance in a foreign language, they would have produced far more questions for clarification than the native participants did.

In sum, the linguistic and communicative surface output in the interactions studied in this research seems to suggest a tendency for native speakers to dominate the conversations and to enhance their self-image, sometimes at the expense of their non-native interlocutors. However, the data also reveal that power-related aspects are not always dominant. Mutual face enhancing, cooperativeness and reciprocal "access" to the Other are also recurrent features in the interactions. Also, part of the data shows that factors other than nativity may and do influence the performance of participants and their face and power relationship. Not all the interactions reflected the same uniform tendency, but personality traits and relative expertise did sometimes reflect the non-native speaker as the party who makes use of a bigger amount of power-related output such as interruptions, amount of speech and questions.

Further research

It must be acknowledged that, for a number of reasons, the above findings and interpretations are not conclusive. First, the present study is limited in terms of the number of recorded interactions and the number of analytical tools. More conversations need to be recorded and studied and more face and power linguistic manifestations need to be included in order to achieve more statistically significant results and an operationally deeper level of analysis. Second, nativity was taken as the pivotal factor, but it was not sufficiently "isolated", as other situational, social and cultural factors might have been at play besides the nativity dimension. Therefore, it is necessary to elicit data from participants from different countries, ethnic groups, social classes, etc. and compare the findings to verify whether there are any generalisable trends in the interaction between native and non-native speakers. Third, the eliciting technique should be more accurate and comprehensive: More advanced audiovisual equipment and techniques should be used in order not to lose any contextual information that might be decisive in the processes of further observation, analysis and interpretation.

Bearing in mind all these shortcomings, broader-scope research into communication between native and non-native speakers would need to elicit a larger number of conversations between native and non-native representatives of different geographical, social and cultural origins in order to make the findings as representative and as generalisable as possible. Also, the physical context should be taken into consideration. For example, to verify whether the country or place where the interaction takes place has any effect, the study should elicit data at least in one English-speaking country and another non-English-speaking one. The comparison of data collected in different countries will probably reveal whether the fact of being in one's own country gives the participants a sense of power. Another aspect that should be taken into account is the possible role of grammatical and communicative competence. There should be a sufficient number of representatives from a wide range of competence levels among non-native speakers to verify whether there is any variation in the power exercised on them and to compare face work enacted towards them by native speakers. In addition to this, it would add to the validity of the study to conduct data transcription, analysis and interpretation with the assistance of the participants themselves and other native and non-native informants. This could be done through questionnaires, interviews and joint transcription and analysis sessions.

To conclude, for a researcher to study such complex and slippery phenomena as power and politeness strategies, they must be equipped with reliable previous research results, adequate eliciting techniques and an interpretation procedure as objective as possible, although the co-occurrence of "objective" with "interpretation" seems to be a contradiction. Whatever the case, at the time of making sense of the data, researchers should resist the temptation to be "hasty to correlate surface features with underlying forces such as power" (Tannen, 1987b:9) and politeness.

References

Almeida, de, G. (1985). "Pragmatic universals and communicative action" in Dascal, M. (ed.) *Dialogue: An Interdisciplinary Approach*, 214–229.
Apitzsch, G. and Dittman, N. (1987). "Contact between German and Turkish adolescents: A case study" in Knapp, K., Enninger, W. and Knapp-Potthoff, A. (eds) *Analysing Intercultural Communication*, 51-72.
Austen, J. (1985). *Pride and Prejudice*. Harmondsworth: Penguin Books.
Austin, J.L. (1962). *How to Do Things with Words*. Oxford: Oxford University Press.
Barnes, B. (1988). *The Nature of Power*. Cambridge: Polity Press.
Baxter, L.A. (1984). "An investigation of compliance-gaining as politeness". *Human Communication Research* 10 (3): 427-456.
Bayraktaroglu, A. (1991). "Politeness and interactional imbalance". *International Journal of the Sociology of Language* 92: 87-117.
Beattie, G.W. (1982). "Look, just don't interrupt!". *New Scientist* 95: 859-860.
Beaugrande, de, R. and Dressler, W. (1981). *Introduction to Textlinguistics*. London: Longman.
Beebe, L.M. and Takahashi, T. (1989). "Do you have a bag?: Social status and patterned variation in second language acquisition" in Gass, S., Madden, C., Preston, D. and Selinker, L. (eds) *Variation in Se-*

*cond Language Acquisition.*Clevedon, PA: Multilingual Matters, 103-125.
Bennett, A. (1981). "Interruptions and the interpretation of conversation". *Discourse Processes* 4: 171-188.
Bierstedt, R. (1950). "An Analysis of Social Power". *American Sociological Review* 15: 730-738.
Blommaert, J. (1991). "How much culture is there in intercultural communication" in Blommaert, J. and Verschueren, J. (eds) *The Pragmatics of International and Intercultural Communication*: 13–31.
Blommaert, J. and Verschueren, J. (eds) (1991). *The Pragmatics of International and Intercultural Communication.* Amsterdam / Philadelphia: John Benjamins Publishing Company.
Blum-Kulka, S. (1997). "Discourse Pragmatics" in Van Dijk, T.A. (ed.) *Discourse As Social Interaction.* London / Thousand Oaks / New Delhi: SAGE Publications: 38–63.
Blum-Kulka, S., Danet, B., and Gherson, R. (1985). "The language of requesting in Israeli society" in Forgas, J. (ed.) *Language and Social Situation.* New York: Springer Verlag, 113–139.
Blum-Kulka, S., and House, J. (1989). "Cross-cultural and situational variation in requesting behavior" in Blum-Kulka, S., House, J. and Kasper, G. (eds) *Cross-Cultural Pragmatics: Requests and Apologies.* Norwood, NJ: Ablex, 123–154.
Bou-Franch, P. and Garcés, C.P. (1995). "La presentación de la imagen en conversaciones entre hablantes nativas y no nativas de inglés". *Pragmalingüística* 2: 37–61.
Boxer, D. and Cortés Conde, F. (1997). "From bonding to biting: Conversational joking and identity display". *Journal of Pragmatics* 27: 275–294.
Bradford, A., Weiner, R., Culver, M., Lee, Y.J. and Thomas, D. (1980). "The register of impersonal discourse to foreigners: Verbal adjustments to foreign accent" in Hatck, E. and Michael, H. (eds) *Discourse Analysis in Second Language Research.* Massachusetts: Newbury House, 111–124.
Brown, P. (1993). "Gender, Politeness, and Confrontation in Tenejapa" in Tannen, D. (ed.) *Gender and Conversational Interaction*, 144–162.
Brown, R. and Gilman, A. (1972 [1960]). "Pronouns of power and solidarity" in Giglioli, P. (ed.) *Language and Social Context.* Harmondsworth: Penguin, 252–282.
Brown, R. and Gilman, A. (1989). "Politeness theory and Shakespeare's four major tragedies". *Language in Society* 18: 159-212.
Brown, P. and Levinson, S.C. (1978). "Universals in language usage: Politeness phenomena" in Goody, E. (ed.) *Questions and Politeness.* Cambridge: Cambridge University Press.
Brown, P. and Levinson, S.C. (1987). *Politeness: some universals in language usage.* Cambridge / New York / Port Chester / Melbourne / Sydney: Cambridge University Press.

Bull, P. (1989). "Psychological approaches to transcription" in Roger, D. and Bull, P. (eds) *Conversation*: 150-165.
Bull, P. and Roger, D.(1989). "The social psychological approach to communication" in Roger, D. and Bull, P.(eds) *Conversation*: 9-20.
Cameron, D. (1992 a). "'Respect, please!': Investigating Race, Power and Language" in Cameron, D .; Frazer, E.; Harvey, Penelope; Rampton, M.B.H and Richardson, K. *Researching Language: Issues of power and method*. London/New York: Routledge,113-130.
Cameron, D. (1992 b). "Not gender difference but the difference gender makes - explanation in research on sex and language". *International Journal of the Sociology of Language* 94: 13-26.
Cansler, D.C. and Stiles, W.B. (1981). "Relative status and interpersonal presumptuousness". *Journal of Experimental Social Psychology* 17: 459-471.
Carter, R. and Simpson, P. (1989). *Language, Discourse and Literature*. London: Unwin Hyman.
Chilton, P. (1990). "Politeness, politics and diplomacy". *Discourse and Society* 1 (2): 201-224.
Clark, H.H. (1987). "Four Dimensions of Language Use" in Verschueren, J. and Bertuccelli-Papi, M. (eds) *The Pragmatic Perspective*: 9-25.
Clegg, S.R. (1989). *Frameworks of Power*. London/Newbury Park/New Delhi: SAGE Publications.
Clyne, M. (1994). *Intercultural Communication at Work*. Cambridge: Cambridge University Press.
Coates, J. (1989). "Gossip revisited: Language in all-female groups" in Coates, J. and Cameron, D. (eds) *Women in their Speech Communities*. London/New York: Longman, 94-122.
Collins, B. and Guetzkow, H. (1964). *A Social Psychology of Group Processes for Decision-Making*. New York: Wiley.
Colom Gonzalez, F. (1991). "Los contornos del poder". *Suplementos Anthropos* 28: 80-88.
Colom Gonzalez, F. (1991). "Sobre la concepción de la política: racionalidad, espacio público y catergorías de poder". *Suplementos Anthropos* 28: 131-135.
Culpeper, J. (1996). "Towards an anatomy of impoliteness". *Journal of Pragmatics* 25: 349-367.
Dahl, R.A. (1957). "The Concept of Power". *Behavioural Science* 2: 201-205.
Dahl, R.A. (1961). *Who Governs? Democracy and Power in an American City*. New Haven and London: Yale University Press.
Dahl, R.A. (1968). "Power". *International Encyclopaedia of the Social Sciences*. New York: Macmillan: 405-415.
Dant, T. (1991). *Knowledge, Ideology and Discourse*. London/New York: Routledge.
Dascal, M. (ed.) (1985). *Dialogue: An Interdisciplinary Approach*. Amsterdam/Philadelphia: John Benjamins Publishing Company.
Debnam, G. (1984). *The Analysis of Power*. New York: St. Martin's Press.

Dolitsky, M. (1984). "Communicative speech and its prerequisites". *Journal of Pragmatics* 18: 183–193.
Drew, P. (1991). "Asymmetries of knowledge in conversational interactions" in Marková, I. and Foppa, K. (eds) *Asymmetries in Dialogue*: 21–48.
Duncan, S. (1973). "Toward a grammar for dyadic conversation". *Semiotica* 9: 29–46.
Duncan, S. and Fiske, D.W. (1977). *Face-to-Face Interaction: research, methods and theory*. Hillsdale: Lawrence Erlbaum.
Durkheim, E. (1915). *The Elementary Forms of the Religious Life*. London: Allen and Unwin.
Dye, T. (1990). *Power and Society: An Introduction to the Social Sciences*. California: Brooks/Cole Publishing Company.
Edelsky, C. (1993). "Who's Got the Floor?" in Tannen, D. (ed.) *Gender and Conversational Interaction*: 189–227.
Ellis, R. (1985). *Understanding Second Language Acquisition*. Oxford: Oxford University Press.
Erickson, F. (1976). "Gate keeping encounters: a social selection process" in Sanday, P.R. (ed.) *Anthropology and the Public Interest: Fieldwork and Theory*. New York: Academic Press, Inc.
Escandell Vidal, M.V. (1995). "Cortesía, fórmulas convencionales y estrategias indirectas". *Revista Española de Lingüística* 25 (1): 31–66.
Fairclough, N. (1989). *Language and Power*. London/New York: Longman.
Fairclough, N. (1995). *Critical Discourse Analysis*. London/New York: Longman.
Fernandes, J. (2005) (ed.). *Academic Dictionary of Communication*. Delhi: Isha Books.
Ferguson, N. (1977). "Simultaneous speech, interruptions and dominance". *British Journal of Social and Clinical Psychology* 16: 295–302.
Fielding, G. and Fraser, C. (1978). "Language and Interpersonal Relations" in Markova, I. (ed.) *The Social Context of Language*: 217–232.
François, F. (1982). Lectures delivered at a graduate seminar at the Université de Paris V (unpublished).
Frank, A.W. (1979). "Reality Construction in Interaction". *Annual Review of Sociology* 5: 167–191.
Freed, B.F. (1978). "Talking to foreigners versus talking to children: similarities and differences" in Krashen, S.D. and Scarrela, R.C. (eds) *Issues in Second Language Research*: 19–27.
Freed, B.F. (1981). "Foreigner talk, baby talk, native talk". *International Journal of the Sociology of Language* 28: 19–39.
Freed, A.F. (1994). "The form and function of questions in informal dyadic conversation". *Journal of Pragmatics* 21: 621–644.
French, J.R. and Raven, B.H. (1959). "The bases of social power" in Cartwright, D. (ed.) *Studies in Social Power*. Ann Arbor: University of Michigan Press.

García, C. (1992). "Responses to a request by native and non-native English speakers: Deference vs. camaraderie". *Multilingua* 11 (4): 387–406.
Gass, S.M. and Varonis, E.M. (1985). "Variation in native speaker speech modification to non-native speakers". *Studies in Second Language Acquisition* 7 (2): 37–58.
Gibaldi, J. (1995). *MLA Handbook for Writers of Research Papers*. New York: The Modern Language Association of America.
Giddens, A. (1981). *A Contemporary Critique of Historical Materialism*. London: Macmillan.
Giddens, A. (1984). *The Constitution of Society*. Cambridge: Polity Press.
Giles, H. and Smith, P. (1979). "Accommodation theory: Optimal levels of convergence" in Giles, H. and St. Clair, R.N. (eds) *Language and Social Psychology*: 45–65.
Giles, H. and St. Clair, R.N. (eds) (1979). *Language and Social Psychology*. Oxford: Basil Blackwell.
Giles, H., Mulac, A., Bradac, J.J. and Johnson, P. (1987). "Speech Accommodation Theory: The First Decade and Beyond" in Mclaughlin, M. (ed.) *Communication Yearbook 10*. Newbury Park, California: SAGE Publications: 13–48.
Giles, H. and Robinson, W.P. (eds) (1990). *Handbook of Language and Social Psychology*. Chichester/New York/Brisbane/Toronto/Singapore: John Wiley & Sons.
Givón, T. (1989). *Mind, Code and Context: Essays in Pragmatics*. London: LEA Publishers.
Goffman, E. (1967). *Interaction Ritual: essays on face to face behavior*. Harmonds-worth: Penguin.
Goffman, E. (1971). *Relations in Public: micro studies of the public order*. New York: Harper and Row.
Goffman, E. (1972). *Interactional Ritual*. London: Penguin.
Goldberg, J.A. (1990). "Interrupting the discourse on interruptions: An analysis in terms of relationally neutral, power- and rapport- oriented acts". *Journal of Pragmatics* 14: 883–904.
Graham, J.L. (1993). "The Japanese negotiation style: Characteristics of a distinct approach". *Negotiation Journal* 9 (2): 123–140.
Grice, H.P. (1975). "Logic and conversation" in Cole, P. and Morgan, J. (eds) *Syntax and Meaning*. New York: Academic Press.
Grillo, R. (ed.) (1989). *Social Anthropology and the Politics of Language*. London/New York: Routledge.
Grimshaw, A.D. (1990). *Conflict Talk*. Cambridge/New York: Cambridge University Press.
Gumperz, J.J. (1982). *Discourse Strategies*. New York: Cambridge University Press.
Halliday, M.A.K. and Hasan, R. (1976). *Cohesion in English*. London: Longman Group Ltd.
Hand, F. and Cornut-Gentille, C. (eds) (1995) *Culture and Power*. Lleida: Poblagrafic.

Harding, E. (1986). "Communiquer avec les moyens de bord". *Etudes de Linguistique Appliquée* 63: 108–118.
Harris, R. (1983). "Language and Speech" in R. Harris (ed.) *Approaches to Language*. Oxford: Pergamon: 1–15.
Harris, S. (1989). "Defendant resistance to power and control in court" in Coleman, H. (ed.) *Working with Language*. Berlin, New York: Mouton de Gruyter: 131–164.
Harris, S. (1995). "Pragmatics and Power". *Journal of Pragmatics* 23: 117–135.
Haverkate, H. (1988). "Politeness Strategies in Verbal Interaction". *Semiotica* 71: 59–71.
Haverkate, H. (1990). "Politeness and mitigation in Spanish: a morphopragmatic analysis" in Pinkster, H. & Genee, I. (eds) *Unity in Diversity: Papers Presented to Simon C. Dik on His 50th Birthday*. Dordruhs, Providence: Foris Publications: 107–131.
Hecht, M., Collier, M.J., and Ribeau, S.A. (1993). *African American Communication: Ethnic Identity and Cultural Interpretation*. Newbury Park/ London/ New Delhi: Sage Publications.
Heritage, J. (1989). "Current developments in conversation analysis" in Roger, D. and Bull, P. (eds) *Conversation*, 21–47.
Herman, V. (1991). "Dramatic dialogue and the systematics of turn-taking". *Semiotica* 83: 97–121.
Hickey, L. and Vazquez Orta, I. (1994). "Politeness as deference: a pragmatic view", *Pragmalingüística* 2: 267–284.
Ho, D.Y. (1975). "On the concept of face". *American Journal of Sociology* 81 (4): 867–884.
Holtgraves, T. (1986). "Language structure in social interaction: Perceptions of direct and indirect speech acts and interactants who use them". *Journal of Personality and Social Psychology* 51 (2): 305–313.
Holtgraves, T. (1990). "The language of self-disclosure" in Giles, H. and Robinson, W.P. (eds) *Handbook of Language and Social Psychology*: 191–207.
Holtgraves, T. and Yang, J.N. (1990). "Politeness as universal: Cross-cultural perceptions of request strategies and inferences based on their use". *Journal of Personality and Social Psychology* 59 (4): 719–729.
Hopper, R. (1989). "Conversation analysis and social psychology as descriptions of Interpersonal communication" in Roger, D. and Bull, P. (eds) *Conversation*: 48–65.
House, J. and Kasper, G. (1981). "Politeness markers in English and German" in Coulmas, F. (ed.). *Conversational Routine: exploitations in standardized communication situations and prepatterned speech*. The Hague: Mouton, 157–185.
Huspek, M. (1989). "Linguistic variability and power: An analysis of YOU KNOW/ I THINK variation in working-class speech". *Journal of Pragmatics* 13: 661–683.
Ide, S. (1989). "Formal forms and discernment: Two neglected aspects of universals of linguistic politeness". *Multilingua* 8 (2): 223–248.

James, D. and Clarke, S. (1993). "Women, Men and Interruptions: A Critical Review" in Tannen, D. (ed.) *Gender and Conversational Interaction*: 231–280.
James, D. and Drakich, J. (1993). "Understanding Gender Differences in Amount of Talk: A Critical Review of Research" in Tannen, D. (ed.) *Gender and Conversational Interaction*, 281–312.
Janney, R.W. and Arndt, H. (1992). "Intracultural tact versus inter-cultural tact" in Watts, R.J., Ide, S. and Ehlich, K. (eds) *Politeness in Language: Studies in its history, theory and practice*: 21–41.
Janney, R.W. and Arndt, H. (1993). "Universality and relativity in cross-cultural politeness research: A historical perspective". *Multilingua* 12 (1): 13–50.
Jaworski, A. and Coupland, N. (eds) (1999). *The Discourse Reader*. London and New York: Routledge.
Jazayery, M.A. and Winter, W. (eds) (1988). *Languages and Cultures: Studies in honor of Edgar C. Polomé*. Berlin/New York/Amsterdam: Mouton de Gruyter.
Jefferson, G. (1983). "Two papers on 'transitory recipientship' ". *Tilburg Papers in Language and Literature* 30. Tilburg: Tilburg University.
Johnstone, B. (1989). "Linguistic strategies and cultural styles for persuasive discourse" in Ting-Toomey, S. and Korzenny, F. (eds) *Language, Communication and Culture*: 139–156.
Kasper, G. (1990). "Linguistic politeness: Current research issues". *Journal of Pragmatics* 14 (2): 193–218.
Kearsley, G. (1976). "Questions and question-asking in verbal discourse: A cross-disciplinary review". *Journal of Psycholinguistic Research* 5 (4): 355–375.
Kennedy, C.W. and Camden, C. (1983). "A new look at interruptions". *Western Journal of Speech Communication* 47: 45–58.
Knapp, K., Enninger, W. and Knapp-Potthoff, A. (eds) (1987). *Analysing Intercultural Communication*. Berlin/New York/Amsterdam: Mouton de Gruyter.
Krashen, S.D. and Scarella, R.C. (eds) (1978). *Issues in Second Language Research*. Rowley, MA: Newbury House.
Kurzon, D. (1998). *Discourse of Silence*. Amsterdam/Philadelphia: John Benjamins Publishing Company.
Ladegaard, H.J. (1995). "Audience design revisited: Persons, roles, and power relations in speech interactions" in Harris, R. and Taylor, T.J. (eds) *Language and Communication* 15 (1): 89–101.
Lakoff, R. (1973). "The logic of politeness, or minding your p's and q's" in Corum, C., Cedric, T., and Weiser, A. (eds) *Papers from the Ninth Regional Meeting of the Chicago Linguistics Society*. Chicago, IL: Chicago Linguistics Society: 292–305.
Lakoff, R. (1989). "The limits of politeness". *Multilingua* 8: 101–129.
Lakoff, R. (1990). *Talking Power: the politics of language*. USA: Basic Books.

Lakoff, R.T. and Tannen, D. (1979). "Communicative strategies in conversation: the case of 'Scenes from marriage'". *Proceedings of the 5th Annual Meeting of the Berkeley Linguistic Society* 5: 581–592.

Lalljee, M. (1987). "Attribution theory and intercultural communication" in Knapp, K., Enninger, W. and Knapp-Potthoff, A. (eds) *Analysing Intercultural Communication*: 37–49.

Laver, J. (1975). "Communicative functions of phatic communion" in Kendon, R., Harris, M. & Key, M.R. (eds) *Organization of Behaviour in Face-to-Face Interaction.* The Hague: Mouton: 215–238.

Leech, G.N. (1977). *Language and Tact.* Trier: Linguistic Agency, University of Trier Paper 46.

Leech, G.N. (1983). *Principles of Pragmatics.* Harlow: Longman.

Leet-Pellegrini, H.M (1979). *Role of Knowledgeability/Expertise and Sex of Dyads in the Perception of and the Linguistic Realization of Dominance/Control.* PhD Thesis (Tufts University).

Leet-Pellegrini, H.M. (1980). "Conversational Dominance as a Function of Gender and Expertise" in Giles, H.; Robinson, W.P. and Smith, P.M. (eds) *Language: Social Psychological Perspectives.* Oxford: Pergamon, 97–104.

Linell, P. and Luckman, T. (1991). "Asymmetries in dialogue: some conceptual preliminaries" in Marková, I. and Foppa, K. (eds) *Asymmetries in Dialogue*: 1–20.

Long, M.M. (1981). "Input, interaction and second language acquisition". *Annals of the New York Academy of Sciences* 379: 259–278.

Long, M.M. (1983). "Linguistics and conversational adjustment to non-native speakers". *Studies in Second Language Acquisition* 5/2: 177–193.

Lorenzo-Dus, N. (2001). "Compliment responses among British and Spanish university students: A contrastive study". *Journal of Pragmatics* 33: 107–127.

Lukes, S. (1974). *Power: A Radical View.* London: Macmillan.

Mao, L.R. (1994). "Beyond politeness theory: 'Face' revisited and renewed". *Journal of Pragmatics* 21: 451–486.

Marková, I. (ed.) (1978). *The Social Context of Language.* Chichester/New York/ Toronto: John Wiley & Sons.

Marková, I. and Foppa, K. (eds) (1991). *Asymmetries in Dialogue.* Harvester Wheatsheaf: Barnes & Noble Books.

Marriott, H.E. (1991). "Native-speaker behavior in Australian-Japanese business Communication". *International Journal of the Sociology of Language* 92: 87–117.

Matsumoto, Y. (1988). "Reexamination of the universality of face: Politeness phenomena in Japanese". *Journal of Pragmatics* 12: 403–426.

McCall, I. and Cousins, J. (1990). *Communication Problem Solving: The Language of Effective Management.* Chichester: John Wiley & Sons.

Meggle, G. (1985). "To hell with speech act theory" in Dascal, M. (ed.) *Dialogue: An Interdisciplinary Approach*, 205–211.

Meltzer, L., Morris, W.N. and Hagues, D.P. (1971). "Interruption outcomes and vocal amplitude. Exploration in social psychophysics". *Journal of Personality and Social Psychology* 37: 865–878.
Mey, J.L. (ed.) (1979). *Pragmalinguistics*. The Hague: Mouton.
Milroy, L. (1987). *Observing and Analysing Natural Language*. Oxford: Basil Blackwell.
Moerman, M. (1988). *Talking Culture: Ethnography and Conversation Analysis*. Philadelphia: University of Pennsylvania Press.
Moya Guijarro, A.J. (1998). "Tematización del discurso: ¿De qué estamos hablando?" in Downing, R.A., Moya Guijarro, A.J. and Albendosa, H.J.I. (coord.) *Patterns in Discourse and Text: Ensayos de Análisis del Discurso en Lengua Inglesa*. Cuenca: Ediciones de la Universidad de Castilla-La Mancha, 129–149.
Murata, K. (1994). "Intrusive or co-operative? A cross-cultural study of interruption". *Journal of Pragmatics* 21: 385–400.
Murray, D. (1989). "When the medium determines turns: turn-taking in computer conversation" in Coleman, H. (ed.) *Working with Language*, 319–337.
Murray, S.O. (1985). "Toward a model of members' methods for recognizing interruptions". *Language in Society* 14: 31–41.
Murray, S.O. (1987). "Power and solidarity in interruption: A critique of the Santa Barbara School conception and its application by Orcutt and Harvey (1985)". *Symbolic Interaction* 10: 101–110.
Nagel, J.N. (1975). *The Descriptive Analysis of Power*. New Haven and London: Yale University Press.
Ng, S.H. (1990). "Language and control" in Giles, H. and Robinson, W.P. (eds) *Handbook of Language and Social Psychology:* 271–285.
Ng, S.H. and Bradac, J.J. (1993). *Power in Language*. Newbury Park/London/New Delhi: SAGE Publications.
Ogden, C.K. and Richards, I.A. (1923). *The Meaning of Meaning*. London: Routledge and Kegan Paul.
Olshtain, E. (1989). "Apologies across languages" in Blum-Kulka, S., House, J. and Kasper, G. (eds) *Cross-Cultural Pragmatics: Requests and Apologies*. Norwood, NJ: Ablex, 155–173.
Parsons, T. (1967). *Sociological Theory and Modern Society*. New York: Free Press.
Pearce, W.B. (1976). "The coordinates management of meaning: A rule-based theory of interpersonal communication" in Miller, G.R. (ed.) *Explorations in interpersonal communication*. Beverly Hills, C.A.: Sage, 17–35.
Perdue, C. (ed.) (1984). *Second Language Acquisition by Adult Immigrants: A field manual*. Rowley, MA: Newbury House.
Quasthoff, U.M. (1989). "Social prejudice as a source of power: towards the functional Ambivalence of stereotypes" in Wodak, R. (ed.) *Language, Power and Ideology*. Amsterdam/Philadelphia: John Benjamins, 181–196.

Radford, A. (1988). *Transformational Grammar*. Cambridge: Cambridge University Press.

Rajagopalan, K. (1997). "Linguistics and the myth of nativity: Comments on the controversy over 'new/non-native Englishes". *Journal of Pragmatics* 27: 225–231.

Rhodewatt, F.T. (1986). "Self-presentation and the phenomenal self: on stability and malleability of self-conception" in Baumeister, R.F. (ed.) *Public Self and Private Self*. New York: Springer Verlag, 117–42.

Roberts, C., Davies, E. and Jupp, T. (1992). *Language and Discrimination: A Study of Communication in Multi-ethnic Workplaces*. London and New York: Longman.

Roger, D. (1989). "Experimental studies of dyadic turn-taking behaviour" in Roger, D. and Bull, P. *Conversation,* 75–95.

Roger, D. and Bull, P. (eds) (1989). *Conversation*. Clevedon, Philadelphia: Multilingual Matters.

Rogers, W.T. and Jones, S.E. (1975). "Effects of dominance tendencies on floor holding and interruption behaviour in dyadic interaction". *Human Communication Research* 1: 113–122.

Rudanko, J. (1993). *Pragmatic Approaches to Shakespeare*. Lanham/New York/London: University Press of America.

Russell, B. (1986). "The Forms of Power" in Lukes, S. (ed.) *Power*. Oxford: Blackwell, 19–21.

Sacks, H. (1984). "Notes on methodology" in Atkinson, J.M. and Heritage, J. (eds) *Structure of Social Action*. Cambridge: Cambridge University Press, 21–27.

Sacks, H.; Schegloff, E.A. and Jefferson, G.A. (1974). "A simplest systematics for the organization of turn-taking for conversation". *Language* 50: 697–735.

Schegloff, E.A. (1972). "Notes on a conversational practice: formulating place" in Sudnow, D. (ed.) *Studies in Social Interaction*. New York: Free Press.

Schein, E.S. (1981). "M.R. Forum: improving face to face relationships". *Sloan Management Review*.

Scollon, R. and Scollon, S.B. (1981). *Narrative, Literacy and Face in Interethnic Communication*. Norwood, New Jersey: ABLEX Publishing Corporation.

Scollon, R. and Scollon, S.B. (1995). *Intercultural Communication*. Oxford: Blackwell.

Selinker, L. (1972). "Interlanguage". *International Review of Applied Linguistics* X: 209–30.

Sherger, J. (1988). "Talk about *tu* and *vous*" in Jazayery, M.A. and Winter, W. (eds) *Languages and Cultures: Studies in honor of Edgar C. Polomé*, 611–620.

Shultz, J., Florio, S. and Erickson, F. (1982). "Where's the floor? Aspects of the cultural organization of social relationships in communication at home and at school" in Gilmore, P. and Glatthorn, A. (eds) *Children in and out of School: Ethnography and Education.* Washington DC: Center for Applied Linguistics, 88–123.

Simpson, P. (1989). "Phatic communion and fictional dialogue" in Carter, R. and Simpson, P. (eds) *Language, Discourse and Literature,* 43–56.

Simpson, P. (1989). "Politeness phenomena in Ionesco's *The Lesson*" in Carter, R. and Simpson, P. (eds) *Language, Discourse and Literature,* 171–193.

Smith, S.W.; Scholnick, N.; Crutcher, A.; Simeone, M. and Smith, W. R. (1991). "Foreigner talk revisited: Limits on accommodation to nonfluent speakers" in Blommaert, J. and Verschueren, J. (eds) *The Pragmatics of International and Intercultural Communication,* 173–185.

Snow, C., Eeden, R.V. and Muysken, P. (1981). "The interactional origins of foreigner talk: Municipal employees and foreign workers". *International Journal of the Sociology of Language* 28: 37–58.

Souza, de, F.D.M. (1985). "Dialogue breakdowns" in Dascal, M. (ed.) *Dialogue: An Interdisciplinary Approach,* 415–426.

Spencer-Oatey, H. (1996). "Reconsidering power and distance". *Journal of Pragmatics* 26 (1996): 1–24.

Sperber, D. and Wilson, D. (1986). *Relevance.* Oxford: Basil Blackwell.

Tannen, D. (1983). "When is an overlap not an interruption? One component of conversational style" in DiPietro, R.J., Frawley, W. and Wedel, A. (eds) *The First Delaware Symposium on Language Studies.* Newark, DE: University of Delaware Press, 119–129.

Tannen, D. (1984). *Conversational Style: Analyzing talk among friends.* Norwood, NJ: Ablex.

Tannen, D. (1987a). "Repetition in conversation: Toward a poetics of talk". *Language* 63: 574–605.

Tannen, D. (1987b). "Remarks on Discourse and Power" in Kedar, L. (ed.) *Power Through Discourse.* New Jersey: Ablex Publishing Corporation, 3-10.

Tannen, D. (1990). *You Just Don't Understand: Women and Men in Conversation.* New York: Ballantine.

Tannen, D. (ed.) (1993). *Gender and Conversational Interaction.* New York/Oxford: Oxford University Press.

Tannen, D. (1993). "The Relativity of Linguistic Strategies: Rethinking Power and Solidarity in Gender and Dominance" in Tannen, D. (ed.) *Gender and Conversational Interaction,* 165–188.

Tannen, D. (1995). *Talking From 9 to 5.* London: Virago Press.

Testa, R. (1988). "Interruptive strategies in English and Italian conversation: Smooth versus contrastive linguistic preferences". *Multilingua* 7: 285–312.

Ting-Toomey, S. and Korzenny, F. (1989) (eds) *Language, Communication and Culture.* Newbury Park/London/New Delhi: SAGE Publications.

Tonnies, F. (1971). *Ferdinand Tonnies on Sociology: pure, applied and empirical: selected writings.* Chicago: University of Chicago Press.

Tracy, K. (1990). "The many faces of facework" in Giles, H. and Robinson, W.P. (eds) *Handbook of Language and Social Psychology,* 209–226.

Trosborg, A. (1987). "Apology strategies in natives / nonnatives". *Journal of Pragmatics* 11 (2): 147–168.

Trosborg, A. (1995). *Interlanguage Pragmatics: Requests, Complaints and Apologies.* Berlin/New York: Mouton de Gruyter.

Turnbull, W. (1995). "A methodology for the study of social factors in language use". Unpublished manuscript: Simon Fraser University.

Turnbull, W. and Saxton, K.L. (1997). "Modal expressions as facework in refusals to comply with requests: I think I should say 'no' right now". *Journal of Pragmatics* 27: 145–181.

Ulijn, J.M. and Li, X. (1995). "Is interrupting impolite? Some temporal aspects of turn-taking in Chinese-Western and other intercultural business encounters". *Text* 15 (4): 589–627.

Van Dijk, T.A. (1977). *Text and Context: Explorations in the Semantics and Pragmatics of Discourse.* London: Longman.

Van Dijk, T.A. (1989). "Mediating racism: the role of the media in the reproduction of racism" in Wodak, R. (ed.) *Language, Power and Ideology,* 199–226.

Vanderveken, D. (1985). "What is an illocutionary force?" in Dascal, M. (ed.) *Dialogue: An Interdisciplinary Approach:* 181–204.

Verschueren, J. and Bertuccelli-Papi, M. (eds) (1987). *The Pragmatic Perspective.* Amsterdam/Philadelphia: John Benjamins Publishing Company.

Wardhaugh, R. (1985). *How Conversation Works.* Oxford: Basil Blackwell.

Watts, R.J. (1991). *Power in Family Discourse.* Berlin/New York: Mouton de Gruyter.

Watts, R.J. (1992a). "Linguistic politeness and politic verbal behaviour: Reconsidering claims for universality" in Watts, R.J., Ide, S. and Ehlich, K. (eds) *Politeness in Language: Studies in its history, theory and practice,* 43–69.

Watts, R.J. (1992b). "Acquiring status in conversation: 'Male' and 'female' discourse strategies". *Journal of Pragmatics* 18: 467–503.

Watts, R.J., Ide, S. and Ehlich, K. (eds) (1992). *Politeness in Language: Studies in its history, theory and practice.* Berlin/New York: Mouton de Gruyter.

Weber, M. (1947). *The Theory of Social and Economic Organization.* London: Routledge and Kegan Paul.

Werkhofer, K.T. (1992). "Traditional and modern views: the social constitution and the power of politeness" in Watts, R.J., Ide, S. and Ehlich, K. (eds) *Politeness in Language: Studies in its history, theory and practice,* 155–199.

Wiemann, J.M. (1985). "Interpersonal control and regulation in conversation" in Street, R.L. and Capella, J.N. (eds) *Sequence and Pattern in Communicative Behaviour*. London: Edward Arnold, 85–102.
Wierzbicka, A. (1991). *Cross-Cultural Pragmatics: The Semantics of Human Interaction*. Berlin/New York: Mouton de Gruyter.
Wolfson, N. (1988). "The Bulge: A theory of speech behavior and social discourse" in Fine, J.(ed) *Second Language Discourse: A textbook of current research*. Norwood, NJ: Ablex, 21–38.
Wood, L.A and Kroger, R.O. (1991). "Politeness and forms of address". *Journal of Language and Social Psychology* 10 (3): 145–168.
Wrong, D. (1979). *Power, its Forms, Bases and Uses*. Oxford: Blackwell.
Zimmerman, D. and West, C. (1975). "Sex roles, interruptions and silences in conversation" in Thorne, B. and Henley, N. (eds) *Language and Sex: Difference and Dominance*. Rowley, Mass.: Newbury House, 105–129.

Index

A

Accommodation: 13, 14, 41, 42, 72, 73, 74, 75, 133
Arabic: 15, 150
Asymmetry: 29, 33, 34, 35, 36, 39, 40, 69, 85, 98, 99, 130, 132, 133, 138, 141, 144, 145, 165

B

Back-channel: 50, 52, 71, 74, 75, 76, 78, 79, 83, 87, 98, 99, 142, 163
Bayraktaroglu: 24, 25, 51
Brown and Levinson: 15, 16, 17, 18, 19, 20, 21, 22, 23, 24, 25, 27, 34, 37, 39, 43, 51, 68, 69, 70, 72, 74, 95, 101, 152, 157

C

Camaraderie: 19
Chinese: 14, 15, 22, 23
Communication: 5, 6, 7, 8, 9, 10, 11, 12, 13, 14, 15, 16, 18, 20, 24, 40, 42, 44, 69, 73, 74, 79, 86, 87, 92, 116, 130, 151
Context: 7, 10, 11, 12, 13, 14, 18, 20, 30, 32, 33, 34, 38, 39, 39, 40, 41, 42, 48, 49, 51, 55, 62, 63, 67, 76, 77, 78, 85, 92, 93, 99, 116, 117, 119, 132, 139, 145, 148, 159
Culture: 7, 8, 9, 10, 12, 15, 16, 18, 19, 22, 23, 37, 38, 69, 78, 80, 117, 141, 145, 147, 157, 159, 160, 162, 163

D

Deference: 19, 20, 21, 22, 34, 35, 51, 142, 159
Distance: 18, 19, 20, 22, 33, 35, 39, 43, 119, 142, 152, 157, 158

F

Face Boosting Act: 24, 25, 34, 51, 96, 161, 163
Face Threatening Act: 17, 18, 20, 31, 34, 39, 51, 71, 97, 153, 158, 161, 162

G

Gender: 8, 15, 29, 31, 37, 38, 39, 41, 42, 43, 67, 70, 72, 77, 87, 146, 154, 155, 157
Goffman: 15, 16, 17, 24, 25, 153
Grice: 16, 17, 23, 24, 65, 68, 73, 122

I

In-group: 21, 74, 75, 87, 96, 153, 154, 155, 156, 157, 166
Intercultural: 7, 9, 10, 11, 12, 13, 14, 63, 69, 130
Interruption: 9, 16, 29, 30, 31, 32, 40, 51, 52, 53, 64, 78, 79, 80, 81, 82, 83, 87, 99, 100, 101, 142, 143, 144, 145, 146, 152, 162, 164

L

Lakoff: 16, 19, 20, 23, 33, 62, 63, 72, 93
Language learning: 2, 12, 47

M

Mao: 14, 15, 22, 23
Misunderstanding: 6, 9, 10, 20, 35, 100, 151

O

Overlap: 29, 30, 49, 51, 142, 143

P

Phatic communion: 105, 107, 116, 117, 119, 130, 153
Politeness: 19, 20, 21, 22, 23, 24, 33, 35, 37, 38, 39, 51, 55, 67, 68, 69, 70, 74, 75, 76, 85, 87, 93, 95, 96, 101, 128, 131, 152
Power: 18, 19, 20, 22, 25, 26, 27, 28, 29, 31, 32, 33, 34, 35, 36, 37, 38, 39, 40, 41, 42, 47, 48, 51, 52, 55, 63, 69, 76, 77, 78, 79, 80, 83, 84, 85, 86, 87, 97, 99, 101, 105, 118, 119, 121, 130, 132, 133, 135, 138, 142, 145, 146, 147, 148, 152, 156, 163, 164

Q

Questions: 32, 33, 40, 41, 64, 65, 66, 67, 68, 69, 70, 71, 74, 75, 82, 85, 86, 87, 96, 97, 114, 117, 118, 119, 120, 121, 122, 129, 130, 146, 148, 149, 150, 151, 152, 153

S

Sacks: 29, 30, 33, 46, 80
Scollon: 7, 8, 9, 10, 15, 19, 29, 31, 33, 35, 62, 79, 80, 84

Second language: 2, 12, 13, 42, 62, 145, 151

Solidarity: 9, 10, 19, 20, 35, 39, 40, 41, 43, 52, 67, 70, 72, 74, 75, 83, 87, 96, 101, 118, 133, 151, 152, 154, 155, 157, 158, 161

Spanish: 14, 41, 131, 132, 147, 159

Speech Act: 17, 18, 19, 33, 74, 161, 162, 164

Speech, amount of: 32, 52, 53, 76, 77, 78, 98, 99, 101, 140, 141, 142, 144, 145, 146, 151

Status: 7, 15, 17, 18, 23, 27, 28, 31, 32, 33, 34, 36, 38, 39, 40, 41, 42, 43, 62, 63, 64, 77, 79, 83, 85, 92, 99, 101, 105, 118, 130, 132, 133, 135, 140, 142, 145, 148, 151, 152

T

Tannen: 19, 32, 37, 39, 40, 78, 79, 99, 148, 170

Topic control: 32, 33, 40, 52, 84, 86, 97, 133, 135, 146

Turn-taking: 29, 32, 52, 64, 101, 142

W

Watts: 27, 28, 31, 32, 33, 37, 40, 50, 51, 52, 67, 83, 85, 130, 135, 140, 142

Lightning Source UK Ltd.
Milton Keynes UK
176978UK00001B/15/P